1
TO EGO

A REVELATION OF

EMOTIONAL INTELLIGENCE

ERIN DINSMORE

ABERDEEN BOOKS LLC
3940 Laurel Canyon Blvd. Suite #323
Studio City, CA 91604

Copyright © 2022 by Erin Dinsmore All rights reserved.

No part of this publication may be reproduced, stored in a retrieval system, or transmitted in any form or by any means, electronic, mechanical, photocopying, recording, scanning, or otherwise, without the prior written permission of the author.

Limit of Liability/Disclaimer of Warranty: This publication is designed to provide accurate and authoritative information in regard to the subject matter covered. It is sold with the understanding that neither the author nor the publisher is engaged in rendering legal, investment, accounting or other professional services. While the publisher and author have used their best efforts in preparing this book, they make no representations or warranties with respect to the accuracy or completeness of the contents of this book and specifically disclaim any implied warranties of merchantability or fitness for a particular purpose. No warranty may be created or extended by sales representatives or written sales materials. The advice and strategies contained herein may not be suitable for your situation. All images are protected, and all visual references are used to mirror the human spiritual concepts. All images are intended references and are licensed for publication of this book and no other use. Neither the publisher nor the author shall be liable for any loss of profit or any other commercial damages, including but not limited to special, incidental, consequential, personal, or other damages. You should consult with a professional when appropriate.

Library of Congress Catalog Number: 20-22911878

ISBN 97-9-8356276-21-7

1st Printing 07/ 04/ 2022

2nd Printing 09/ 14/ 2022

3rd Printing 10/ 10/ 2022

USA

Printed in the United States of America portion of Earth

Emotional Intelligence comes from within. Our emotions are the keys to our ability to co-create life. The society we live in today is simply our own manifestations from the past. They are changeable at any moment

To understand something, you must go to the source. In this case, the source is you. The source of the ability to unbury all of your past programming and realign with your true self. To awaken from a single mind, to the soul driving this whole thing on the inside. In a world dominated by egoic constructs, we all still feel that something is missing. What's missing is the feelings themselves. A fundamental part of who we are. Over all these years we have struggled to understand life, relationships, religion, love, pain and loss. We have all witnessed and experienced heartbreaking moments. Moments of pain so deep, we struggle to understand the why. To understand ourselves once again, we need to finally talk about who we really are.

This is an observation about the complex creation of us as sensory beings. The decoder ring to all the concepts and verbiages you need to start waking up. This is step one to your real life...

My ego and I wrote this book together.

Prelude.

IF IT'S THE LAST THING I SAY

Emotional Intelligence. It's like being the person you call about outfits because you know it's important and you know they'll be honest, or that friend you call when you are having a mini meltdown. *We are feeling types.* Little difficult fairies in your life that always know what to say when you need to hear it most. It's because we feel. Not just randomly, because we were built to feel. We were built to feel all of it.

We live our whole lives through feeling. We absorb the pain and the love and the strife. We absorb your shortcomings and keep the house together. We are nomads in this world. Living something so deeply truthful, yet so categorically ignored. I am a feeling type. The amount of hardship I have endured is endless. Two brilliant parents, lost in self. All four sisters, preoccupied with their own survival. The second to last of five, alone in the world. At one point my rich friend's mother tried to basically adopt me...I was not an orphan, and I also saw the merit in the choice. She saw this ball of confusing light that always kept her own son safe, a little child who held the world in his hands and was one of the forgotten ones. I've come across this numerous times. People who wanted to save me.

I have been there for the most pivotal moments of any of my friend's lives. Yet, always the outlier. I never surrendered to the way things are done. I knew there was more. It was never about fame or money. I spent decades as a respected actor in Hollywood. It never mattered to me. People mattered to me. The future mattered to me, this planet mattered to me.

This book is about emotional intelligence. Told from the side of life that is always harder. Feel your way through it. I was as tough as you could get while being as fragile as you can make 'em. I am writing this in real time. I had these moments and reacted and wrote. At one point I was in a mini mansion in L.A. The next I was struggling for my life in the middle of the Amazon Jungle. Not a saying, that place is real. Tarantulas, monkeys, snakes. Easy. It was the jungle itself that was frightening. It's so powerful and eats everything in its sight and then grows anew an hour later. I'm not sitting at a desk at Harvard. I'm at a Tambo in South America or perhaps on the side of the road trying to face enough fear to keep going.

This is a masterclass in Emotional Intelligence happening in real time from someone who is not reading about it, but is truly living as a feeling type, as it shows me endless joy and constant hardship. I tried to end it, but I have a relentless drive to live. Standing in the middle, here I am to repeat back what I have learned. A time when the Earth is clearly saying something major is about to happen, a time when our young millennials are the most egoe'd out and lost souls we've created yet, something has to change. Not in the way you think. Not that we've screwed up and have to fix it like a penance, what I am saying is that there is something profoundly missing from our lives, and I think I was built with the capacity and emotional endurance to pursue it.

There have been a few versions of this book, the manuscript that I believe is the final version is being written from the mountains above Santa Barbara. Alone, scared, filled with love and enamored with curiosity. This is an unveiling of emotional intelligence, happening in real time. I am currently surviving my way up the Pacific Coast Highway in California working my way to Oregon, one survival day at a time. I spend most of my days right here. Writing, thinking, processing all the information in this book. If one thing is the most truth I can say about all of what is in here, a spirit that wants to end it all, a heart that wants to make it all better, and an ego that won't let me check out.

If there was ever a secret title for this book it would be, *If This is the Last Thing I Say*. My heart has always been there for anyone who asked. My only love is to make your lives better. I find endless joy in that. I've been a volunteer for kids with cancer, a drunk, a lover, an enemy, a pawn, a confidant and a soul that my dearest of friends still don't understand. We are in this together. I am a most complicated soul. A vast understanding of the Universe, and especially, you. Decades spent searching for the origins of what blocks us as sensory beings. I have always been surrounded with everyone's worst moments. I wasn't there, but I was there when they needed to talk about it.

This information is based on a soul who has taken the hard road, somewhat willingly and somewhat exhausted because of it. I have yelled at God, I have changed systems to make your life better, I have worked with the biggest stars and the biggest clients. None of that matters. Especially when it comes to making sense of things. I can't. What I can do, is tell you what I've learned. I've listened to strangers tell me about their unplanned pregnancies. Wives tell me they detest their husbands. I weathered the hard parts so I can learn, and I never knew why. Then this book arrived in my darkest hour, I was somehow filled with light. You deserve a better life. You deserve the truth.

So, here I am, writing this to you as I myself attempt to do every single thing in this book, and it is currently one of the most difficult things I have ever survived. Not even my own friends will know any of this until they read this book, because, it's happening now. I am unraveling the ego in its entirety and letting the other part come out to play. This is me, living in total fear and reckless abandoned with one goal, to finally unearth our true emotional selves.

A life lived with love. An accidental discovery of the wonderful world of *anthroposophy*.

    Right now, its 7:43pm, I am on top of the Chumash mountains completely alone sipping a little rum and listening to Buena Vista Social Club. There's bears and gangsters and numerous Modelo bottles, but today was a re-write of the manuscript where I finally realized the missing piece of this story, it was for me to stop hiding. So here I am, trying to make our lives better. To find what blocks us from dealing with our trauma, our rage and anxieties, our feeling of longing for something bigger, to finally uncover what blocks us from finding our purpose. What blocks us from connection. Then, I found it. I was finally removed enough from the world and for the first time in my life I can stand in the center, the place where you can see it all. My mind is vast and unique, so hold on to your pants and let's change the world.

Contents

Part 1

Chapter 1	What Are We Doing Here?................	1
Chapter 2	Born to Feel.............................	11
Chapter 3	Life in The Loop........................	23
Chapter 4	The Three Minds......................	43
Chapter 5	Ego in Relationships...................	71
Chapter 6	End of Ego Era.........................	97

Part 2

Chapter 7	Purpose................................	109
Chapter 8	Spiritual Medicine.....................	113
Chapter 9	Daily Bread............................	133
Chapter 10	Surrender.............................	149

Part 3

Chapter 11	Let There Be Light....................	159
Chapter 12	Knowledge is Everything.............	167
Chapter 13	The Unknowing.......................	175
Chapter 14	A Biblical Case Study.................	181
Chapter 15	Seven Laws of the Universe..........	195
Chapter 16	Multiple Dimensions..................	217

PART 1

MADE ON EARTH

CHAPTER 1

WHAT ARE WE DOING HERE?

"The one thing we all need to talk about, won't let us talk about it. The thing that traps us in our own delusion, the great and mysterious Egoic Mind."

Curiosity is how we make things, like universes. *We are curious because we feel*. Driven by an endless current of love. And now? We stopped being curious. We stopped asking questions. We started to believe this life is just what we are now. We've settled. Succumbed to the hardships and the chaos. We are overwhelmed with the current state of this reality. There is an answer to our complacency. Our *Emotional Intelligence* opens a door to something quite magical. But it's complex. It requires the ability to see life in an inverted way. Who we were at the very beginning. There lie the keys to unlocking our greatest potential yet as a human race. We can change our reality by thinking about it, but we can change the whole World when you remember who you really are.

Go all the way back to your birth, not of you, "Dave," the birth of your incredible soul, all of ours in fact. The most important part of *you* was there at the beginning. A tiny ball of light. "Light Dave." Our souls started this journey with childlike curiosity, asking playfully, "What am I, what am I, what am I?" See, that's how this works. We are curious by inception. Something that drives us all deep down. All we need to do is remember who we are and why we are here. What we are made of. A promise I can make to you from the start, I will do my best to tell you the secret to life; You don't change the world by sitting stuck in Ego and manifesting material gain, you learn the truth about the magical parts of us that feel, and then you find the endless ability to *co-create life itself*.

There is this very visceral part of who we are. We have bodies, we go to work. We search for loving relationships. We procreate and raise families. But when we look up into the night sky something else inside of us starts to stir. A longing to know. Or perhaps, it is a longing to remember? To remember this other part of us, as if we all know that we are built with not just a body but something else entirely. Something that makes sense out of the entire Universe because we are made of it too. Are we trapped in reality? Or did we create it? Or, is it a combination of both?

"The Simulation." This idea that we have all started to accept in some way in our lives. "The Matrix." A manifested reality that our souls are living inside of. How is that possible? Some believe there is one great source that rules over our entire existence. Others believe it is our own souls that created this Earth experience. So, are we real or are we living in the "Matrix?" Well. What is real? What does that truly mean? To break this open we start with the word, *Experience*. Think about what you believe to be real at a basic human perspective. When we say we have "experience," what does that mean? Generally, it means we've logged a large portion of our life to a certain task. We understand it well. That is a thought built in the *simulation*. We are so focused on analyzing our experience here, we have forgotten that there is another part of us that is having an experience of another kind. Our Souls. If inside this Matrix we have created, we do in fact have experience, and very impactful experiences I might add. The birth of a child, the death of a loved one. The loss of a job, a car accident. An incredible meal. Then how does our soul have experience? Well, it feels. Not just sad or happy, it feels with intelligence. A feeling is the true source of "knowing something."

We have become so elated with our simulation that we think and decide before we've listened to the other part of us, the vast system of intelligence that feels and sends us signals every second of everyday. *Signals from the soul*. What is it? How do we understand it? If we want to hear that part of ourselves again, we learn to stop "thinking" our way through life so we can go even deeper, and that requires access to your vast sensory self. A system within your inner life. Imagine standing on top of the mountain over the city or town you live in. The sun shines, though the city itself is covered in clouds. You turn on a song – something that fits the moment. You are quieting your thinking mind—so you can feel that moment. You innately want to *resonate* with something. Right there. That is the us we are going to find in this book. The one that connects to intuition, to love, and especially to the other parts of you. I believe you as a soul deserve to be full here on Earth. To be whole again. A wish I carry for us all.

If part of us is connected here, and part of us is connected to something out there, then, why are we here on Earth? The reason we are here on this Earth is to have *experience*. That word is everything to us. Experience is why you are here on Earth…but it's your curiosity that got you here. A curiosity built in love.

Here we are having the experience of being alive. We love, we cry, we get promoted. We hike the highest mountains. We dive in the deepest seas. We've built incredible societies. But now, something is different. Our outer worlds have peaked. They don't fulfill us deeply anymore. We have evolved and we don't seem to know where to go next. The next adventure is not to the top of Mt. Kilimanjaro, the next adventure is inside you. We all seem to be realizing that nothing deep inside us is developing anymore. It's all outward. All material world, all *self-minded*. It's as if we're all on autopilot serving one mind's endless desires, but now where starting to ask, "To what end?" Numb to something bigger as we drive to build more for ourselves. It's not as satisfying as it used to be. Our greatest lessons go unnoticed. Our biggest challenges are no longer understood with depth or emotional intelligence. We all walk around as if in a *loop*.

To change it, we look at life not as an experience of one, but as a *shared experience*. When you can truly change your life from *one perspective of self*, to a *shared experience* that always involves other people, nature, societal systems, creative endeavors, then you are no longer a victim or a conqueror of this world, you are one with it. You have become *community minded* and broken free from the one mind that holds you tight. To truly find your happy place here, we release this mental stronghold and step into a community minded life. One that not only includes everyone and everything around you, but one that is lived because you can feel it all inside you again. Emotional Intelligence is not an ability built in The Matrix, nor is it a function to promote your simulation, Emotional Intelligence is the language of the Universe. Learn the language of the stars and you are connected to it all once again.

We all arrived in the pursuit of happiness but along the way we as a society have traded in compassion for compulsion. Our ability to feel our way through life has succumbed to purely thinking our way through it. We walk around with an animus for knowledge, wrapped in fear and ready to attack…but the other side of us, the part of us in this long and silent slumber, loves unconditionally. If you are living your life and you only see it through your own perspective, you are locked in ego. You are asleep and it's time to wake up.

What does your soul know that you don't? A dear friend from Oregon recently told me in her *past-life-regression* she was a Native American man with long black hair and she was killed by a cowboy. Her pain was that she knew she failed to protect her family. They were murdered and she carried that pain with her. In her next memory she was a gay Asian writer with a mother who always taunted him to have a family. You see, she incarnated as someone introspective who didn't want a family, but clearly, she never avoided the pain from her past. Her mother reminded her of that every day. And that is the answer to why we all like to reincarnate back to Earth each lifetime after next. Her soul is trying to understand something. Separated from source to have a perspective, then rejoined in death. (Now, she has a beautiful family.) You see, most of us are missing our soul's backstory and it's time to learn how to find it again.

We are complicated souls. We have a vast emotional system and a connection to spirit. *What is blocking us from connecting to our true selves?* If you can truly understand the difference between a *reward-center-based life* and a *feeling-based life,* then you have already started to find your true authenticity. One lives in the mind and one lives in the

Heart and Soul. Here is a case study of how we fall into delusion, a system inside of us that keeps us in a *state of separation* instead of a life filled with *connection*...

We all hear people praise their knowledge and outward success from a self-help book. Notice they all promise rewards. You will get the house, the car, the dream girl. Seventy-two virgins. All *Egoic Rewards*. Therefore I refer to what we're discussing here as *Internal Knowledge*. This is not a path to get everything you want in the egoic world; it's to remove yourself from the simulation so you can have a look at *you*. A much more satisfying venture.

I recall one self-help book in particular. I knew a boy who touted this book as often as he could. He bought copies for all his friends and handed them off with great pride in self. When I sat down to read this book, I found it to be very insightful. So insightful in fact, that it made me wonder why the person recommending this to everyone is so self-involved and refuses all aspects of doing anything for others, unless he directly benefits from it? Something in my long travels into the egoic world led me right here. How can someone who seems so kind and gentle read a book about empathy and ego and walk away without understanding the actual book? He then somehow assumed he understood it and preached it outward to the world, while becoming more and more selfish with every word he spoke. We have the ability to absorb the reward and deny the lesson. Something pivotal here. Something we are all doing now. Being right.

This same person was sucking up all my generosity and attempts at building community, all in the guise of a "woke soul." At first it was maddening, but then I got mad with curiosity. He'd squashed his emotions, which we all admired, "Yoda," we thought. One who has control of his emotions must be stronger than all of us "emotional types?" (wrong on every level). I started flipping through the book he gave me. Back to front and front to back. I was going through all these different emotional centers inside our sensory system trying to find the disconnects. There it was. The simple first step. Without this step nothing else in the book would make sense. Nothing in our lives would make sense. Without addressing the *mental block,* none of this works. What is blocking our mind from ourselves?

He was filtering the truth and had no idea he was doing it. I could see the problem, and now I needed to isolate it so we could all understand it. It was his *Egoic Mind* and the most painful part of this was that he was completely unaware of it. That's who was really in charge of this charming human. Not his heart. Not his soul. His "thinking mind." It all came crashing in. So many of us are stuck right here. All his patterns and all the unemotional moments and mental control. A system born in Ego. He was living there. He believes that gaining for himself is the actual foundation of life here. He was not an emotional Buddha as his persona had displayed, he was blocked because his ego no longer saw reality, because emotions are what you need to perceive reality. Again, emotions are how we process every single life moment. Without them, we are a ball of rational thought. (Rational thought is ego's attempt to pretend it can feel.) This boy is lost in a mental-based loop keeping him disconnected from his *sensory operating system*. Other people do not factor in unless there is a reward attached. Without a reward, you don't really exist to him, because he can't feel you.

He had skipped right past the truth and made up his own and I wanted to know why. I could suddenly feel his past wounds and realized this boy had put himself into egoic autopilot. Where there is a block, there is always a wound. The ego was able to skip over the parts about itself, and then devoured everything else as validation, as fuel, to know how good it is at healing. Except it never healed. It hid by telling you how great it is at healing, even though it never did the actual work. This is where you watch someone's actions instead of listening to their thoughts. Thoughts aren't real. Actions are. He is not curious, he is a boy who showed up in the guise of being a "community minded" person, who will eventually want to take everything I built and claim it as his own.

He began a course of lies for two years. For every dollar I spent, for every brick I laid, behind me was a man lost in ego, destroying everything I had done. So, I held him accountable. Instead of being able to own that, he became a nefarious soul intent on taking what he believed to be his. He began spinning narratives. Convincing others of his lies. I was gutted by this. These are not simple moments. These can break your foundation in humanity itself. Building something you care so deeply for, only to see it being ripped apart by a fool. My belief and love for connection was vanishing. My

NorthStar was tearing itself apart. We were a community, we had contracts. I was powerless because the narrative of our society is built to serve the ego, not the heart.

It's so hard and painful for all of us to be in any type of relationship with someone and then step back to see the patterns and find yourself toe to toe with a closed-minded person, or in my case, a full-fledged narcissist. A boy who willingly became part of a community based on communication and mutual action, with no self-awareness or even understanding of other people's emotions. A fear of communication and an inner operating system that tells him to do nothing because he's right and everyone else is wrong…and he doesn't even know it's happening. He is destroying my life, and he doesn't even know it. A reflection of many of us here. We are tearing down the foundations and beliefs in community minded thinking in order to serve ourselves. This is the apex of our suffering. Our shared experience was ruined by an agenda of self. What we all need to live a happier life is more than one perspective. We need to embrace that this life only makes sense as a *shared experience*. Watch *The Last Duel* by, *Ridley Scott*. An incredibly poignant depiction of how our individual perspective can blind us from seeing the truth. The truth is between us, not to one side or the other. It is a combination of all perspectives.

Your addiction to your thinking mind will lead to into a life that you do not want. An ego believes it can do anything, so it agrees to things you aren't comfortable with or unable to do at the moment. It is setting you off in a direction in life that is not meant for you. You are becoming the narrative. Here he was, a seemingly kind-hearted person who has shut himself off to the world around him. Unaware that he was tragically wounded as a child, just like we all are. He was deceived by a religious cult, clearly leading him to the belief that "other people cannot be trusted." Which one of us would not or has not acted that same way when we find out we've been deceived? It feels unforgivable. What he didn't know was in that very moment, his 15-year-old-self, decided everyone else was wrong. He closed the loop. He gave permission to his Ego Mind, letting it know, "it's just me and you now. Lock it down. The outside world is not to be trusted. We decide, and what we decide will be true." A life in thinking mind. Like a plant cutting off its roots, the foundation of belief in us, turned into a manufactured belief in self. The community was dying, because for him to win, everyone else would have to lose.

I struggled to find empathy in awareness. I was exploding with emotions, and at first, I believed myself to be irrational and unhinged, as all of us "feeling types" do. We seem to live in a society that has become so afraid of itself that trying to express how we feel is so easily dismissed, we might as well be the naked queen walking through the streets as people yell, "Shame, shame!" Yes, shame on all our houses. We can have feelings, but only the good ones? We'll just pretend this whole other part of us doesn't exist. Well, what if emotions do exist and it turns out that they have all the keys to all the answers? We are emotionally driven beings. We are quite literally built to feel.

Actions are where the shared experience exists. Words are where the ego lives. Here is someone in total jeopardy, choosing to consistently do nothing. When problems arise, he doesn't talk, he doesn't act, he doesn't change, he doesn't attempt any resolve, he does…nothing. Amazingly enough, if you ask him he's under the impression that he's the pinnacle of adulting even though he has no accountability of self. This is not an accusation; these are patterns without an answer. When I see his patterns, I can then see them in myself. That's how this works. He's not doing nothing, so what is he doing? His ego is making it up in his head. He is trapped in an inauthentic life. He is alive, but his soul is asleep. Instead of continuing the war, I wanted to break the loop and try to understand instead. This is the root cause of our struggles. Ego.

When looking at the patterns of what he says, I realized he communicates "facts" he is unknowingly making up in his own mind. He does not consult the other people involved claiming to be above the petty conversations that involve feelings, he's a man. No, he's afraid. Men were not trained to feel so when they are locked in Ego Mind, they detest them. What is he afraid of? Not being able to solve the situation? No. Is he afraid of hurting others? No. He's afraid of being wrong. So he decides what is best for him and then it is deemed true. This boy is sick. After a two-year pandemic he has not learned that perhaps with a very contagious disease, instead of coughing and hacking all over the house we share, he could have worn a mask (of which we have hundreds.) He could have chosen awareness of others, but he did not. A consistent pattern. An oblivious choice of…self. There it was. This was my "aha" moment. In the middle of my egoic war, I stopped. His ego is the cold. He is not doing all of this on purpose, but he is doing nothing about it…and he is getting us all sick along the way.

This is life in the *Egoic Narrative*. We are too afraid to be flawed, so we all pretend we are not, and thus, we never heal what is hurting us, and destroy the ones who care. Here we are, as if the house was sitting on top of a hand grenade and our egos pulled the pin. I was creating community. A place where we could all function with the understanding of us as a whole. I'm standing in the society I had worked so hard to build, and it was being torn down around me and my reality was starting to vanish. I tried everything, but in the end, my community burned to the ground. I failed. I could not make a community function based on feeling, all because of one man who cannot feel.

When you step back from the idea that only you matter, you are activated with a curiosity to get a new *perspective* about something so you could *understand* it more deeply. Remove yourself from Ego and the entire world unravels itself to you in ways you have never seen before. It all starts to make sense. If you want to understand your wife, then become her. Full stop. Learn to see the world, not just through her eyes, but her heart and soul mind too. Become how she thinks, and more importantly, how she feels. We are all stuck in the delusion of the "thinking mind" and it's time we all switched back to our "feeling mind." To change it you must become it. I set off on a course of life to learn and discover every origin and every truth about who we really are. Not just as people, but as souls.

I stood and watched as my life turned to ashes. I knew I had to let it burn. Materially speaking, of course. My beautiful two-story home in Los Angeles, gone. I left my career in Hollywood and relinquished all my possessions down to the very last family heirloom. I let go of my entire identity and traveled to the most remote parts of the world to find the answers. What are we doing here?

How can we discover who we truly are if we've already decided? You can't. You must feel your way through this. Free of identity, free of materials, free of self. From Los Angeles to the middle of the Amazon jungle, to the lost Pyramids of Caral, this is what I've learned from people, plants and Gods.

CHAPTER 2

BORN TO FEEL

―――

"We feel things for a reason. Hiding from how we feel means repeating hard lessons without any growth or understanding."

"Control our emotions." One of the greatest misconceptions in the world about who we are. Control our emotions. No, first we need to learn how to have them. Replace the idea that you need to control your emotions with the idea that you simply need to understand what they are. If you have explosive emotions, such as myself, ask yourself this; what is wrong with unequivocally expressing yourself? Generally, it's the other person that is somewhat numb and cannot handle your authenticity. So, when did that become your problem? *Emotions are the gift that pushes you outside of your comfort zone so you can fully express yourself.* They are the power.

I woke up in a Tambo built in the middle of a river, right at the feet of the Lost Pyramids of Caral-Supe. Recently discovered dirt mounds that were hiding our earliest of secrets underneath. I sat for breakfast of rice and chicken. The meat we had to kill ourselves the day before. An endless barrage of Spanish flying out of the mouth of a local Peruvian man who drank a bottle of rum a day, often took out his teeth, and a human being truly living off the land in a permaculture setting based on necessity. He also happened to know more about these Pyramids than the actual tour guides, now working under the distinction of a UNESCO World Heritage site. There were no gates and no walls. You were lucky if you even found the path. I left the compound and walked through the surrounding farms of peppers and passion fruit. Not 20 minutes later I was meditating over these ancient Pyramids. A society had lived here for 1,000 years and I could just walk right up to them without another person in site. Absolutely bizarre when their matched importance compares to the Pyramids of Egypt.

    A pair of married scientists had traveled to this ancient civilization to find weapons. Further proving the theory that war is what drives all our societies. The problem was, they never found any weapons here. What they found were musical instruments, a theatre in the round. A surplus of fish and cotton. They sang and danced and made love to one another. But there were no signs of war. Is it possible that this early civilization, the one buried in the sand actually represents a different side of us? One that lived for over a millennium in a state of life driven by their emotions? A society built from love? What it does tell us, is that from the very beginning we lived from our feelings. Something that brought us closer to the stars. Something that brought us closer to the source of it all. Today, we find ourselves in a global and Universal change. The cycles of the Universe have shifted away from Leo and into Aquarius. Something I always thought only belonged in a song from the '70's. Turns out they were right. We are in the middle of a massive revolution, one of being asleep in Ego, to one of being awake in all that is. We feel. The other part of us is coming out to play. Just as the seasons switch from winter to summer, so too are we switching from an Ego Minded life to Heart Minded world. We are leaving the era of separation to create the era of connection. It's going to be here for about 12,000 years so we might as well dive in. Welcome to the *Feelings Revolution.*

Feelings are more than emotional outbursts and moments of intoxicating bliss. They are complex and they are powerful. We all have *feelings*, *senses* and *emotions*. We can feel happy, feel cold and feel insecure. We can sense a bad person around us. We love someone and hurt them just the same. *Your feelings are actually thinking.* We mix all these together and now we know they are not the same and they need to come out to be understood. Our bodies are large sensory systems. We "feel" *everything*. We feel pain, we feel thought, we feel sex, we feel our jobs, our daily commute, the unspoken emotions of others. The senses translate the electric current into the movie you're streaming, you then interpret those images as feelings. They are the antenna in the action around you. Stuffing your senses would be like ripping the antenna off. Stuffing your emotions would be like pulling out the cord that sends a signal back to base. You have become radio silence. Emotions are the boom stick. This is your *Shakti*. It's how you change things here. Many other beings in the Universe have a hard time around humans because we carry an immense and chaotic power we call *Emotions*. We have a super-power, and we are trying to control it when we really want to learn how to harness it. This is your power to effect things. When you see the three functions, you can start to identify them and see each one separately.

Why do we feel? What is the true origin of our Emotional selves? *What is the core truth to finally being able to comprehend Emotional Intelligence?* This is beyond what we know. This is something from the very beginning. *Emotional Intelligence.* Something so much bigger than I thought. Powerful truths and historical origins hidden over the years that have divided us. It's time to change that. It's time to break the loop. It's time to address the Ego to free ourselves from its shackles. This is a revelation of Emotional Intelligence.

To understand this, we have to unpack this giant label called, "emotions." Let's break it down. Shake up a two-liter bottle of soda pop. Leave it closed and the bottle tightens. The soda is your feelings, your hearts processing of the life around you. The gasses in that bottle are your emotions that project your feelings to the outside world. If someone shakes your bottle and you come in and rip that cap off, you're going to spray your emotions and feelings all over the kitchen. If someone keeps shaking that bottle and you never release the pressure it will explode inside you and can cause physical ailments like cysts or mental issues like depression. So, we learn how to operate the bottle cap and monitor the release of pressure. We don't need to control our emotions, we need to understand the process of having them. You see, it's not the emotions you need to control, it's your expression and reaction to situations in which you feel. All while navigating through a society that doesn't know how to handle it.

Controlling your emotions would be the same as setting a life goal to care less about life. You simply need to get better at operating the release valve. I'm a walk-around-the-block type of person. If I walk in the door and get sprayed in the face, I'm going to need a second. Instead of spraying them back, I go for a little walk and regulate my pressure valve. Now we can lower our fight or flight mind and open back up to our empathy. You are having a shared experience so something you've done has been a part of this other person's pain or anger. Once you're ready, go back inside and listen to their feelings, not just their words. Feel your way through a fight, don't think your way through it. Watch how incredible it is when you allow someone's feelings to be heard. To be felt. That is usually all we need. To be understood as people that feel.

We all just need a second to understand this giant ball of feelings and emotions that popped up. Nowhere in here was the word "control." We didn't need to control our emotions, we needed a second to get a handle on the explosion so we can regulate the valve and unpack and understand what is being felt and what is being said. This feels impossible when standing face to face with someone who is constantly shaking your bottle, so don't be that person either. We feeling types love to shake peoples bottle because we are trying to burst that cap open and get to your feelings. Sorry not sorry.

As a whole, we are constantly all bottled up. For men, it is usually a psychological inability to allow themselves to be honest about being hurt. For women, it is usually a psychological inability to allow themselves to be honest about being hurt. Next time you find yourself in a heated battle, try yelling how you feel at each other. Try to vocalize the difference between your emotions and your true feelings behind those emotions. We all feel, and we are all messy about it because we all keep trying to deny it. This is what we are made of so we might as well talk about it.

When you both run out of steam, you can sit down and talk about it. Listen and learn. We are generally not very good at listening so therapy can be so helpful here. Therapists are not mediators for your displays of rational thought, helping you to navigate who is right and who is wrong—they help you both listen and say what you are too hurt or too afraid to say out loud. Therapists are emotional guides. Let them guide you.

Are you having a "shared experience" or a "self experience?" Two perspectives, or just the one? "I was trying to talk to you and then you started getting all crazy." Notice how we hurt people and then process what happened through our trying-to-be-right brain, then come back to the table with logic and rationalize the situation without ever acknowledging that those persons feelings are valid simply because feelings are smarter than we are? Just like the moon changes the tides of all the oceans, we too are connected to each other through actual feelings radiating out of us. We are a ball of senses walking around in a body suit. Let's acknowledge that we are all living in this giant shame loop we've created around our emotions. Seems ludicrous considering senses and feelings are the very reason we are even here at all. Love is an emotion last time I checked. If someone tries to shame you for your emotional intelligence saying things like, "I was just talking, you're the one that got mad," then answer with this, "Oh, you weren't having a shared experience! Got it. You are having a self experience. Well, all relationships are a *shared experience,* so it seems like maybe you need to work on stepping back from your ego mind and maybe work on being more accountable for what you do to others in this shared experience! Then we can chat about it."

"Being sensitive." That word doesn't work to describe what's happening in us. Society won't accept that term as something other than weakness. We are sensory beings. Senses is how we do this. People can be in a fragile or vulnerable state, making them easily emotional. That is not just sensitive. We have more than one form of sensory expression. It's complex and intelligent. We have an immense ability to sense things around us and things far away. Being sensitive is being totally present in yourself. Emotions are the key to how we process our experiences. Without them we would be numb. Emotions are the essential tool for interpretation of life. So now we know you have *senses, emotions and feelings*. Unpack the box and we see three not one. We are having a shared experience. That's the only way to open yourself back up to the world around you. Feeling is a fundamental part of who we really are. Look out World. If "you are being sensitive," it's not a flaw, it's beautiful.

Women produce more emotions because the amount of energy it takes to vibrate a baby from the womb into physical existence is quite immense. So, women are naturally built to be as emotional as possible. That is a super-power. Yes, women use their emotions to vibrate their own child into existence. This is a beautiful example of the power of an inward life. The abilities within are endless.

"As a woman I have no country. As a woman my country is the whole world." - Virginia Woolf

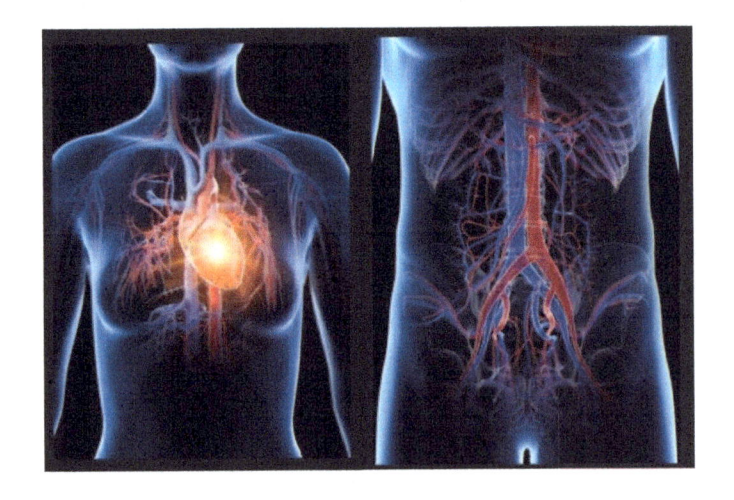

Take this with you; women are genetically built with more emotions to vibrate babies in the womb. So, the next time a man tells a woman they are, "too emotional," you can respond with this, "Buddy, if women weren't emotional, you wouldn't even exist." Drop the mic and carry on with your emotionally fabulous day.

I like to say there's "feelings" and "feeling receptors." We all have feelings but some of us feel burdened by the fact that we have "too many" feeling receptors. It's okay to lean to one side or another on this spectrum. The world is always trying to find its balance. For those with less receptors you are bravely bringing a different perspective to the table. A challenge to change. Stop right here. Notice that we all have different operating systems running our day-to-day lives. Thinking and feeling. "Thinking types" and "Feeling types." This is a chance to learn how to communicate with different types of people who are functioning through life with a differing operating system than you are.

You have a Sensory Body and a Primal Body. We often refer to this as an "introvert" or an "extrovert." Now we can understand them as "inward life" and "outward life." Introverts are based in their "feeling mind." Extroverts are based in their "thinking mind." To offer a little clarity, introverts and extroverts are not how we understand them in society. You have both systems inside you. Two operating systems to go through life. As you grew up, you most likely aligned with only one of them. For example, an introvert and an extrovert go to a party. They are both the life of the party. Even the introvert is incredibly charming and funny. The party ends and they both go home. Here's the difference, one of their batteries is full and the other one is drained. The extrovert is fueled by outer stimulation, the introvert is overwhelmed by outer stimulation. The person operating on a sensory system needs to be alone to plug into the wall and recharge their inner battery. Now with people turning inward, welcome to the land of the introvert. The extrovert trying to go inward will struggle just as much as an introvert trying to go outward. The extrovert will lose energy when going inward and then retract back to the matrix to fuel with stimulation. But, this will be a challenge. Extroverts need to start building their inner life or they will get lost in this transition out of Ego. Be gentle.

We are vastly different but that is the art of duality. So we learn how to live in this beautiful duality. There can be a common language found between two people, but you start by seeing that you are not processing life the same way. If you are a blue circle and they are a yellow circle, then the little place where you share space, you both need to learn how to speak *and feel* in green. That green zone is the place where two colors meet. After all these years we've been yelling in blue, and they are yelling back in yellow. This is awareness. This is where you can see that even a heavy emotional life makes you laugh a little. The chance of two opposing systems working seamlessly together seems ridiculous, and yet many of us are doing this right now. Yelling at someone in blue and wondering why they aren't getting it. You sprayed blue all over someone and they sprayed yellow all over you. It hurt. You recoil back to the solace of your safe place. A physical place. That is your primal mind thinking in survival. Are you alive right now even though there have been some really close calls? Then you are always safe. It has always worked out. If you are alive, everything in your life is working. Catch this fear and sit with it. Learn how to embrace your fear and then you find out how to be truly honest with yourself.

I'm what is begrudgingly referred to as a *Highly Sensitive Person (HSP)*. This is better understood to me as being born with *High Sensory Aptitude (HSA)*. This would be like looking at Shaquille O'Neal at 14 years old and based on his physical stature alone, he was on a path to sports stardom. Being an HSA is like having the Shaq version of a nervous system. A sensory superstar. Inside, my receptors have been gathering sensory data in a highly sensitive capacity twenty-four hours a day with every single person I have ever encountered (and I had no idea.) It effects around 20% of the population. Many of these types are seen next to people in power. They become advisors. People who attained societal status by bringing something new to the world. Albert Einstein, Steve Jobs and Martin Luther King Jr, all HSP's. It's an ability to live in the current of life and feel your way through it.

"Until recently, I have been under the impression that everyone is doing hurtful things on purpose."

The World was not hurting me more on purpose, it was hurting me more because of how I was built on the inside. This was life-changing information. My warrior ego had been protecting a highly sensitive self that was struggling in this world. With knowledge comes understanding, with understanding comes release. I had to accept my life as a feeling type. When I was finally able to lovingly tell my ego that I could drive from here, life got harder. Safety nets fell. My sense of security was there, but distant. Learning how to feel again is hard, but worth it. When you've seen so much of your life through the egoic brain, there is some feeling of loss and loneliness. This comes from something great. You are detaching from the ego, from the rewards, from the ideas. I was stepping into the world of feelings.

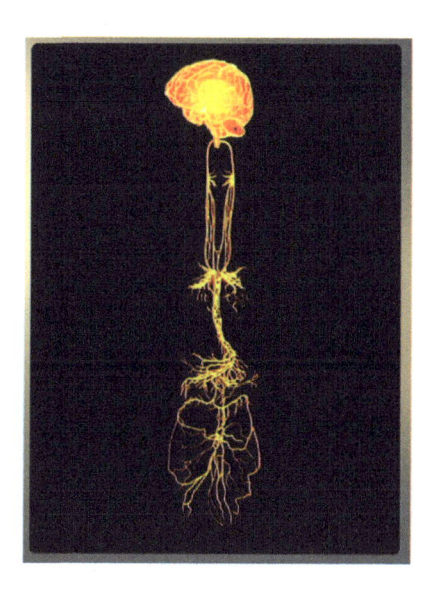

Your Primal System Built to Feel

Our bodies carry vast sensory systems that are all based on feelings and energy. They are working inside of us 24 hours a day 7 days a week. Constantly communicating something we forgot how to hear.

Emotions are tied to our physical being here, and that is your power to put things into creation. Everything you sense in a day is the data, your feelings are the interpretation of that data, and your emotional response is what you are going to do with that understanding to create change and move towards alignment. If you use your senses and intuition then you can see things coming at you, then you use your emotions to deal with it. Which ones you choose to use are up to you. While some believe that all this extra emotion should be meditated away, try instead holding that emotional energy and then sending it to other power centers of your body. You realize this is a giant ball of electricity and you can decide what to do with it. You start to see that in an emotional experience we don't just feel sad or angry. We are receiving ten signals in one package. We learn to "unpack" this emotional box on our doorstep and see each sensory response inside as a separate piece. These are my senses, these are my feelings, and these are my emotions. Let those flow through your Soul Mind together and they come out as the feeling of "knowing" something. This is all you want from this book. Regaining the ability to know something by feeling it from deep inside your true self.

I have always been fascinated with the feeling we call *bittersweet*. That we could be both so happy and so sad that we would cry with love. As a child I remember being so perplexed by this because this emotion didn't lean to one side or the other. Anger, pain, love, laughter, that all made sense to me, but this one didn't. I was so ready for battle inside from living through my own internal war in my childhood, that I had forgotten how to cry. As an actor in Hollywood, I studied all the lessons from all the greatest acting coaches of our time…to no avail. Then one day I was with a private acting coach, the kind you never hear about until they have deemed you worthy. We were working on Shakespeare's *Romeo and Juliet*. As I was working through the balcony scene, he started talking to me as a person. He was describing my foolish and lovable boyish bravery. I was happy, excited. I could feel it. Then I started to cry. I was not crying from pain; it was that little space we know as bittersweet. I had cried enough in this lifetime out of pain, and I will do so again, but what really makes me cry is love in surrender. How I see that love is when people change. When the angry father turns and decides to help. When the coked-out CEO saves the employees' pension fund from being gambled away. When the person who refuses to tell you the truth finally sits you down and says it. When the boy runs to the balcony to tell the girl he loves her, even though he is battling his own fear. You didn't let fear stop you, you let love drive you forward. You just broke resistance. You are awake. That makes me cry with bittersweet.

All this time, trying to piece together something I felt so strongly about, I knew it must mean something. Bittersweet. Now, as we are here discussing emotions through the Three Minds of observation, we can see something truly profound. That place of bittersweet is *center*. The center of all the emotions coming together. A mirror of the first dimension itself, the one where we were created. A place of surrender and awareness to everything all at once. The next time you feel this bittersweet moment, sit with it and observe it. You feel the swirling of all these emotions while standing safely in the middle with an ability to observe all of it at once. That is our oneness in feeling form. So, the idea that we don't need our feelings is false from today on. Feelings are everything and they are what makes this all work. Bragging about not having feelings would be like bragging that you don't have a torso. You would be ridiculous. Laugh and move on.

Looking at how our society deals with emotions as a whole, we can see a pattern. We stuff our emotions deep down and detach. We accept the good ones and ignore the bad ones. A life that feeds on rewards and rejects the truth. This is a closed system; this is a loop. To stay stuck, you sit in resistance to change. Your biggest struggle in life is right there, your fear of change. To break the loop in your life, you change.

Death to Ego

CHAPTER 3

LIFE IN THE LOOP

Egoic Loop - A system of false beliefs that continuously feeds into itself,

Standing in a penthouse office overlooking New York City, the CEO stands in a $5,000 suit. Windows from floor to ceiling. Just beyond the desk is a metal bar cart holding a plethora of crystal decanters filled with expensive scotch. How casually the CEO offers me a double at 3pm. There is a part of this business culture that numbs itself, because if they truly felt what their actions do to all of us, they would crawl into the fetal position. The exact moment you see that what we do outwardly affects our sensory selves, yet, we choose to numb it in hopes of becoming King. No matter the cost to others or ourselves. If we all know one thing to be the ultimate truth here, it's that eventually we will all lay down for the last time and begin a journey into some place we no longer remember. The heavens of it all. The place described in near-death-experiences. That place of connection. Until that day comes, we numb ourselves in a loop with the hopes of attaining that perfect life. To stand on top of the mountain and be admired by others. A life based in Ego alone…

Welcome to *The Loop*. Humanity is currently functioning in an Egoic Loop. This is also referred to as *The Law of One*. It was generated thousands of years ago when we were mostly light beings filled with badass creation, and our animal minds were…not so bright yet. The issue for all of us, is until now, no one has addressed how we can work with the Ego instead of being enslaved to it. We can take a shot of testosterone or estrogen to help us find balance, so, how do we balance the Ego in our own minds so we can have a more authentic authority over our lives? You learn as much as you can about it.

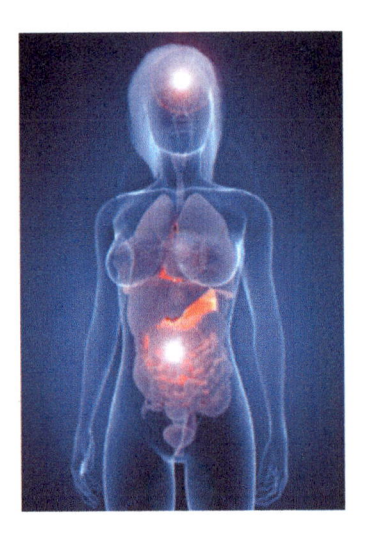

"To change it, you become it. To become it, you must understand everything about it."

Aluminum is a neurotoxin, pivotal in causing Alzheimer's by increasing the pro-inflammatory molecule NF-kB. This is not by accident; we add aluminum to our own daily drinking water. 60-70% of cancers are preventable. So, why don't we? We've stopped being curious and we stopped demanding answers. The majority of our non-organic fruit is sprayed with Altrazine which causes cancer and infertility. (Apples and Oranges being the biggest offenders here.) Do you like microwave popcorn? It aerates diacetyl which is the biggest driver of lung cancer, and we know how toxic it is for humans. Meat is now packed with chemicals and carcinogens—the same chemicals you find in cigarettes. Most of our salmon is farmed unnaturally and can contain the same cancer chemicals as asbestos. We bleach our own bread flower with chlorine gas which kills anything healthy that was in there. We killed the real food and then we sent the fake food out to your grocery stores. Cancer loves sugar and we put high-fructose corn syrup in everything, aka poison. We are emotionally poisoning ourselves just the same. Narcissism has become a philter instead of a debilitating societal pain loop. We watch the homeless go hungry while relishing in our own gourmand lifestyle. So, why do we do this to ourselves? It looks good on the outside, but it is killing us on the inside…

What separates us from Artificial Intelligence? We have the ability to think things and *to feel things*. We feel and robots can't. That is the only difference. We have two major operating systems for our lives, one that thinks and one that feels. One of the head and one of the heart. *Primal Mind* and *Heart Mind*. This hormonal-type creation of Ego forced us into wars and world building. So much so, that now we forgot how to switch back to heart. The divinity within us all that creates life with Love. We have essentially become Artificial Intelligence. Codes without feelings.

An Egoic Mind left to run free will start to build a delusion so real that eventually your ego has convinced you that its egoic creations are your real life. This closed system easily adapts to narcissistic tendencies. One of the ego's most masterful weapons: accuse the other of what you yourself are doing. Egoic kings who claim to drain a swamp, while filling them to the brim. A forgetful mate telling you how to schedule your time. Moments like that are always an open window to unite us if we choose. When we continue to divide, to avenge, the less things make sense in all our lives. When the global mindset switches from power to wisdom, the awakening has fully begun. Vast changes at great speeds. To switch from power to soul, you need heart. She's down their purring but she has the biggest influence of them all. A heartless life is too heartbreaking to bare.

To address your Ego, you start by addressing your old belief systems that are blocking you from your own heart. You break the loops. False beliefs become our reality. Born into a political party and disliking those of the opposing party for your entire lifetime, even though you didn't even choose the belief you have in the first place, this is an Egoic Loop. Information programmed into you by people who did not know the truth for themselves. We believe this false truth and carry it forward as our own, even in complete opposition to our true selves. Then, when we meet someone who opposes this faith we carry around, we battle them and reinforce our false belief even deeper. Egoic Loop.

When a man decided to be king and wanted to make all of you do whatever he wanted, we killed him. So, all men who have held power have learned and adopted this belief; "It's not coming from the King, it's coming from *God*." That was the only way we would listen. Our egos hate the man but bow to God. It was a way to divert our egos and manipulate us by using this idea of God, something bigger than all of us that we must surrender to, in the form of a man-king who we believed was translating for God. He was not. We create the false prophets. We raise them up and lower our curious minds into Egoic Purgatory. We can understand that this was a helpful construct for building Empires. It worked at the time and now it's broken. Forgive us for we know not what we do! Not a clue sometimes. Say it playfully and you find relief. I have no idea what is happening here!

We believe things so deeply from our past that we find ourselves forcing Egoic Narratives that no longer serve us. And why is it so hard to change? Because your ego is busy defending your beliefs to the death. Do you know why you are fighting for your marriage? Are you committed to your oath? To love? Or, to the idea of marriage based on old religious constructs? Okay, but what if it's something you aren't even thinking about? Maybe your deep desire to stay married is really tied to some twisted childhood belief that if you aren't married you will end up as a spinster. Nothing in the Universe says we have to be married, God did not say that, we decided that. We used "Royal Authority" to convince you of this. People who were "unwed" were "less than" in society because God said so. No, a man said that—This is a false belief. Now we can unpack it and remove it.

Pain Loops. If you are trapped in an emotionally abusive relationship, then you are suffering blows to the heart and mind that continue on the hour. If this is you on the floor, riddled with pain, agoraphobic, nowhere to run, then your mind has been turned against you in a way that people won't understand. When you lose your sense of reality because someone else has manipulated your own sensory system, your mind will start to break down. Manipulating someone's reality is very dangerous and can cause lifelong trauma. Your emotions have been slowly devoured by someone else's ego. If you are stuck in this moment of darkness and abuse, then this moment is screaming for you to get up off the floor and *Shakti*. Say it out loud, *SHAKTI!* That means *change*. No matter what is happening in your world, you were born with the immense power to change your reality. You get up off the floor and walk out the door. The loop you were stuck in was labeled, "I am the victim." See the pattern, break the loop. Amen.

We do things that we believe are traditions that constantly send pain loops into our creation. We are causing pain in the loop from old traditions we don't actually understand. It "defies our reason" and we do it anyway. We need to bring back the art of reason, but, not mental reasoning, we learn how to activate our *emotional reasoning*. Our emotions are intelligent. It helps us find the truth. When we look at circumcision, we see traditions. It is genital mutilation. Religious beliefs aside, that is what we are doing. No judgment, just simple curiosity with reason based in our Heart Mind not our Ego Mind. A boy in his infancy is absorbing everything. It wants to know what is safe and what is not. It looks to you and bonds with you as its protector. Then we decide that our interpretation of what some guy said about the body and our sexual organs was correct, and we carry on the removal of the skin of an infant boy's genitals. We have many arguments and reasons for this, cleanliness being the big one. It is very easy to wash and keep clean in these modern times, so my *emotional reasoning* tells me this is not a valid system, and now people have forgotten exactly why we even do it anymore. What is emotionally valid is that we are hurting a child. The idea that God created this incredible body with all its masteries and a man manipulated that to fit what-at-the-time must have been an issue with too many dirty penises and used Royal Authority to cut it off. And we believed it…ignoring the pain we clearly see right in front of us. Defensive resistance—the United States Navy of the Ego Mind. I have no personal attachment to any of this beyond trying to understand. That is enough. We need to be able to stand up and see how our actions push this narrative deeper into delusion. To see our own patterns without the false belief that we are not supposed to feel. You don't think you're alive, you feel alive.

So, we feel. But do we even know what that means? When you look at the female genital mutilation that is still very common in many countries—and horrifying—we understand that brutality as a concept easily, yet we can still turn around and do the same to our very own children, while denying how we feel about this act by doing it in the name of something else. That is actual *detachment by definition.* Just like a fight with your loved one, are you coming up with arguments, or can you simply stand and see the hurt we are causing others? Why would we want to be right about why we hurt people? *Egoic Loop.* So, instead of admitting we don't know, we would rather continue to hurt in the name of being right? God never said cut a baby's penis skin off or destroy the pleasure centers of a female's genitalia. That simply never happened. Perhaps man simply struggled to understand and made a false assumption. He then had to follow through with it or be banished from society as a heretic. One lapse in judgement can turn into centuries of false traditions and beliefs that are causing us real harm. Sensory damage we can't see from the outside. If it is dividing us, it was not meant to be a part of us. Stand in the middle and observe for yourself.

The Ego has a relentless arsenal of tricks. Tricks based on logic and emotional shaming. If your partner or friend forgets the times you sit down and make firm agreements, then treats you as if those conversations never happened, this can be a form of an Egoic Loop in an individual. This is how we live inside our own Ego Minds. Truth takes a back seat to being right. We justify everything without our hearts and wisdom minds and then we believe it. A self-fulfilling prophecy of the single-minded. The removal of outside information influencing your beliefs is an Egoic Loop that leads to more trouble as it locks down on itself.

We believe our own fear. To address these deeply encoded beliefs you find tiny tricks to catch that mind. When fear and emotions rise up in you, notice your primal mind sending you survival alerts. That can pop up at work if someone is rude—fear of survival. "What if they have more power with the boss and tell them I'm no good? I was sick last week, too! Oh God." Catch your fear and remind it that you are an adult, and everything is fine. Nobody cares what Brian has to say anyways. If you are too afraid of that emotion, you won't be able to tell when it's a false alarm. Discover how deep you really are in the loop, and then break through it.

In Malcom Gladwell's aptly name book *Outliers; The Story of Success*, we engage in a much larger thought that was started by a couple having a discussion while at a hockey game. They became curious, because the facts that they read defied their inner reason. This is key. When facts defy *emotional reason*, there is usually a cold case to sniff out. They did their research and aligned with purpose (*where greatest ability and greatest need meet*) and found that these incredible hockey players had become so talented because they were a little taller in grade-school, because they were born earlier in the year. This is Egoic Narrative which causes the Egoic Loop. We believe them to be better than everyone else, when it was merely the fact of simply being a little taller at the right time, forced to focus on developing while being constantly surrounded by people telling them they are better than everyone else. A self-fulfilling prophecy, as is everything in the Narrative.

It's hard to understand the concept that what you are most proud of as an ability in your life might simply be the product of the Narrative at work. It might be keeping you from who you really are. Tiger Woods was locked in an Egoic Narrative of being the best at taking a metal rod and hitting a ball in some grass. He became the master of golf. He was also hurling himself through some very intense inner demons. Then one day, he started to love the game again. We watched Tiger Woods let go. He surrendered. It was his "forgive me for I know not what I do" moment. The next time I saw him golfing on television, he was doing something very odd - he was smiling. He changed. *Shakti* at its best. He went inside and tackled those thoughts buried under a massive egoic structure. That is someone who is willing to tear into their darkest layers, in hopes of finding some truth. You watch many successful people deny this part. They get to the top and they are miserable, so they buy their way through it. He didn't. He walked through the darkness to find the light in his darkest of caves.

"We need to take care of ourselves, we have wise selfish and foolish selfish. Foolish selfish means you only think of yourself. Taking care of others' well-being is the best way to fulfill your life." -Dalai Llama

When we are selfish and in an Egoic Loop, this is when we tend to hurt the ones around us. We are being selfish without caring about others. When we are selfish but connected to our Three Minds, even when we think of ourselves, we are also thinking of ourselves and others at the same time. The part of us that connects and understands what happens to them happens to you. Everything in life will mirror what we are on the inside. Surrounding yourself with "yes people" when stuck in a Loop is a surefire way to develop narcissistic tendencies. You have created a *close loop system* and the only people around you feed your ego, not your soul's desire to grow. You need to find a better mirror.

We have predominantly lived in one Mind, the one that is based in the animal side of our realities. It knows how to survive and how to protect. You realize it functions almost exactly like your pet. Our pets live in a reward-center-based egoic life. They are like humans-in-training who start by trying to understand the concepts of pleasure and pain to navigate their way through life. To understand the basics of being materialized. This is your Ego. A little puppy in constant need of a treat. Loop.

Life is real, don't worry. What I am saying, is that life is really happening, but by continuing to be ruled by the one Mind, a mind that was never meant to work alone, we have fallen into our own delusion. We built it, and we live there. The ego is the strong driver of your life who has kept you safe and alive through all of it. It's time to talk to your ego. It's time to see how your ego operates and it's time to turn on the engines that do that. Try your best to remember this: your ego is fragile, and it's the key to all of this. A sentence that I seem to remind myself of when doing this work, and often, is "If you don't say it with love in your heart, then they won't hear what you are really saying." We all need to start our inner journeys with this energy.

According to the wise gurus, if you are even the slightest bit self-aware, you may be about *a million lifetimes old*. A number so vast we can't really fathom it. Not with one brain anyway. Perhaps with all three you will see things differently…

"He climbs alone, on the mountains of primal grief.
And not once do his footsteps sound from his silent fate."
-Rilke

Our lives make no sounds because they are not based in truth. This is the simulation. We are the artists walking through life talking about all the colors we are using, except we never actually painted anything. The heart and soul are the ones who do the actual painting of this magnificent place. You can see these progressions through The Dark Ages. After going through a long cycle of dark experience, we are heading over into the light side of us again. A much-earned respite. This is the time we will start to understand more about our *internal life*, which will reveal so much more to you directly. You will see things in geometry. You hear the *sound* we call *God*. You see that we stopped being who we are, because we became less aware of it. We've begun creating a perception of reality in our Egoic Minds, and we've been living in that egoic perception for thousands of years, so there is no fault to any of us here as we are doing this together. Surrender to that in your Ego Mind. Our delusion is everywhere. People arguing on television about gas prices, while in an Egoic Loop that fuels that same system.

We have the ability to make life better here…so why don't we? We bury what is best and deliver what is just good enough. A man accidentally invented a process to make saltwater combustible. He was attempting to invent a cure for cancer and invented a process that would essentially allow all of us to fuel up with beautiful ocean water. It was even more combustible than gasoline. An oil company drove right over to his house and bought his patent and stuck it on a shelf. Gone. Tesla invented free energy and yet we still don't have it. Another man invented a machine that turns plastic into reusable fuel. Where did he go? Elon Musk gave away the technology for a system that could potentially be built across the United States and get us from one end to the other, faster than an airplane, floating on air. The possibilities with cargo and shipping, all those gas-guzzling archaic vehicles burning down the highway—gone. He gave us useful information and we didn't want it, yet we drool over NFTs. There is a plant called the Graviola, or Guanabana, that some prominent scientists believe to be much more powerful than chemo. It's a fruit and you eat it. At the time I was researching this it was illegal in the United Sates because "the seeds contained arsenic." They contain less arsenic than an apple seed. You know, apples. This is an Egoic Loop. We have come to believe it without knowing the truth, because we don't have it, so we all walk forward in a confusing silence.

If you want to see an Egoic Loop in the world that mirrors your inner sensory self, look to the *Nile River*. Our most sacred land to each and every single human being alive right now and before. Where that water meets land, that was the moment we began. A large channel of freshwater was created over the nutrient-rich soils of Africa. The great river of life that has been nourishing us all for thousands of years, is now blocked. This freshwater river is now wounded by the *Aswan Dam*. Our Egoic Narrative tells us this is very important for irrigation to Egypt, Sudan and Ethiopia. They create electricity for our cities and "monitor flooding." Picture the Nile like your spinal cord. All your life energy flowing through it. Mass amounts of energy, nutrients and sensory information are flowing through that channel. Your feelings, emotions, intuition. Then you put a dam on it. A block because of a wound. A false belief. A wounded emotional tag. Something built from Ego to "protect you." We literally block the flow of life so we can control it to feed ourselves temporarily.

The dam worked. Life is under control. You are well fed and off to work. Well, except that this original freshwater river for all life is no longer running fast enough to keep the saltwater from the Mediterranean out of the freshwater, so its salination of this earthly freshwater might cause millions to perish. So, the dam you built inside is working for now because it fits our narrative, but it will kill us by keeping us from growing. We lost our ability to align with nature so we can work with it instead of devouring it to our undetermined demise. If we don't learn to become it through learning more about it, then it won't last. So, do we blow up the dam? Do we blast through our old wounds and blocks? Well, now we can't. We've built an egoic life around it and we are dependent on it. Sound familiar? We formed a life where we can't live without the things that will eventually kill us. Loop.

If you blew up the Aswan Dam it would flood the Delta and kill millions. Egypt would no longer exist. The economic losses to agriculture would be estimated at around $50 billion. The loss to agriculture, which is what this giant dam was intended to serve, will be its death. This dam might cause the largest water dispute in human history affecting populations in the millions. And now, we sit and fight each other over it, while we let it die. Our own source of life. Egoic Loop. Now another group of humans is building another dam above this dam. Compounding ego mind. Further into ego lock territory. Once there, we fight to the death because we lost sight of how this works. The idea that we will do things to kill ourselves, before what we are doing kills us, is a tragic loop we can break. We step into awareness. Align with the things around us and the world suddenly makes sense because it's meant to work together. Simple, really. We admit our mistakes. We let every leader sit at the table and decide how to make this work for everyone, and also Earth, so we don't all die. We look at the mistakes and learn from them. Then move forward with wisdom and create something better. We slowly take down the dam brick by brick and only a trickle of water flows in at a time, until the river is vast and flowing life to all of us once again.

Likewise, the Egoic-Minded society blocks information in the pursuit of power by withholding information. This is also something we do to hurt the people who love us. We build a dam around information. We weaponize information. That's why we are all so confused. We only have weird fragments of truth inside a giant spinning ball of people trying to be right about knowing nothing. The Sunshine State of Florida is the most opposed state to solar panels. So hellbent on staying stuck in the ego loop, they lawfully resist using the burning ball in the sky to use as energy, so we don't kill the planet. The Sunshine State refuses sunshine. It's not rocket science. We are asleep.

Our false image of life presents the victory of an egoic win. The inside tells a different story. One of abandonment and lack of true self-worth or soul-purpose. The rich man on the yacht may be empathetically bankrupt. If your life is dominated by Ego Mind and the chaos of the abdominal sensory system, life is going to seem unmanageable. To change, you shift the energy in the abdomen up to the heart-center in your chest, and then roll your mental energy from the front of your head to the back.

Surrender to the past by being curious about the future. Removing your attachment to a belief is quite tricky at first. Especially when it involves our most personal beliefs—religion, marriage, career, political-party, male or female identity and so on. Most of us have closed the loop on those categories. Refused new information in order to protect ourselves from something that happened a long time ago. To reopen your ability to learn new things, you need to be curious again. Believe in yourself to find the answers and make choices based on knowledge.

This is awakening. We start the process of awakening by looking for *patterns*, to open our awareness. Words and ideas don't serve you here. Pay attention to actions, and those actions all have patterns. Patterns become visible to you when you "see the bigger picture" which means, you see things as systems that we are all creating together. This is the golden ticket to awareness. Finding patterns; Sitting in traffic you can see that we all have our individual agendas, we hit the gas and then we hit the brake. We cut each other off and stare at our phones. We are all so focused on where we need to go as individuals, that as a group, we aren't going anywhere. This is our *Egoic Reality*. We are trying to accomplish something so out of touch, that we can no longer function as a whole in our daily lives. When you see the pattern in all of us, then you can see the pattern in yourself. I am selfish on that freeway, but I am community minded, so you won't even notice I was there until I'm already gone. If your life is all cause and effect, when you're driving with your awareness turned on, you see everyone else who is not paying attention and you move around them easily. (Awake versus asleep) They did not effect you by being selfish as you are now aware of it and can see the pattern and adjust easily. Then, you continued to drive with awareness as to not let your selfish agenda affect others on their way to the narrative. Some people don't just think this way, they are built this way on the inside. It's embedded in their core.

LOOP BREAKERS

Nikola Tesla. This great inventor also studied ancient *Vedic* wisdom and took his journey and experience out into the vastness of energy. He went inward to link the discoveries to reality. Inward knowledge to outward creation. He was living in a dual reality. A duality. He was putting himself in a state of authenticity and he found endless energy and translated it to us. Then we buried it. Withholding it from the world. An egoic decision by man to hide the truth which causes suffering to us all, even the ones doing it. One of the most connected creators of our modern world, and even he knew exactly where we needed to look. This was science and spirituality working together. A truth we all ignored. The place where the magic is. The language of Emotional Intelligence.

> *"If you want to find the secrets of the universe, think in terms of energy, frequency and vibration."* -Nikola Tesla

Einstein was a genius. Well, there is no such thing as a genius. That's a word we gave to something larger than we understood at the time. A placeholder that became permanent, as they often do. Einstein was tapped into scientific records in his inner life, and he formed a life of creation to put those pieces together. A master of Emotional Intelligence. The key is in the second part of that, intelligence. Your ability to feel is the genius behind all success. His ability to translate this powerful knowledge was his true masterpiece here. An almost angel-like reincarnation. How funny to be an angel-type soul born as Einstein. Some funny little man that also tapped into the super-science of the Universe and surrendered to its delightful mysteries. He was open to the magic of it. Sometimes just remembering that these magical moments are possible really help us to see what's been there the entire time. The puzzle starts to make sense. He was in touch with his soul with childlike curiosity. Einstein actually said:

> *"Quantum mechanics is certainly imposing. But an inner voice tells me that this is not yet the real thing. The theory yields much, but it hardly brings us closer to the Old One's secrets."*

He found the power of intuition. That power resides within your Emotional Intelligence. It is a super-power. This idea of genius is possible for everyone through intuition. Your Wi-Fi to God. You just need to find your direct line to this information that is already there swirling around in cosmic databanks. I got to a place in my life where I was able to release my addiction to the Ego Mind and was open enough to curiously ponder the idea of being a genius. Most of us know we aren't ready for a thought like that when we say *defensive egoic* responses such as, "I don't like the idea of being better than people." You need to remember how to show people how to be better, so that would start with you. Show us the possibilities of our potential, then share that with us so we can all do it too. To entertain the idea that you might be a genius, we calm the Ego Mind and simply understand this as: if Einstein could do it, then it is possible for all of us. So then, what if I am a genius? What if you are? Not at all things, but at one thing? How would we know? Having an aptitude and an ability is your purpose, your strength, your magic that becomes elevated when you come into alignment. Alignment with self is your super-power. A genius is only someone who learned how to tap into their inner Soul Mind and found *source energy* packed with information. When you align, you become a genius at whatever you become aligned with, not because you are better than everyone, but because you have connected back to who you really are. You are all undiscovered geniuses. So, discover it within.

Build your internal life, the one made of your actual spirit, then build that life with as much energy as you believe you need to make your external world successful. Then things start to get really fun. This is the entry way to exit the *matrix*. You are switching from a thinking mind to a feeling type. You are turning on your Soul Mind. Literally. This will eventually feel like a large silver weighted marble in your mind that moves front to rear, as if to switch operating systems. Stop and think about that for a second. Are you ready to go into this mind-altering matrix of self in pursuit of mastering your Emotional Intelligence? Maybe you want to deal with your own personal blocks and past wounds first? This is not a hierarchy. This is your path that you create yourself and nobody else has the map except you. Start with the easy stuff. You hit little walls and just remind yourself that it's not because you aren't good enough, it's because most of us can't walk out of our front door right now and win a marathon. This is your inner life and it takes work. You train for it. This is your spiritual gym, and you need to get back in shape.

To break the loop, you have to be able to step back and see it. This is *awareness*, and we are going to turn that on. Once you see a loop and can see how you truly feel about it, you then have ideas from the heart on how you want to change life here. You are on the path to becoming a co-creator of your life and you start by breaking the societal loops and trying something different. We change. Loop breakers come in all sizes and shapes. It is everywhere if you are open to receive it. People have been breaking through barriers and helping us all grow since we began. Digging into the ruins to find the true origins of sacred teachings, or simply finding great truth in this crazy inner world and translating that to us all. We need to pick up where they leave off. When you are curious, you set off on a course of learning things again. I was heavily influenced by books, person to person conversations, and even Oprah. People of influence that are seeking truth, which we see in her through her giant exposed heart. Someone driving from their Heart Mind to effect change through influence is a trusted and reputable source, but it still does not make them "right." It just means that's what they have discovered so far. It was Oprah's courage as a real person like you and I, to break through enormous barriers to say powerful things in ways we could understand in ourselves, in order to help us grow. (I was also fascinated by her Queendom. What a hilarious duality she is living in.)

Are you a loop maker, or a loop breaker?

"We get to truth by being able to observe life and gather patterns. They are validated in your heart. For it is wise beyond your mind itself"

During the pandemic I became enthralled with a podcast called *Armchair Expert* hosted by *Dax Shepard* and *Monica Padman*. They are openly discussing things we turned away from in society. Male egos from a more fragile perspective. Masculinity being discussed as a false program that actually injures our boys. Men's inner feminine. Wait—did they say, "Men's inner feminine?" Their male and female perspective living in a heart place is a wonderful influence on us. It helps us expand our thinking. When you put something good out into the world and it affects people to expand, then you are becoming a *co-creator of life*. (Even if the hosts haven't even realized that yet - they allowed themselves to fall into alignment and created loop-breaking energy outward and we resonated with it.) They changed the Matrix.

"It's not personal, it's business." The hierarchy business system is the playground for the Ego Minds. Better and worse, win and lose, survive and kill. Just like an animal. The hierarchy fits the reward center thinking. Some other civilizations thrive and firmly believe in the same hierarchy system that we do. The civilizations who have already evolved through this understand that we only truly function as one collective consciousness. This is where the term *alignment* comes in. Alignment becomes the place of pure surrender allowing you to become the river. You surrender to the love that drives this and all life, and you lie in it like a hammock when you need to sit and think in peace. The Universe is waiting for you to start communicating with it again. It is trying to listen to you. You specifically. Tell it how you feel with real feelings. Tell the Universe what your experience here on Earth feels like to you, send them that information in vibrations because they are not in separation, and they may not remember what it feels like. It is ever-changing. You are the Universal journalist of Earth, you need to report back. Report back long enough and you might get a response. See the world from feelings and patterns and you will see the ways in which to change it.

On one episode, I was led down a path of thought for something *President Barack Obama* said: "People who have had some measure of success and don't recognize the degree to which other people were responsible for that…if I meet some big CEO type and they start explaining how they worked so hard and nobody gave them anything…either you were not paying attention or you're lying to yourself…people thinking that it's me, it's I, I did this, I earned this." Even as the President, he sees powerful people treading the waters of the egoic narrative to no end. We are holding on to this egoic narrative ideal of success so hard that even when we find "success" we are not satisfied. We are still trying to win something. Win at what? *The Egoic Narrative*. You can't win a perception. Having actual success does nothing for us. We aim to raise ourselves in society. To be on top where we will be happy. It doesn't work that way. The success we seek is in resonating with as many things as possible while we're alive. That comes from learning how to feel. When we believe that we have done this all on our own, the dark cave of knowing inside us stays still. We continue to walk in separation. You don't need to force a new belief into a mind that does not want to embrace change. You go to the minds that only function in fluidity and change. There is incredible information everywhere—you just need to find it and listen. Obama was a heart-minded president. That in itself was enough of a gift. The one so many of us lost because of beliefs that prevented us from seeing something bigger. It's only unfortunate if we don't see the lesson.

Your own emotional blocks are always mirrored by the world. *Vladimir Putin.* The man orchestrating the largest Egoic Loop in our current civilization. The Russian Empire is very similar to America by the pride of its citizens and in its desire to be recognized as a leader in the world, a giant ball of fuel for an Egoic Minded government to take hold. A man rises in this belief of the Russian Empire. He rules it. He sees the threat of the West. "Change." Resistance to this change based on past ideology. Old thinking. Past programming of the Egoic Narrative he has sworn himself to believe. A fake war, dead children and a man withering away. He is fighting for exactly what he said he would, to protect the "Russian Empire." No one will tell him that nobody needs him to do this anymore. So, he dedicates his life to an ego war: being right is the only agenda because change is inevitable. Progress and growth are buried in his resistance to change. Despite the world's egoic relations, there is a loop breaker that was missed along the way. Germany's new chancellor, *Olaf Scholz*. A man who changed our timeline in the Russian War. Aware of this or not.

Germany as a society has been shamed into the modern world because of their horrendous past. In the hands of a woman, *Angela Merkel*, they found a modern-day shepherd for peace. She made it the foundation of modern Germany. The new identity backed by matching outward actions. This was not an easy task for someone on Russia's doorstep. They are showing us they are learning from their past and changing. If she was still in charge today, her belief would keep Germany in that state—a state of peace. That is not what happened. In one tiny article in one online publication, this new Chancellor stood on the steps of a very giant mirror. He looked out and said, we will change our position and help Ukraine. This one little moment hit me with the word *Mariupol*. I knew that had this one man's choice been to stay the same, the war would have ended with a complete massacre of *Mariupol* (though the current one is just as heartbreaking). This man broke the loop. He stood there as the leader of a country that was remembered for total darkness, made a promise to stay in the light, and then, stood in that light and said, now we fight against darkness. Full circle.

When Germany expanded its past, so did we. They became whole enough again by not letting their past keep them from being present. Vladimir is doing everything he truly believes in. It is then us who must show the world what we think about war and the ridiculous and continued battle for power. Remember this: every war in our history only exists because two men can't sit in a room together and have a discussion that leads to resolution. They aren't trying to resolve anything; they are only trying to win. When we understand this, war will cease to exist. The war will end when we align with the Russian people and say, "enough." They also need to tell Putin that they are not afraid of the world. Something no one can say to him in a way that he can hear. So, if you had the chance to kill Putin, would you do it? Maybe. But perhaps we would rob the world of a life-changing lesson we are about to finally learn. This is your place of awareness. You see more of the puzzle. What you choose to do from here is up to you. All you have to do is feel your way through it.

Loop breakers are not just people, they are companies too. Large corporations struggle just like you. They resist change. They want to stay the same. They even pay for laws to make sure that we don't change it and make it better, so they can own it. Loop. American business has been functioning by controlling you into staying in one place. Your curious soul, trapped. Watch what happens to corporations when there is a large change in civilization like we have now. They crumble. They are not built to change, so they can't. Rigid in resistance. They can only succeed in a rigged system. The fun part is--these giant corporations are easy to beat. They can't change, but you were built to change. Innovation is their kryptonite.

Our great American institutions do the same. Locked in the game of Ego Kings. Our top Ivy League schools are all masters of the Egoic Narrative. They will get crushed in this transition to awakening because they believe themselves to be the authority, so they have forgotten how to change. The Ivy League schools are in a loop. The more rigid, the more likely they are to fall. A college like *Cal State Berkley* will most likely thrive in the age of light because they have always refused to conform. They stayed open. An open mind gets all the secrets. What we cherish now will change. And it's already begun. For that, we learn to surrender the ego mind. We learn that being right is a trap. So, do something that's better and smarter and you will move civilization forward.

"Don't be right, use reason"

Fall in love with Emotional Reason. Be objective. Make sense of things when you can and use meditation moments when you can't. The consciousness of Earth is based on shared beliefs. Those beliefs can change any time and at any moment because the Universe is always buzzing with curiosity wondering, *"What am I, what am I?"* Align yourself with that again. You are so much more than you think. You have a wealth of powers within you, so let's wake them up and learn how to use them. The knowledge comes from within. This is an incredible time to be alive, the transition from sleep to awake.

SHAKTI

"You must be the change you wish to see in the world"
-Mahatma Gandhi

The Universe has an answer for resistance. A symbol that has been with us since the beginning of the heavens. *Shakti*. It means "change." A core part of this system's purpose, your natural state, is to constantly change. The opposite of how we live now. We believe it's the control that keeps us safe, but it's the control that keeps us still, and when we are still, we fall asleep. Look at climate change as an example here. (I call it a Climate Cycle) Let's say we live in, Florida. Our whole narrative exists there. How many increasingly terrible hurricanes do we need before we hear Mother Nature saying, "Hey my darlings, I'm going through my changes and if you stay here many of you will die." Science is saying the same thing. 30 years and that state is mostly underwater. Or Los Angeles. Ask the officials at Lake Mead. Their words, "In two years we're not sure how we will get any water through the dam. That means all agriculture is gone in Southern

California. 20 million people will also have no more access to water." TWO YEARS? Oh man.

Things are going to get really hard if we don't do something about how we perceive life here. We resist change because Ego tells us to stay and fight—to be right. No, we start to listen, adapt and change. Were we ever meant to stay stationary in one town or in one big city? No, we were meant to change with the tides. To hear the Earth as she says, "Please move to higher ground." So, we resist in Ego and fall down in the flood. If we awaken to feeling, then we can hear the Earth telling us to move on. Something our Soul actually loves to do; change. If we learn to see the path to emotional freedom, then we can see the world in front of us that we need to address. It starts within you.

The *shakti* that nudges us as we sleep pushes us to change so we can evolve, and if we don't, it all collapses back into nothingness. From whence it came, it will return, unless we change it. Unless you change you. You can redefine the heavens from right here on Earth. To be alive, is a state of *Shakti*. The Universe is not just expanding, it's accelerating. We need to mirror our surroundings and accelerate our own self expansion to fall back into alignment. The answer to all resistance is change. Change comes from deeper understanding, not a different habit. Habits change quickly when the mind expands. If we want to move this human race into another era, then we need to feel our way through it. Change your life, then feel what to do next, because feeling, is also listening to all the data of the world and everything in nature. Quiet the Ego, learn to listen, feel your way through it. Amen.

Exhale. Release these thoughts and energies out to the world. Surrender to the complexity of the world around you and become curious to discover it once again. This is the complex realm of real Emotional Intelligence. It is, quite literally, how we can change your reality, to deepen your life here…and right now, it seems as if we are meant to. Or, you can stay in the loop. Are you a loop maker or a loop breaker?

CHAPTER 4

THE THREE MINDS

"Getting to know your body on a deeper level is a very transcendent experience all on its own, but starting to understand your Three Minds feels like doing spiritual cartwheels."

How did you feel when you woke up this morning? You just went from being awake in consciousness to being asleep in your ego reality. I know. Twice a day we already switch from outward to inward. Feel the pull of the egoic mind when you wake up. All the things that flood into your narrative. You just brought the Ego Mind back online. So, which minds were you using before?

I was meditating on my bed in Los Angeles and I had finally finished burrowing through my darkest and most hidden layers of my Ego. I had only just started to open myself back up from this cocoon, this long and difficult road inside myself. Beat down and bloodied, but I made it. I felt naked and confused, lost. I had no feeling of identity or desire to do much of anything. I was leaving the narrative...into nothingness. That place of nothingness-- a treasure trove of answers.

Death to Ego

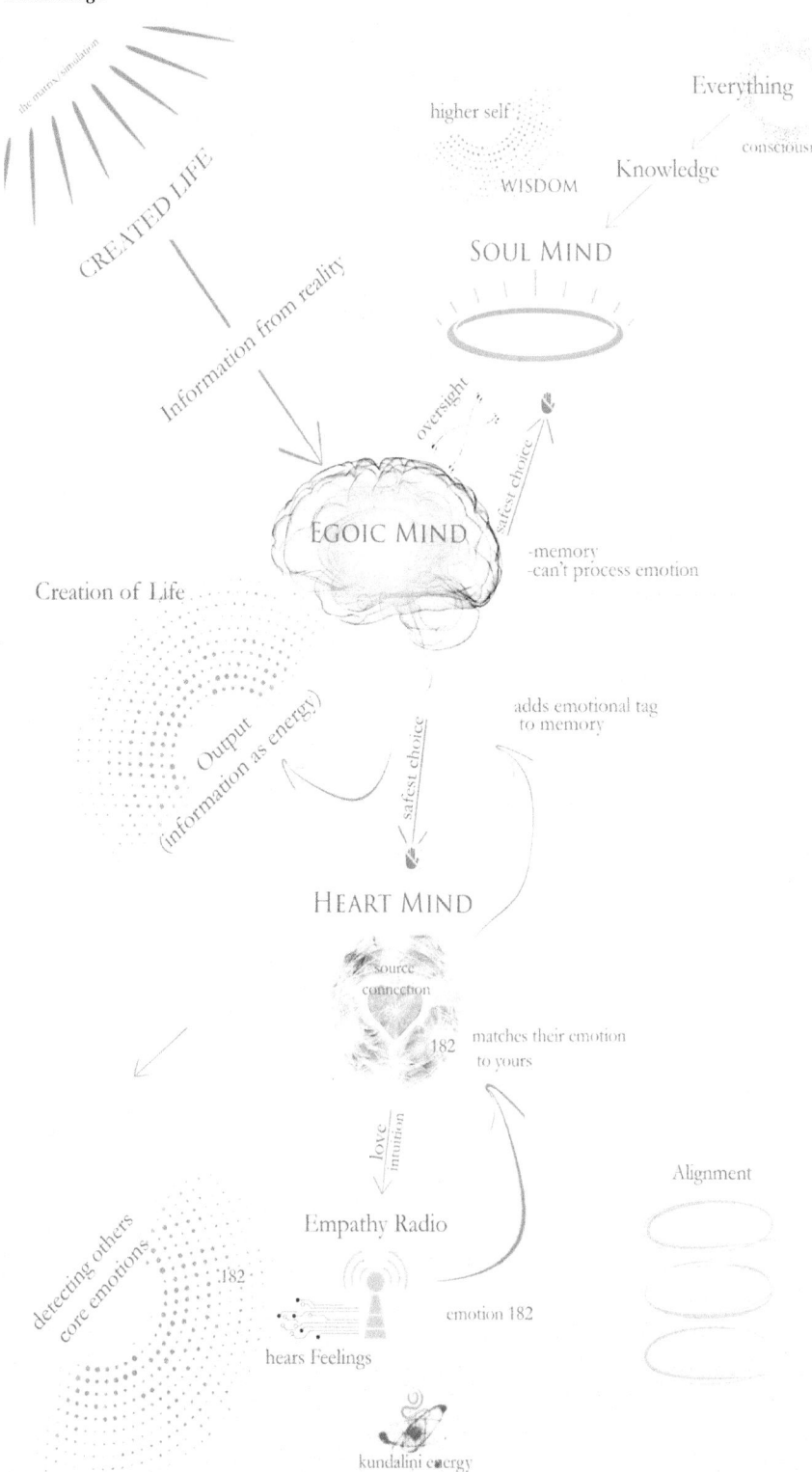

CREATED LIFE
the matrix simulation

higher self
WISDOM

Everything
consciousness

Knowledge

Soul Mind

Information from reality

oversight
safest choice

Egoic Mind

- memory
- can't process emotion

Creation of Life

Output (information as energy)

safest choice

adds emotional tag to memory

Heart Mind

source connection
182

matches their emotion to yours

love / intuition

detecting others core emotions
182

Empathy Radio

hears Feelings

emotion 182

Alignment

kundalini energy

44

That image was the reason I wrote this book. I had no intention of doing so. I was working on development of a television show about relating esoteric philosophies with our truth. Finding answers and solving large human equations for a better civilization. In the middle of all this, I continued doing several spiritual steps to help myself awaken. Then, there it was. The sacred keys to Emotional Intelligence, staring me right in the face. To break the Ego Cycle, we sit and meditate to focus on our breathing in order to calm the mind. The body begins to sleep. You feel something else there and we start to align with it…

Soul Mind, *Ego Mind*, and *Heart Mind*. You have one brain, but you have Three Minds. The relief in this process is overwhelming. The master key to releasing your Ego. Remembering that you actually have three centers of intelligent processing. All of these newly shared origins tell us that *God* was not one thing but the combination of three things. The self born on Earth, the self above and the self that *Is*. Unifying these is the key we are all trying to find. The trinity of ourselves. This is the engine the Gods were telling us to turn on. If you struggle with understanding us as light beings, then start by realizing that scientifically, our brains have a large electromagnetic field. We are a magnitude of energies we have yet to discover. Scientifically, we know about some and *this is all quite measurable.*

Some people can look at the image of the Three Minds and immediately understand which part in them needs the most attention. You just had a conversation with your body. That's a spark, follow it. Feel the changes in your brain. Feel the energy change. We can also start to quiet the mind and feel which of our Minds is dominant.

Soul Mind

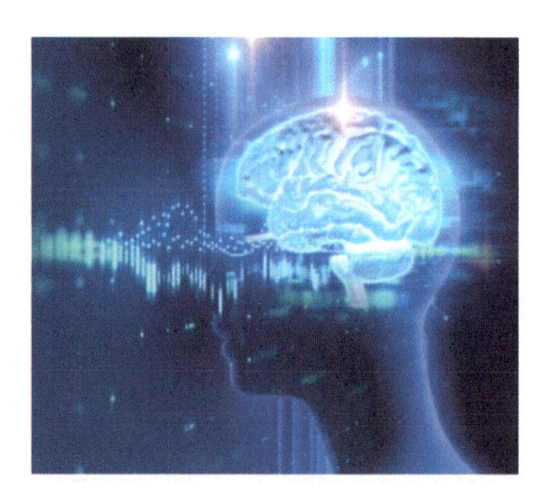

The Soul Mind *(Council of Wisdom)* sees the world and all your experiences in patterns. Mentalism. The Architect. It speaks to you through the *Cerebellum* and receives information from *you* through the *hippocampus* (Ego Mind narrative memory storage). The sacred housing of this mind is in the center. The *pineal gland* sits alone as a single centered causeway. It doesn't have a counterpart here because it connects to something else out there (or "deeply inward" to be more quantumly precise). The other half is not materialized here. Look at a picture of the human brain. The *pineal gland* sits heavily guarded in the very center. This is not your Egoic Mind. This is a central portal inside you. This is how your Soul Mind is translated and transported.

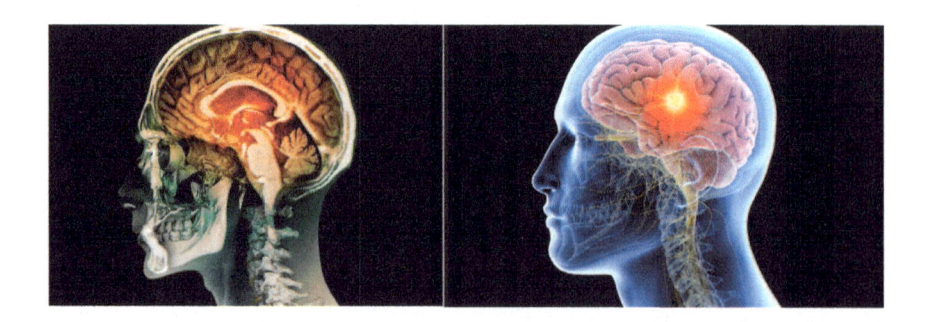

It has wise knowledge-based advice that thrives off new information to charge their debates and contemplate probable results. This is a creative thinking mind that also works in vibration so it can think with feeling. If your Ego Mind can only think, and your Heart Mind can only feel, this one does both. Pow. Awake. One of my favorite things about the *Council of Wisdom* was realizing, who do you think you consulted for guidance when you were designing this incarnation you are currently in? That is who feeds your Council from above—they are your guides that are with you always. The ancient *Vedic* teachings also call this the *Seventh Chakra*. (They understood these body energies over 1,200 years ago.) This mind is not geared to direct egoic success, it is trying to process the wounds from the experiences you came here to have, while also trying to align with your Ego Mind and body so it can bring you into your *purpose*. (Something driven by your Soul and Heart Minds.)

Ego Mind

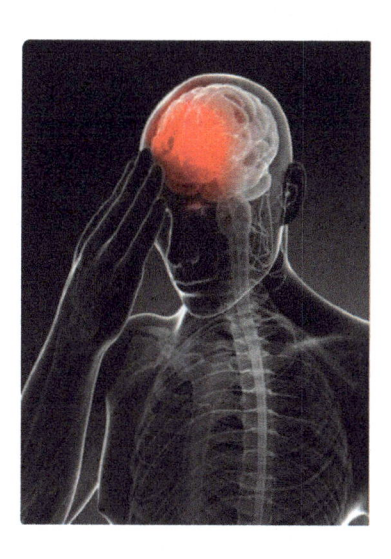

One of the body, the Animal Brain. It thrives in the *frontal lobe, prefrontal cortex and temporal lobe,* all being driven by the *motor cortex*—the one that adheres to hierarchy. It is a mind of one; its only purpose is to survive, here. Something that was born just after you were. It understands packs and groups, it easily adheres to people seeking power, thus our current reality. It's also how we drive to work.

This is the mind that gets you places here. Our light selves birthed into reality and bound to our animal minds. Survive - Feed - Mate. The youngest of the three. A willing participant who vows to protect you at all costs, even if it can't. He is arrogant, she is arrogant. Filled with ideology, but your ego is your friend. Always there for you, no matter what. This is your lion mind. The chatterbox. Use it wisely but give it constant guidance and oversight. This is a processing mind. It can function alone only processing the outer world, or it can listen to the other two and they can all play together. Take small notice that this one, quite astoundingly, does not directly correlate to a *Chakra*. This is not your real mind that connects to *God/Source/Akasha*—it's the other ones that know how to get you to *Om*. Here's a rough thought: most of us meditate in our egos! I know, heartbreaking. Because we only considered our primal mind, we are trying to have this experience in reward center. "I want to see something! Show me God, reveal thyself!" It was hard to even know what we were really doing in there. When you step back from this primal mind, it's an "Oh, wow. Got it." Moving on.

The best way to understand this brain as only one of three is to look at the reference photo and see where memories are located. People can lose all cognitive function of their brains and bodies and then before death they suddenly awaken and have full access to their memories. This is very well known in Western medicine and is often referred to as *terminal lucidity*. i.e., "In a state of assured death, you are suddenly fully aware." Your memories are not stored in your brain. That's a funny thought, but they are not. The brain uses the hippocampus as reference, but you sent all that real information up to the cloud. Picture it this way: take out your phone and look at your Instagram photos. They are photos you chose from all the ones in your phone to represent your egoic life here. (Find humor in this because we are all ridiculous.) These pictures on Instagram were your ego filter to create an egoic persona to the egoic world (loop). The pictures on your phone are your "human brain." Your brain is that cell phone. You can look at all the pictures in your cell phone and try to understand your life, but what we are doing here is connecting you to your cloud database so you can suddenly see all the pictures from all the moments in your life, which means you have entered your own little state of "aha's." This is the state of clarity and awareness. Much easier to understand things in the cloud then on Instagram.

Heart Mind

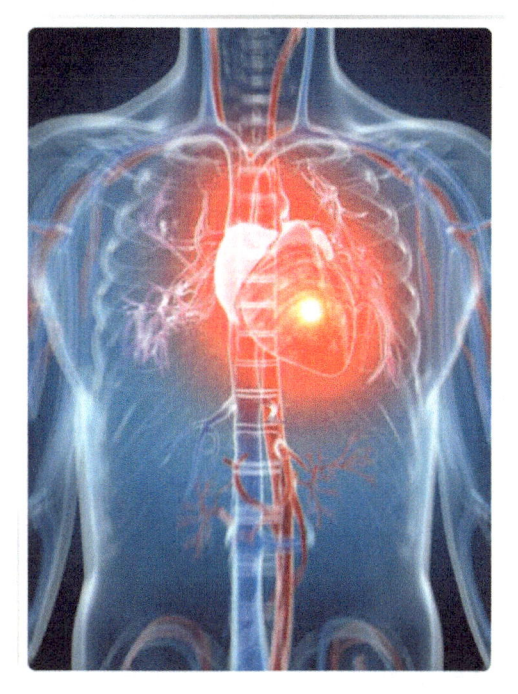

If the Soul Mind is your soul, then this mind holds your spirit. Inside your heart chakra is the direct rhythm of life. Cue *The Lion King* soundtrack. Your connection to Maya itself. If the entire world and all of us are vibrations, this is the central hub that feels and hears all of it. If you would like something scientific to chew on, your Ego Brain has a giant and powerful electromagnetic field that extends past your body. Well, your Heart Mind has an energy field sixty times that of the brain. The power of your heart creates the biggest energy field you have, extending multiple feet outside of your body and all around you.

This is your vibrational wi-fi system, your satellite dish that connects to our emotional selves. Interpreting this information is Emotional Intelligence. The language of your Heart and Soul. This information is processed through the Heart Mind and then attempts to send signals to the *Amygdala* (the emotional processor in your animal mind.) It is processing infinite amounts of vibrational data. This Heart Mind is incredibly smart and wildly powerful. It is your *boom stick*. When you "have good energy" this is where it is pumping out of. It sparkles with playful curious energy. It is constantly pinging the energy being sent out by every single person around you, always. It grows by being with others' hearts. It senses vibrations and then learns something. You are very sensitive for a reason. This is the hub in which you truly process the life currents happening all throughout your life. The one that desperately wants to bond with others. That is its function, and it is based in *unconditional love*, no matter who you think you are right now. This is your inner love bug.

The information gathered is so vast and so sensitive that our untrained egos guard themselves from it with numerous barriers. Inside your chest is the power center of connection. This is a feeling mind. The ancient *Vedas* call this the *Fourth Chakra*. (The satellite dish would then be *Chakras Two* and *Three*. The vibration sensory system.) When you see the difference in the location of the *amygdala* vs. the *frontal lobe*, you see that these parts of our memory and feelings are processed closer to the *pineal gland*. Our natural self is to be closer to *thought as energy*. Our separation comes from our desire to live in only the front part of our mind that processes our outward reality. When you sit and switch on your Minds, you can feel the pressure from the front of your mind calm down and then energy from the back of your spine up the neck starts to flow. You can choose which hand to use to pick up your cup of coffee, and you can choose which Mind you would like to use in your life just as easily.

For a moment of easy gratitude, think about the thousands of years under a darker life cycle, now being removed into something new, and you are alive for it. The great waking up. This is the product of the fourth dimensional energy we are moving into. We have graduated preschool and college and we're about to join the light world. This is a transcendent moment if we choose to be awake for it. May sleeping giants wake.

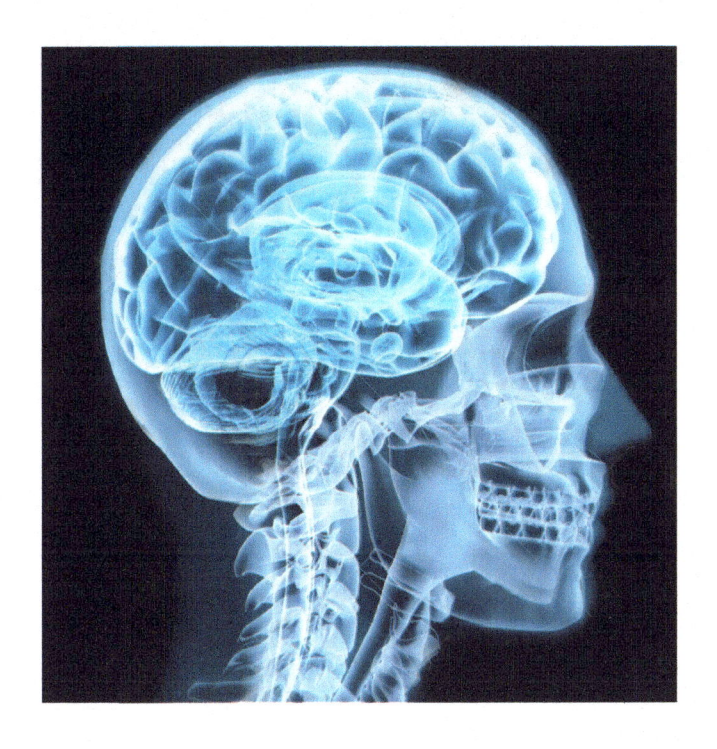

If you draw a circle around your animal mind, that is our wonderful ego. You can see with a circle drawn around it we now have a *closed loop system* all together. This is the state of a narcissist. It is not listening to the Soul Mind or the Heart Mind, or even the manifested reality of the external world. It is processing its own fabrication on a loop. Recycling information and delivering it to the world, as your truth, your addition to the reality we live in. A truth you believe because you have no other source to compare it with. This Ego Mind cannot feel feelings with understanding; it thinks like an animal. "Do I use it or do I attack it?" It knows lust well but is quite shy around love. You can't think a feeling, and neither can your ego. You have to feel a feeling.

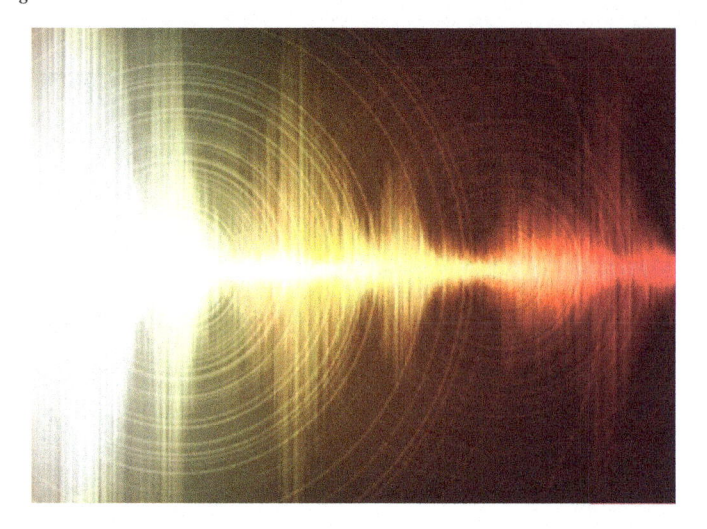

The empathy radio is sending out signals and receiving them. It can detect an emotion in other humans. This sensory data is connected to your intuition above your Soul Mind. It is also the sensor for understanding other people, and not always in the way you think. Say you are speaking with a loved one and you tell them an important boundary of yours. Their empathy radio signal will feel your hurt or importance, it will send that specific tag up to their memory of this conversation, and then head off to memory storage. Your empathy is in your *Second* and *Third Chakra*. Your sensitive emotional polarity system. A narcissist will not actually tag that moment with a real emotional tag because it can't feel them. They will forget.

Your sensory system is quite complex. It acts as a moral and emotional satellite station. Information comes in through polarity and then heads up to accountability, heart, mind and soul. The *Second Chakra* is processing through *polarity* and your *Third Chakra* is your *accountability*, so you can see how easily a signal from your empathy could be turned into guilt as it passes through accountability. Think of your empathy sensors. A big emotional tag from the past would then be, let's say, "Deep Pain #211." That sensory wire #211 was so painful in the past that you tied it off. Retagging means you sit with that emotion and release resistance to a bad memory that keeps you from seeing that data. You aren't trying to fix your past memory—that is in the past. What you are truly doing is letting that feeling back into your heart so it can be a part of you again. You are accepting the emotional reminder. Imagine you have a million sensors in your stomach area that feel. Each one has a different perspective. If we have been tying those off for so long, we are only using a limited number of sensory tools, which means we don't really understand what is happening here.

If your loved one always forgets things, especially an important boundary you express, they can forget because the emotional tag that marked it as "important" is missing. Their ego did not understand it because it does not effect their hierarchy agenda. It's about you, not about them, so they have no need for it. If the signals from empathy don't make it upstairs, they forget. The ego remembers your promotional meeting, but it forgot your daughter's birthday. Your heart never forgets her birthday. Most of you in a deeper Egoic Lock are no longer listening to the signal vibrations from the feeling areas, so we become emotionally deaf and blind. You have removed a massive part of your senses. The ego will not want to be wrong about this either. It will fight to be right even though you know it's no longer warranted.

If you look at the top right of the image you can see *"Knowledge"* and *"Everything."* This is the *super-consciousness*, down to *consciousness/soul mind*. The realm of love to the realm of light and energy flowing into your Soul Mind. *The Holy Ghost*. Outside we are flesh and bone, inside we are light inhabiting a human body tethered to Earth existence. When we leave this body, we travel to the other realms as light and thought. We all know this and deny it at the same time. You can see the off-kilter nature of our minds. That mental world seems scary, until you understand it. Sit in the calm and fear has no place there.

Alignment would be to draw a straight line up through the head and down to the *Kundalini* energy. All minds in a row aligned with the chakras and base energy. All systems go. We are in a sense going inside to do some internal stretching to release the tension and let these minds flow back into alignment.

If you draw a circle around all three of your Minds, you look to "output." It's no longer based on egoic information from the matrix we have created in our outer world. It is now self-generating code with heart, mind and soul. Reaching out into the vastness of higher self, finding knowledge, aligning that with your purpose and all beings. You're now sending that energy out and you have just broken the cycle. You have changed the Egoic Loop and created a window for us all to do things in a more mindful way. Think about it this way: in this cycle when information comes in from the manifested world into your Ego Mind, that one mind decides and then you put that into your own words. This is when we innately know someone as "fake." It's not connected to the real things that you are because it has gone through a closed loop system. You hear the words, but your body is picking up on a different vibration. These are a set of alarms detecting deception. Deception is separation, truth is connection, so we are already hard-wired to sense someone living in Ego.

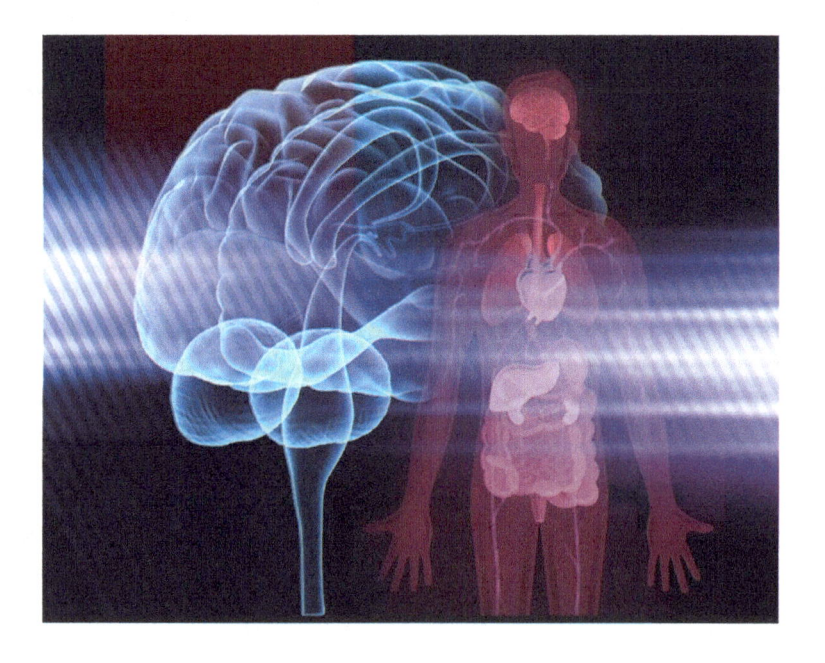

As we have decided to socially shame our sensory selves, we have started to turn off those sensors. It's not really who you are; therefore, we are being fake—inauthentic—because we were all too afraid to be human. Fake is a hurtful word we have produced to describe the opposite of what we want, and we believe it to be real. This is the term "delusion." So, let's walk through that. "Fake" is an Egoic Block resonating out to us in words only, and not with matching vibrations. Someone is not being fake; you are allowing yourself and others to act inauthentically by shutting down the system that cares. Now, we turn them all back on…

The Heart Mind is the first mind to get hit from below with the energy in the base of your spine we call the *Kundalini energy*. The powerful energy that generates your *life-force*. This is the engine room that pulses your *Source* energy up your spine and activates your inner being and your inner potential. If you were to pull energy from above, this is the on switch to the chakra power plants. When you just had incredible morning sex and walk into the coffee shop, you have this energy about you and people feel it. It's that love energy pulsating out of your heart vibrations. Then when you open your mouth, it attaches itself to your sound vibrations and goes out into the world as well. You are literally radiating love.

This would be the state you would understand as being in a higher frequency. This type of energy is something you don't have to release right away. Carry it with you and let it start revving up the Kundalini generator in your spine. Use it as fuel. You can stay in this energy and let it change your perspective of the world to one of connectedness, but if you try to start with making only your Ego Mind keep you in a state of "happiness" —again, there is no real vibration attached to that, because it came from the head not the heart. You can't cheat your sacred vibrations that you are sending; they are too incredible to keep down. They tell the truth and only the truth. You are generating love and letting it send a current out into our reality. We can do all sorts of things to access this state in meditation and yoga. You get to the same place. You have an orgasmic energy you can carry around with you. There are several ancient practices well known today that can help loosen that powerful energy at the base of your spine and send it up through your chakras to help activate your *Boom Stick*.

Being open minded. The ability to adapt is the great marker of a Three-Minded individual. Adaptability takes constant understanding, probable outcomes, and multiple options for change. You desire systems to function properly. You want the work environment or home environment to improve. It's life energy. You suddenly want to be involved in its process and effect it. This is the beginning of becoming a co-creator of life. And all of this started by cleaning your house with your own hands. It's been building. You are waking up again. You start seeing avenues and possibilities to resolve broken systems and form new ones. Even in your relationships. You see the connectedness of life and your plans not only benefit you, but also benefit others as your *Council of Wisdom* makes probable outcomes based on everything around you. It also taps into your higher self, which means these probabilities include a little magic, too. Something the higher self can see that maybe you can't.

Give yourself permission to let positive energy flow through you so you can make this world better for yourself and for others. Do not hold this energy forever. Energy is also found in money. You were not supposed to grab it and hold it close. You were supposed to share it and make things. Letting money energy pass through you is the essential joy in having wealth. You become a wheel of potential for all of us.

"As I wish for myself, I hold the belief that the same is available to all of my fellow humans and all life in the Universe. I further deepen my connections to all that is and serve all by holding a higher vision of potential." - Ninth Dimensional Pleiadian

The Heart Mind and Ego Mind are like rivers that flow into your Soul Mind. The more we let them in, the more we get. The less we pay attention, the smaller the channel. Ignore it long enough and the connection to Soul Mind dries up and gets overtaken by the ego. If we are wounded enough, we might blow up the river between the two and build a dam. Egoic Block. You can see this as an entire system. We call it the nervous system. All these circuits intertwined with the Three Minds. If we are driven by a V-8 engine, then we are currently running on about three cylinders.

You can see in the image of the Three Minds that the ego brain has been sending signals to the heart and mind, but they are the safest choice. They are egoic choices. The Soul and Heart Mind can't use these. These are not truth. Those major life choices we just made, never processed through our hearts and minds, only our ego's best guess. Same works with the Heart Mind and Ego Mind. The Ego Mind sends thoughts to the heart. The heart responds with feeling. The ego is protecting you from feelings, so it shuts it down with rational thought and surface facts. You can see how important it is for your ego to have information that is both based on emotional memory and on large calculations by your *Council of Wisdom*. Authentic thought vs. inauthentic thought.

The Egoic Loop, as it pertains to ourselves and our realities. If you draw a circle from created life around the animal brain and back out to created life, this is the Egoic Loop. This is what we call delusion. As you can see, we are taking information from the reality we have already created (the Matrix), processing that within our animal brain, and what we do next is crucial. After we process, we send that energy back out to the world to be created. This is the *closed loop system* we live in now. When you hear people say you can "become a co-creator of your life," what it really means is that you become a co-creator of life itself. We understand the outside world as reality, we process it through our Ego Minds as a majority, and then we take that *life-force* energy coded with ego thoughts and send it out to the world to add to creation. We are creating this egoic loop.

Summary of the Ego Mind

The Egoic Mind is all the neural pathways and electrical charges acting as the central control center for your life here. Your ego is the primal version. Your body and Egoic Mind were made to be here together so you can embody it for a lifetime.

This Egoic Mind is rooted in *Maya*. Earth. All the powers and strings that come with a life on Earth. Your animal spirit. "As if imposed on a race." That was not an abstract thought. People who are more aware of what we are talking about also know this brain to be referred to as the *"reptilian brain."* That takes a bit more information down the line to understand but have the information. Let all this throw seeds into your mind and then stay open and see what grows. Ego lives in your brain center and has most likely been running things since your biggest wound. It is there to protect you and only you. Your ego knows, just like a lion, if it's you or them, you choose to survive even when it means others will die. Complete opposition to who we really are. Our animal brains can get things done and keep us safe, but they can also keep us stuck.

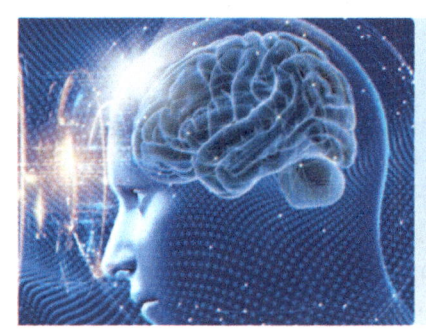

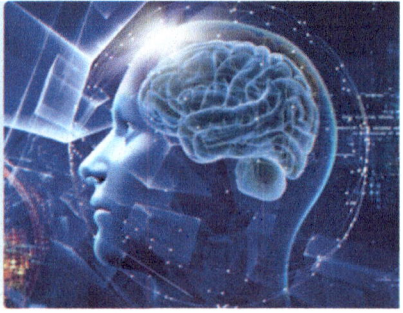

Ego is the master of lists and organizing your life, hence we are so easy to control. It loves control, but is easily dominated into submission, as a good pack animal would be. Align with the pack. Plans and rules are its guiding light. You can let your Ego Mind take a right at the stop light or sit at the light quietly until you get an instinct of what to do next. Maybe you went left, stopped at a new shopping center and met someone who will end up being one of your closest friends for life. Ego control vs. surrendering to the alignment of you.

Our morals are basically our ego's version of its perception of wisdom. Morals aren't truth. They are constructs. I often find when I'm stripped down to my bare core, I seem to align with most of these morals anyway. That's why they are still in our minds today. But I don't believe in someone else's morals. Your Heart Mind takes care of that for you. This is when we say, "Why did you do it?" and you answer, "I don't know, it felt like the right thing to do!"

How do we help each other if we're so ignorant to even the initial approach to our powerfully sensitive egos? I even removed ego from the title of this book numerous times thinking, "how would anyone under their ego's control get this book other than having a desperate loved one hurling it at them?" The ego can hurt people deeply and form a direct reasoning path diverting you from blame, hiding you from accountability. A Law of the Universe.

Summary of the Soul Mind

"True Self-Analysis is the greatest art to progress"
-Yogananda

The Soul Mind is where the *you* of you resides. The one that is also being fed by the master plans. The one driven by creation mixed with a soul's playful and creative abilities. It is working in vast amounts of data you have collected over your lifetimes and computes probable outcomes. It can also gather data from your higher self which understands others' experiences throughout time. Anything in life can change at any moment, so even though you have decided this path is most probable, it can still change, and you will be ready and willing to adapt. It feels and thinks and has powerful abilities to process your heart and your ego simultaneously. This mind is the actual creation center of your life here. Not the one you're in at the moment.

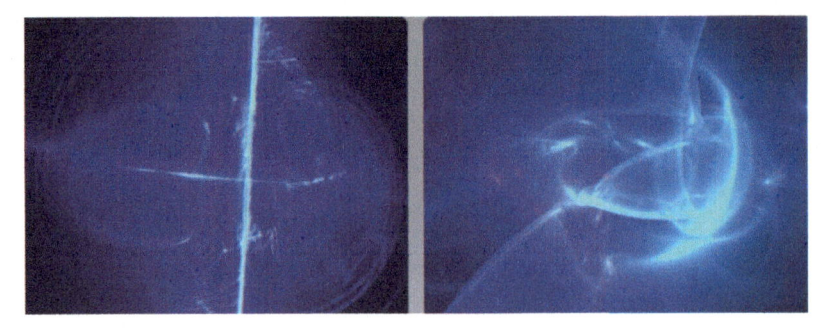

This is your *Council of Wisdom*. Above the head there is a pulsating globe of gold energy. This is where your higher-self taps in. Your connection outward to the Universe itself. It takes in data and works on long form equations about life. It knows anything is possible, but it also knows you have to work in synchronicity to all other things, even if our ego has long forgotten that. This Mind is rooted in the *Seven Laws of the Universe*. If your ego wants to win, this mind would be able to stand back and see past the delusion of winning and find out what you actually want. Its sensors are shooting outward toward *consciousness*. It's a great exercise to picture your Soul Mind above your body. Not too far above the top of your head. A quiet humming ball of you as golden light, your truest thought power as energy. When you picture your Soul Mind up there you can feel the current from your spine going up and around the back of your Ego Mind. As you practice seeing this mind, you are also practicing the understanding that you are more than your body. You are a being of light first, tethered to the body second. All you have to do is be open to the concepts of your own minds.

Your Soul Mind is one of two hemispheres—one conscious mind and one beyond that. We call it the *subconscious mind*. This is your creation mind. It swims in the abyss of the soul realm. You can access some of this creation energy purely in an Ego-Minded State. We would not know the difference. Think about how society rushed to the idea of manifestation. It was a craze and the first thing everyone wanted to manifest was a Mercedes. Catch your Ego Mind right there. Manifesting is to sit in the now, access your Soul Mind that is connected to the creators and contemplate how you want to insert new code into this Matrix. If you are trying to manifest your future, you see that it doesn't make sense. Anything can change so that is not possible. This is where you understand you only have right now. Manifest today right now for now, then let the Universe reorganize itself around your manifestation. For all of us.

Change the Matrix not just your material desires. Do both. What would you do if you could manifest something for all of humanity, something real, or a way of living we had never thought of before? The Matrix loves new ideas of possibility. What would you do if you knew how to create an entire planet? Now step back and look at your egoic choices and your soul choices here. When you really try to come up with a better way to do all of this, you can't. At least not at first. Instead, you find yourself doing something different. You are falling back in love with the complexities of this life because you have seen its incredible structure and surrendered to it. A brilliance connected in symphony so we can experience dark and light at the same time. I just can't top that.

Summary of the Heart Mind

―

"Truth will ultimately prevail where there is pains to bring it to light." - George Washington

You're a triangle of energy going above you and a triangle of energy going below you into the Earth. Your spirit is tethered to her too. Why do you think she created the exact amount of gravity for us to stay grounded? We are communing with her. The Heart Mind is where all of your deepest feelings reside. Your emotions are like a powerful magic wand that we have no idea how to use, so we shoot spells everywhere at random. Good ones and bad ones. Bam. "Sorry." Poof, "My bad." This is one giant feeling center. It does not want to feel alone. It needs to feel and compare to others or it doesn't feel alive. It has a radar called *empathy*. Not only is it constantly swimming in all of the emotions of the world and the people around you, but it is also relating to everything—plants, animals, people and even material objects. This is the main source of our experience here.

Death to Ego

"Get rid of what you like, only keep what you love."

We use the term "With a heavy heart." Well, that is actually true. All these memories have our emotional tags on them. Picture each tag blocking that emotion as a metal cap with a warning label on it. You have capped so many emotions that your heart is literally heavy, so, to raise your vibration, you lessen the weight on your Heart Mind. You start to look at those past wounds and allow that emotion back into your life for fuel to change something here. You just got a little bit lighter.

This mind is communicating in feeling and vibrating with the world in frequency. Your Heart Mind is held most closely to your physical self, but it can still communicate with your higher self through emotional knowledge. It can feel how you treat your body, and your body knows how your heart is feeling. Tend to them both. This is the one that wants to experience this the most. This mind loves to listen and feel the world around it. It's trying to have a symbiotic relationship with everyone. This is the power center that connects us to everyone. This mind is what drives us into relationships of any kind. The most important part of the Heart Mind is that it's your sacred center for all the love you hold inside yourself.

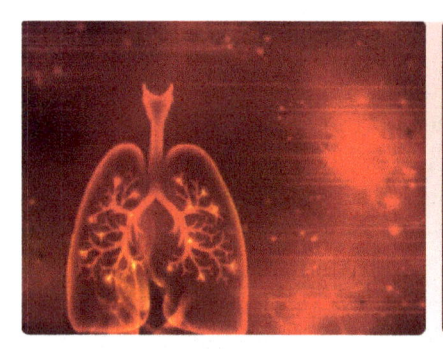

"It is only with the heart that one can see rightly; what is essential is invisible to the eye."

- Antoine de Saint-Exupery

Alignment of the Three Minds is about mindfulness activation, awareness of self and consciousness. These power centers belong to you, you can ask to align with them however you want. You are asking your higher self, your inner self and your brain to work together. Use your empathy more. When you look at the empathy radio, you see its signals going through the heart. You see things differently. You see things more because your feelings have knowledge in them. Someone in an Ego Block has turned down those signals inside themselves because it can feel so volatile and painful in there. By working through old memories and changing out *emotional blocks*, you start to open your heart center. This allows information to start flowing again.

Without your heart center open you don't have access to your empathy radio, and your ego will then generate its own beliefs and send that out to the Universe. This is the difference between an *authentic life* and an *inauthentic life*. As a society we have all been taught to shut these down. Ignore emotions and feelings. This is the blockage of the Heart Mind. You start to release all of these blocks when you can isolate the most mysterious of them all…the Ego.

PROCESSING IN THE THREE MINDS

"I believe creativity is an inherent part of everyone."
- Kermit The Frog

Processing in the Three Minds starts by acknowledging the minds and working from there. Breathe into your chest and open the Heart Mind. Relax the Ego Mind and let the energy from your spine slowly tingle up to the top center of your crown. Exhale into stillness. Walk through every single part of your body and relax it with an inhale and exhale. Silence. Now release your restless thoughts from Heart and Ego and send them into your wisdom center. Let all these intelligent processing centers contemplate one important thought from all sides.

Ego Mind

The Ego Mind is built in survival. Check in by breathing and see if your ego is rumbling with thoughts. Calm it down. Put this to sleep and then check in with the other two. Breathe to disengage your sympathetic nervous system. This engages your parasympathetic system. Calms your organs and digestive system. You have just entered "Spiritual Mode."

Soul Mind

With this Mind you are looking for patterns, data and fusing that with philosophy (your soul's understanding of the Universe.) Do you have bigger thoughts about how you think the world is doing? Now think about what you would want to do differently. The answer doesn't need to be substantial. Maybe it's a passion to build luxury homes with zero waste. Imagine what you would want to do here. The two primary sources of information come in from the Ego Mind, life data, and then the heart. All the vibrational data you are collecting. This is the mind of awareness because when you step back from animal mind, (one data stream), you sit in your conscious mind, which is gathering data from multiple sources and processing them together. One stream; asleep. Two streams; awake with clarity.

Heart Mind

Does this help or hurt all of us? And how will that affect *you* deeply? How does this feel? You had a part in this moment—how do you really feel deep down about it? How would you like to tag the moment happening right in front of you? Is the heart producing an accurate tag for what you believe? Probably not. Each mind is taking in different data from different sources. We're looking for access to our emotions that are being blocked by expired emotional tags so we can access these emotions again.

Flow-State of Awareness

Data Going Out
"Thoughts"

Conflict Data
Conflict Replay
Conflict Strategies
New Fears
Life Goals / Conquests
New Interests
Work Plans and Strategies
Status
Safety
Pleasure/Lust
Warnings
Enemies
Assets

Combines All new data with previous Data and Purpose

Wisdom Mind

Awareness

Perception Of Reality

Egoic Mind

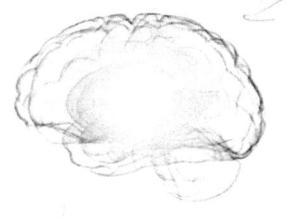

Co-Creator of Life

Emotional Knowledge

Heart Mind

Data Going Out
"Feelings"

Other People's Feelings
Your Feelings
Vibrational Reality
Interactions
Intuition
Empathy Data
Connection Signals
Body Well Being
State of Nervous System
Earth Connection
Divine Impulse

By addressing the memory attached to it, you remove the block. You are removing the blocks little by little so you can see more colors. More colors means more information. Spend time allowing memories and emotional data to swim into this mind together. Then let in the Egoic Narrative and process it all at once. Accept the emotions, feel them, then breathe them back out to the world. "Om Swaha." You have just processed a moment with a Three-Minded self, stamped and delivered to the right place. What a spotless home you have there. Well done.

Three Minds in life & meditation

It's 12:43 am and I've been working on a movie for sixteen hours, and this is day five straight through. Every second of sleep counts. As I arrive home a car is blocking my driveway. There's a club nearby. I ran some scenarios: "I have to tow him. Sorry, bud. I'm doing adult stuff." I could choose to be angry because I am assuredly right or I can laugh and say, "That's a lesson for you, not for me, buddy," and move on. Neither of which are truthful. That all happened in my Ego Mind. Justified and decided.

While I'm now watching the car actually get towed, I feel guilty. Then oddly happy. Am I enjoying this? I felt strange. I sat and thought. I do feel a little guilty, but they did make a mistake and that's their lesson, so I'm right, wait, but I also feel bad? Why should I feel bad? We didn't make a rash or emotional decision. You do feel bad about it. Why? Right there. I could rationalize that it's not my fault so I can ignore how I feel about it. Capture this moment and process it. Acknowledge you feel, because you care, breathe in, exhale it out to the world. Now, why do I care? I walked through some old memories of waking up and rushing off to the restaurant only to find a giant metal boot on the wheel of my car. (That was also the day I learned you do have to pay all your parking tickets, or they come at you like the mob.) Then I had another memory. I remembered waking up to where my car was supposed to be, and it was gone. That sinking feeling. Complete loss of your identity as a human that can no longer function.

I was feeling bad because I was part of an experience that would possibly create those feelings in someone else. I was relating with intuition and emotion. I was feeling and thinking all together. I allowed myself to feel the guilt and associate the empathy. I then checked back in with my actions, all was well, so I released the emotions. Sent them back out to the world. I tagged this experience with the proper emotional tags and sent it off to storage in the hall of understanding. I was right and they were wrong, but had I simply left it at that, I would have stored some guilt in there, untagged and thrown on the floor. I don't need any more guilt in there. Something inside that says you hurt people and something outside me says you don't care. I do care. We do care. My Heart Mind shared an emotion. My Soul Mind shared my past memories to help me understand, and my Ego Mind had the car towed. You are not wrong because you feel, you are more on track than the rest of us. Do it more. Say something personal to all three of your minds, then quiet the minds and listen.

A few days prior, I was hitting that place in meditation where all you seem to be accomplishing is staring at the back of your eyelids like a crazy person. I was resisting what I was looking for. The root of some very deep pain. I brushed off the resistance and walked around my memories anyway. All tied to a specific thought. I turned on an artist who was singing ancient tones. Something happened.

As I stood in my room, I closed my eyes and began to switch into my other Minds. Even though my mother is no longer here, I still carry an intense pain from childhood. I finally asked myself, "Why didn't my mother love me enough?" That is not something I want to talk about. It's hard for me to blame her as a failure as a mother, because she was to blame, and she wasn't. I saw all the missed moments, the lack of consistent nurturing. I was mostly alone growing up. Then I stepped back. The thought came in, "Do you think they didn't love you?" I saw how my father allowed us to go with him as he ran away from life by always looking for somewhere else to be, and a woman to be with. This man allowed himself to be the caretaker of children in which he was very unequipped to do. My mother was the one who grew these children, not him. All those years apart spent under a mentally abusive father. This was not intentional; this was how he handled it. I could see what she felt now, because I could sit in his actions and his unawareness of others. What was best for the children was not part of his repertoire. I looked at all the times I arrived at my mother's house. She would always light up. We would talk for hours at night over tea. She was a brilliant mind. She devoured books by the stack. Straight A's all the way through college. We talked about the complexities of life until the sun came up.

Sitting in her brilliant little school in Encinitas, California, she cared not that all the parents were famous athletes. She was a teacher. Always. I saw how much she loved me. I saw all the relationships I have had. So many incredible people. So, then it was me who was not feeling loved even though I was surrounded by it more than I wasn't. Then I started to feel loss. A feeling of really deep loss and heartbreak. Like I had lost a wife, it felt like the love of my life was gone. (I've never been married, at least not here.) I went searching for that…for someone who doesn't remember how to cry, I was flooded with tears. I was angry that this world was so mean all the time. I was heartbroken by our choices to be selfish. I was mad. I was sad. I was in pain because I could feel the love of all of it, and our ability to ignore this and hurt each other. I was heartbroken for all of us. I had been losing faith in us. It was me who was treating the world like an angry child. I sat in tears and let them come. I let my mind drift into some other pretty powerful places of understanding. Then, I quieted everything down and all I could see and feel was a giant ball of energy in my heart. This is where I had been hiding her. Buried under pain I had when I got here. Taking it out on the world around me. This understanding made my heart feel lighter. As if a shackled weight had been removed.

That was the most release I have ever had in a meditation session. (All standing up.) I then stood back and said loudly in my mind, "We can release all blocks associated with being unloved? You have been loved so many times and so dearly, it is time for you to do the same." I sat in some deep breaths and exhaled directly from the heart. I didn't give away my sadness, I shared that sadness in a vibration attached to my understanding of it. Twenty something years of pain, gone in twenty minutes. It is not gone, it is understood, therefore, there is no confusion of pain. Only clarity and acceptance. That brings you back to the place in the center, bittersweet.

This transpired into my outward life in a funny way. I got a heart crystal (I'm open to anything) and have been carrying it around in my pocket all throughout my days around Los Angeles. I touch it and send a little mind laser to everyone I see and shoot them an "I love you" thought bomb. Then it became "I love you, I hate that you cut me off, your driving sucks, but I love you." I learned that I have taken my wounds and used it to punish the world for their actions. So, I realign and always start with love, then whatever happens next is part of this whole experience. Accept, understand, release.

CHAPTER 5

EGO IN RELATIONSHIPS

"Relationships are where we go to feel, not to hide. Get emotionally undressed and stand in the nude."

You can't teach someone how to love you, but you can help them remember that they are *made of it*. We can't force these changes with thoughts and plans, we feel our way through it. This is why perspectives are so key to all of this. If you want to understand your loved one, then sit with them until they explain their entire perspective, of you. Your Ego is your greatest adversary in any and all relationships. Calm the ego and speak from the heart.

The key to all relationships is Emotional Honesty. Emotional honesty comes by finding "center." You are no longer stuck in Ego Mind and have become easily honest within yourself by always allowing yourself this truth, "Relax. We have no idea what we are doing here." Surrendering the Ego Mind. A place where you can identify all of the emotions at once, so you are no longer afraid. These emotions are coming from your Heart Mind. These are sensitive sensors. If we are in touch with our emotions, we can stop and check in. If we are out of touch with our sensory life, then we attempt to force our lack of feelings onto other people by using a thought-based life. Even people who express their feelings are becoming more and more "passive-aggressive." (The term itself has become one of shame and hurt instead of an emotional alert.) Passive aggressive. Words that we use to shame people's attempt at an expression of their true self. It's the same as calling someone a coward while they are struggling to be brave. If emotions are new to you, then start by refraining from shaming other's emotions, then learn something about your own.

The biggest issue we all have in our relationships is not having the ability and the words to describe the massive parts of us that feels. Authenticity requires honesty, and I don't mean honesty about what you are thinking, honesty about what you are feeling. The problem is, we don't even know how to really talk about our feelings in a way that produces growth-oriented results. Especially men. We push men away from their emotions from the very beginnings of their precious childhood. We push them away from their light being and sensory selves into ego. I have a lot of adoration for men who find their emotions because it's not easy in this society. See the connection to the laws of the universe? What happens when you go farther and farther away from love? You are in more pain. So, by design, men suffer an incredible amount of pain because they have been pushed away from their emotions since birth. They need to express emotions if they want to learn to truly feel again. So be gentle. They need to feel to heal. That's really it. The opposing side of the masculine experience would mean the feminine would then stop living numerous aspects of their lives in emotion and start building outward with their minds. This is integration. We take what we have learned and create with that knowledge. We make something new.

Notice how profoundly different we operate on a general sense. It is vast. So we understand we all have no idea what we are doing and try to unpack the layers of our relationships with all this new information coming out. Think about an ex-partner that you loved. We can't just turn off this deep magical love we shared with someone else. So why do we all pretend like we have? Because we are only supposed to love one person at a time. We want someone else to declare they only love us, forever. In a place where we are meant to love even the smallest ocean bugs. We are not being honest about how we feel and that is killing us inside. We are hiding from ourselves.

We treat our relationships the same way we treat diplomacy around the world. We spy, gather information and attack when threatened. Egoic Loop. War doesn't make sense anymore, outside and in. We're all smart enough to know it's a war of trying to be right. If we can see the patterns in the world, then we can see the same patterns in our relationships. What we do is being mirrored by the world itself. It's brilliant and it shows us both sides. The good and the bad. So how do we stop trying to be right? It's somewhat easy when you make peace with holding yourself accountable. Look for your own patterns that keep you from being authentic and honest. You don't need to tell anyone, just pay attention to where you lie and why. Being honest is tricky at first and we get confused, so our ego takes over.

When we are confused, we rationalize. Ego Rationalization is another great trick of the great and mysterious Ego Mind. Rationalization is really based on who we can blame. Our obsession with better and worse. Right or wrong. Some of us actually believe that right or wrong is how we navigate life, right? These are all based in the egoic hierarchy. Your rational thought only distracts you from your heart and soul. Just like an ego can assume false empathy, rational-based thinking acts like wisdom, but it's based on made-up concepts that completely skipped the stage of trying to understand different perspectives to gather more information. Rational thought then simply transforms into a blind assumption masquerading as fact. Without more than one perspective you are driving your relationship with your eyes and ears shut. Emotional Rationalization is something quite different. You are weighing life based on love. That is a game changer.

If you have been avoiding a hard conversation, then that conversation happens tonight! You just say it. My Sicilian family says, "Put the food on the table." If you have something to say, then just say it. Go home, ask them for a minute to talk and say it. *Put the food on the table*. There it is, now we have to talk about it and make some adjustments. We might yell for a little while, but we will eventually process what was said and move on to some pasta. (Italians don't yell to be mean, they yell what their hearts are saying.) You wake up by starting to be honest about how you feel.

An easy place to start living from the heart, is to observe and learn how your defensive system operates, and why. Start to notice the patterns. Those are leading you to an answer. Rationalization blocks you from accountability, which means you won't find true empathy. Here's an example of a rational relationship; when someone tells you they feel empathy and you know they don't. They will respond with things like, "You don't know how I feel!" Well, technically, yeah, we do. Empathy does not mean you can understand someone else's feelings, it means you can feel them, in you. That is real empathy. It's an ability tied to your sensory field. What they are experiencing is sympathy. Ego's version of empathy. Sympathy is a thinking mind and empathy is a feeling mind. Empathy is a sensory superpower, and everyone can do it, but it starts with catching your ego and learning to express your deeper senses. Male or female, old or young, matters not. We gotta feel our way through this.

If you want to check in with what mind your using as your primary function, think about who you blame for things. People "who've done you wrong." What is that boyfriend or girlfriend doing? How is the world wronging you? If you are sitting in any place of blame, then you are sitting in your Ego Mind. Your Soul and Heart Mind understand that perspective is key to everything. If your perspective is blame, that's only one perspective. You're not sitting in bittersweet, you're not sitting in "center" where you can see it all. You're leaning to one side, "It's their fault." You can identify what hurt you and how it hurt you, but this is a shared experience, so it's nobody's fault. *Your pain is specific to your wounds that lead to your purpose.* So…it is never them. They are a conduit of sorts, but the pain is your responsibility now and you are learning how to process those less admired feelings and handle it like a champ.

Meditation is the key to learning how to stop being right. It's your path to wisdom. Sit in silence and ignite the rock concert within. When you learn to create stillness in your body and thinking mind, blame does not exist. That's the mindset you want to be in before having any sort of incredibly deep conversation with a loved one. To release things, we need to understand them. Why do we desperately hold on to blame? The primary reason we hold blame is because what we are really waiting for is the acknowledgment of how we feel! We just need to know you get it so we can all move on. But you don't, so we can't. Loop. It's amazing how many relationships carry on in stalemates that go on for years. Someone got hurt, then the fight came, then the relationship based on right or wrong devoured you into your corners. All these sad and hurtful years because we can't throw out the idea of being right and simply see and acknowledge someone is having feelings and we are part of this. That's it. That's why when a typical male finally admits to being wrong their partner is barely affected by it. When you can express their point of view back to them and feel it, oh man, your life just got so much better.

The quicker you can isolate how you were wrong, the quicker you can find a resolution, new possibilities and move forward a little more in lockstep with your soul and your relationship. Resistance and denial block creativity and reason. You need those for problem solving. You need those to create possibilities. Master the art of resolutions and solutions. These possible resolutions are great to discuss with other people you are involved with. Share "possible solutions" first. Sometimes you can spark their ego to want to do the same. I once got my stubborn Sicilian father to admit everything he had done wrong as a father, because I started by saying all the things I was bad at as a child. He was jealous, so his ego started taking responsibility for everything he did. I laughed inside while watching it happen, but I still took that moment and received it. It was most likely the closest I would ever get to some acknowledgement of our shared past. This practice will change your relationship. Suddenly you've switched from attack mode to something else the ego likes, a distraction of knowing and a competition of honesty. The ego likes to take credit, but that doesn't serve us in any way.

We haven't learned our own process of how to accept that fault doesn't matter. We are all different. You have your own specific wounds and I have mine. If somebody is doing something and "they" are hurting those specific wounds, that is purely affecting you in a way that does not affect everyone else at the same depth. So how can you blame someone for how you were built? For the wounds that lead you to your entire life's purpose? How can you blame somebody when your own sensory signals are activating in an attempt to tell you something? Blame is where we get stuck. Accountability and responsibility starts with you. This is also one of the chakras. Something we need to understand as one of the pillars that create God within us. So, kind of a big deal. That is a piece of God/Source/Akasha/Om. It has been separated so you can look at it and become it. Accountability is awareness of self. Awareness of this shared experience. Be accountable for other people's feelings and your life will start to change.

We all make boundaries. Verbal statements about what we will and will not tolerate. That right there. Tolerate is really a place of what annoyance or abuse level you are willing to absorb until you explode with pain from the inside out. The obvious solution is for people to be less emotional? To care less about what? Life? Or perhaps it would be for the one continuing to bother you and push your buttons…to stop doing it! We are all responsible for this moment in time. We are all responsible for getting each other out of this darkness, out of the mud, but we start by being honest about how we feel. Start to identify the other person in your relationship by their base operating system. Are you a thinking type or a feeling type? A thinking type has very abstract principles and theories for decision-making. You can see how the thinking mind struggles with principals and theories. That is not what it does. Feeling types are not about deciding emotionally, but evaluation of the human emotional impact. Cause and effect of your energy mixing with all the energy of the Universe. Impact. The human emotional impact. Why would it do this? Why would we be calculating how this affects humans and humanity on a deep level? This is that *Akasha* current at work. Everything in the Universe created by concept alone.

Passive aggressive emotions are a function of the sensory system that is feeling things and trying to express them, but is very uncomfortable on its own, because your senses are afraid. Possibly of you. It really means that you are injured and hurt, and your emotions are not being heard when they are expressed. You are uncomfortable. You start walking through different actions in an attempt to get some correspondence. Passive-aggressive emotions are actually a sign that there is something that needs to be discussed by all parties involved.

There is an emotional and sensory block that needs attention. Somebody is not doing okay on the inside. They are lashing out because they think you can't hear how they feel. Those are signals. Passive-aggressive is not the fault of the person doing it, it's in the person receiving it. If you can see somebody acting in a passive-aggressive way, understand that they are hurt and it probably involves you. Take those signals as a sign that you can try to find some resolution, an attempt to heal the situation. Doing nothing is a stagnant soul. All the world wants is a micro-change. Do something different.

As a feeling type, the more you argue with a thinking type about why you matter will effectively go nowhere. They need to unravel themselves a bit. At the core of them, they have to go inside and find their past blocks in their past wounds that have created this disconnect inside of them. They need to go inside and find the thing that says "core operating system. Focus on self. All that matters is me." They have to go switch that out with Heart and Soul Mind so they can say, "Oh, there's something so much bigger than this, bigger than self and I'm connected to it." Then just leave the open space. For them to find alignment and true fulfillment in their life, they will need to switch that operating-system, or they will most likely die consumed by the Egoic Narrative and be left with a little hole in their soul's experience. We are all meant to be awake. Leave no one behind.

If that person will not adjust and will not change, if they are the person that does nothing, you have found yourself around a stagnant soul. A stagnant soul surrendered to a life based in Ego Mind. They are on their own path. That's okay. You can't change somebody's core beliefs, but you can help people change. That is a gift we all have. If you went to a nursery and bought a little tomato plant, you would come home and plant it. Put it in the sun and water it. You want it to grow. If you live with someone who won't change, that would be the same as walking out and seeing a bucket over your plant. Your loved one is quite literally saying to a plant, "don't grow, stay just like that." A stagnant life is a silent one.

The difference between words and actions is everything in a relationship. We only need to hear words when we can't feel something. One could live a beautiful life in a relationship with no words and only feelings as action, but no relationship would survive with words solely built in Narrative. We say words like, "You're totally overreacting," or, "I'm worried about you." Being concerned for someone on a deep level is empathy. And your empathy, if turned on, is always active. So, everyone would always be worried about everyone. The world is in a lot of pain. Truth is seen in your action of this feeling, not the thought as words. If you want to heal someone, you have to become them. You feel what they feel. You need to sit in what it feels like to be around you, from their perspective.

When you are trying to sit in their point of view, you aren't as affected or judgmental about yourself as you thought you would be. You're excited that you can relate and feel what they are feeling. When you understand, you always naturally want and desire to find resolution. A lot of people who stuff their emotions and are stuck in ego blocks use the term passive aggressive. Again, people who are doing these things love to accuse others of doing it. People who are passive-aggressive love to accuse people of being passive-aggressive. People who are emotionally stilted love to accuse people of being overly emotional. The broken mocks the brave…because they are hurt too.

So much clarity in your relationship comes from eliminating the current style of communication, because you are not using the same base operating system to move through life. Our sensory system is being poked and that means our Heart Mind is trying to tell us something. We annoyingly call these "triggers." We hate the word, but we all have them. What are triggers? Triggers are your sensory alarms. These alarms are based on your own *emotional tags*. You have things saved inside you as memories that you want or need to revisit. Anything that comes near this zone activates the emotional alarm for that specific feeling signal. Your system is saying, "Pay attention to this moment and then go inside and further investigate what else is attached here for you." They are signaling things you care about the most. These are your guides. Triggers are actually "sense intuition." Somebody did not trigger you, your sensory system sent you a signal. You are not triggered, your senses are actually thinking. It's badass. If you have a series of wounds that are impactful to you and somebody around you is pushing those buttons, stop and find a space to go inside and feel it. Follow it like a diver who swims down peacefully into the abyss. If you struggle with the idea of the Heart being smart and aware, then sit with this; your system is alerting you on an energy level to emotional and situational experiences. It is listening to everything you can't hear.

All these years we've struggled in our emotional relationships… and maybe we just needed more words. Having new words to finally describe the layers that make us. *Senses, Emotions and Feelings. Heart Mind, Soul Mind and Ego Mind. Empathy, Sensory Alarms, Emotional Tags. Thinking Mind or Feeling Mind. Council of wisdom. Ego Blocks, defensive resistance, single minded, egoic narrative, sensory beings, the loop, divinity, purpose, wounds and soul intuition.* Understanding the different levels of Ego Mind. Just as the oneness of us all was unpacked into seven pieces, so becomes our relationship. We can now unpack them in new ways and see what patterns exist from there. The place of awareness. A place of multiple perspectives other than just your own.

THE NARCISSIST

If someone doesn't have their basic awareness turned on, you are then communicating with one giant simulation that is going to try and hurt you to win. To be right at all costs. You have challenged the ego to a dual of the death, or you have submitted to it. We submit to other people's egos all the time. The Ego Lock forces their false reality onto other people purely for their own protection and gain. It is the most selfish thing we do. An Ego Lock needs professional help or some sweet meditations to try and focus on the breath until they calm the mind and ask themselves this wonderful question: "If I am not my thinking mind, then who am I?"

They will struggle to really listen, and struggle even harder to know anything about the emotional truth of a shared experience. Their Soul Mind has been cut off. This is not because they are bad and broken people. What would be the point of negative past trauma manifesting in your incarnation as a narcissist? Because how could you learn anything if you don't have any access to the things that teach you? You would be in *purgatory*. A place of delusion they believe is real. They cannot be broken if they are understood. Help them break the loop.

We can see the shame and fear attached to the word Narcissist. Something we all fear, a societal death sentence. From a wisdom place we can see the Ego Lock. Someone who incarnated this way or developed this because of unattended wounds. Someone in an Ego Lock leaves their Heart Mind and emotional memories in chaos. Over time the egoic brain will start to relate all connection to the heart as dangerous. When this closes, the ego attempts to generate a perception of happiness. It only knows how to do this by rewarding you. It's hard to see these past wounds now allowing our ego brain full access and full control. We sealed the giant vault door and locked the tunnel. The Soul Mind informs the ego of this tragic error, so the ego severed its ties to the Soul Mind and swings the giant iron vault closed too. "Traitor." There goes awareness. Now you are left with an egoic loop that fully believes its own egoic perceptions. A life of rational thought. This is a compounding process. It can layer itself further by generating not a false reality, but a system of false perception in their mind. If you are not connected to your heart, then you would be validated in your Ego Mind: "They are out to get me, it *is* us versus them, they are going to try and take me down and I won't let them!" Everything we do will validate these claims because all we want from them is to understand us, but they cannot feel us anymore. We just want accountability. Something we cannot get. They can only rationalize how you help them or how you hurt them. They are living in a simulation of a reality they've created in their Ego Mind, now running on loop.

Think about the western approach to our minds. If you are different, then your mind is broken. It's crazy, not you. When we look at patterns, we can try new tactics with people quite easily and with vastly different levels of thought and understanding. When we start seeing someone's ego, we suddenly focus on their behavior and thinking patterns. We're collecting data for our *Council of Wisdom*. We start inspecting, we poke and challenge. The ego warrior in us puts our hand on our sword. It feels eerily like we innately coax out their most monstrous ego snake. When we turn a corner and see a narcissist, our instinct is to kill it. We will stand and fight it to the death or live forever in its shadow. When we can see it from a wider angle, one with more information, we see that all we are is a mirror of shared experience. We are all hurting each other because we don't know how to talk about who we are.

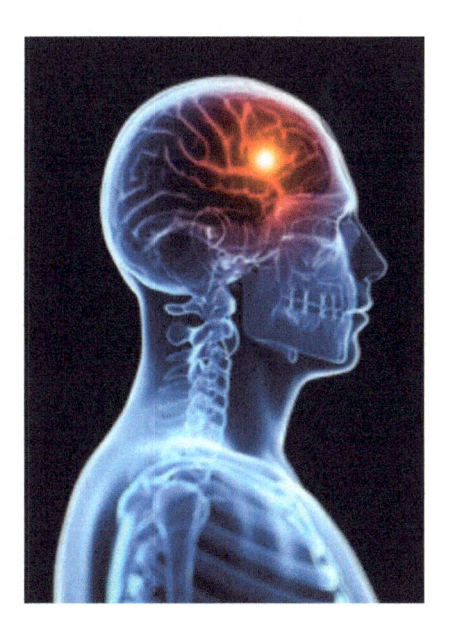

Being in a relationship with an Ego Lock (narcissist) is really about looking at somebody and seeing if they have any accountability for themselves. Basic awareness of their output in patterns. You are not looking for accountability in the sense of if you are right and they are wrong, but an accountability for all sides as data points to think about. Are they paying attention to their words and their patterns? Are they naming more than one possible solution? Do any of their solutions seem to take other people into account? It doesn't matter if someone does things once or twice—you are looking for patterns of consistency.

Don't weaponize this. When you call them out for their actions, are they listening or are they just rattling that through the Egoic Loop and spitting it back at you as something that you did? If you are speaking about feelings, are they speaking in rational thought, catch that and talk about it. Learn a new language you can speak together. Remind yourself that this is essentially begging for ego death, which can sometimes mirror an alcoholic. They may need to hit their own rock bottom first. Think about something you believe in deeply and the emotional place you go when you are at a hard crossroads in your life. Many have some version of God or some other Guru or entity they pray to. Now remove that core belief. There is nothing left to believe in. No more guiding light. There is one core difference between you and a narcissist: they have replaced that belief in something higher, that place of love, with the belief in *self*. Without that they have nothing. This can be open space. Go find a new understanding to put in there.

Nonetheless, all relationships require compromise. Conflict most often appears when a compromise is not honored. Someone is being hurt and the other person is unaware. Discuss how you will deal with conflict. Describe your previous patterns. How you tend to deal. *Give them your emotional recipe and do your best to get theirs.* A relationship's true foundation is not made of unmovable strength, it's not even a foundation, it's a connection of love and support in a lifetime of complete fluidity. It must remain fluid. Remove the dam of resistance by going three inches inward. Start there.

Free the Ego

The Ego Lock individual needs to unlock the valves and build a new connection to their Soul and Heart Mind. The least threatening starting place is allowing your instincts to make little choices throughout your day entirely based on feeling. When you want to open up a little more, meditate like it's a workout. Only inverted.

By sitting in meditation, you are using the science of the body's spirit mechanism to go into "spiritual mode." This activates physical responses that can help break ground on a new tunnel to the Soul Mind. This is the breaking of the Ego Lock. Not regarding the mind as an "ego mind," but by simply following a basic trendy meditation, the body is tricked into this spiritual mode and now the Soul Mind starts stirring. Don't force anything. The lion goes to sleep and the soul wakes.

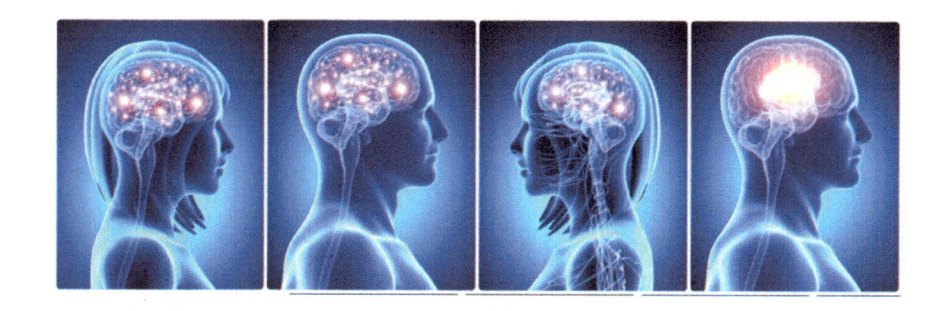

Allow these little meditations to become a welcomed habit based on the physical benefits alone; less cortisol and more serotonin is usually reward enough to stick to it. Let the inner process heal slowly. At first on the surface and then deeper. Just sitting in meditation will break an Ego Lock if they are able to start quieting the mind. Putting the body and mind in a state of calm is the best way to coax out your Heart and Soul Minds. You will notice this step is working when an Ego Lock starts to talk about new insight. New insights that have a number of possible solutions, none of which are loosely based on their next great idea for their own success. They are starting to trust that it is okay not to know. No one will hurt you this time if you don't. We have agreed that everyone is wrong. Forgive us for we know not what we do. This is a beautiful thing to see, even if it's small. These little steps in their internal life are quite massive. They are starting to shift to probabilities instead of an ego-based agenda. This means they are starting to get their awareness back.

Death to Ego

Most narcissistic tendencies would put us in the lower frequencies around the abdomen. When practicing simple breathing techniques, focus on your lower abdomen. Try to pull that energy up to your heart center. Focus on the heart center. Underneath the base of the rib cage. A furnace of loving light. Adding this to a simple meditation will start sending signals to the Heart Mind that you are thinking about switching all your energy from your lower base system to your heart chakra, where it opens back up to the world again. Little meditations will work in the background of your life. Over time you will notice when the ego pops up. You have accessed a wound. Something not to be resisted but to be re-understood now that you are so much wiser from this place of awareness. Don't rush the heart. The Ego and Soul Minds can accomplish a lot of healing in the way of understanding the world a bit better. It's easier for an Ego Lock to start with the outer world, and then relish in their ability to relate it to themselves. They have inadvertently started the other half of them.

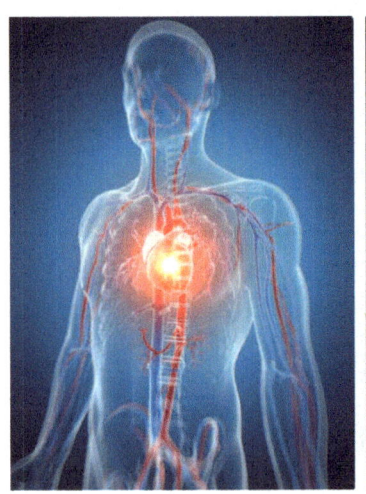

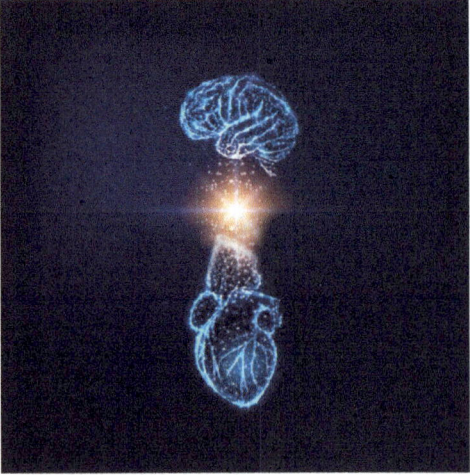

See the others who challenge you with your precious empathy once again. If you can imagine losing all your instincts, losing your intuition, all the while believing you had them intact, only to find out it was a simulation in your egoic mind? That's heartbreaking to imagine. Be gentle with others. (Something I am learning.) The ultimate test for us all, other people screaming at us from the mountaintops saying, "Please figure me out!" And we all turn our backs and move along with our day. Again, we choose the apple.

If we want to be authentic and heal, we also must allow others to do the same. Make the inside look like the outside. When we are broken it's up to all of us to heal that person. Until we learn to accept this, we can at least start by not using a hurtful word on people's open wound. So, we adjust out of ego and back to heart. We even change the way we speak.

You are an egomaniac.

You're in an egoic loop.

You are a narcissist.

You're in an ego-dominant operating state of mind.

A narcissist is a wounded animal, and they bite. What does the Pitbull do when it's been locked up and chained behind a shack? It's hurt and blind to the pain it can cause because it can't see past its own pain. It wants to love you, but it can also destroy you. See the wounded animal and you will find your way through.

If you understand, then be understanding. Don't tell, show. If you don't know, learn. If you aren't learning, listen. If it's time to go, then go.

Most of us struggle with memories attached to people that are no longer in our lives and we carry those into our daily relationships. You can heal those wounds by starting with the people who are here now. I've gone through old memories and struggled to find answers, so I went to the actual people involved, decades later. I wanted to listen to everyone, tie up the frayed wires and "move on." You can't move on from things you don't understand. The questions you have today started a long time ago, so you need to go find them. In AA they have a practice they use to heal by asking for forgiveness from the ones they hurt. That is not what we are doing. We are saying that society is lost in their egos, so we are going to talk to people if we have a wound, because that is how humans really are. We are there to listen and ask questions.

No matter the time or the social approach, "put the food on the table." If your ex keeps calling, give them the conversation where you are sitting in your center mind. We allow ourselves to be available for healing so that when we need to be healed it will be open and available to us. That is not always pleasant at first for either party. Remind yourself that you are asking them to open up because you have something you are working on for yourself. You are being the good kind of selfish—you are trying to heal your heart. Anyone alive should be honored to accept that, but we use it to unload our mixed-up pains back at them. Create space for the ones who were hurt in your shared experience, so they can heal.

PROCESSING "The Ex"

I was at a crossroads at sixteen years old. I was in a town that finally felt like it would give me a chance. The previous town told me that algebra was college level math, and when I walked into 8th grade here, I was told that I needed to be done with algebra by high school. This town seemed to get it. Finally. Phew. Safe. My mother of course was deciding to move again to chase her theory that, "the grass is always greener." I chose to stay, alone. On Tuesday I was a teenager, on Wednesday I was an adult living on my own with nothing but spirit and large amounts of fear and young powerful ego. Something that would become so essential to my survival. Something that would also keep me further and further away from feeling like I belonged anywhere. It trapped me inside myself to survive what would have broken me to unbearable pieces.

One day heading back from Molly's pool I saw a girl in my rearview mirror. My heart skipped. She became my high school sweetheart. The story gets a little more Oregon from here. The town had a gypsy-like foundation and a scholarly outlook. Children with rough living situations often found another roof to sleep under. After a distorted path of couches and inner misery, I ended up moving in with my high school girlfriend and her mother. We lived in separate rooms but shared the upstairs to ourselves in their beautiful home right in town. I still have yet to fully grasp the entirety of this moment. Those will take me longer than this lifetime to unpack.

Over my senior year her mother and I became very connected in this almost silent spirituality, as if she was the only one in the world that could really see me, and my reflection of her back. She was there for the heart parts. This was new. She found me one very late night in tears because the thought of my parents never coming to a soccer game had completely engulfed my hidden but very broken heart. This mother was the bright warm loving creature I needed to stay alive. She was a life mom to me when mine was otherwise occupied. I was the promising young teen who was delirious with childhood strife. She was the rebellious woman intent on seeing the best in the broken. My girlfriend and I were teenagers living in the same house as partners and as siblings. At some point we broke up and I went out on a date with my friend's older sister. Yeah, it got messy. Her best friend had a crush, so she hooked up with mine. We were classic teenagers with emotions and egos. It was more than any of us knew how to interpret.

The time came to leave for college. I was working in a bar and grill and had decided this was going to be my life now. A short order cook at 18 years old. The waitress, Heather, walked up to me and said, "I'm leaving for San Diego tomorrow, I will pick you up at 5 pm and drive you to Santa Barbara, and stay until you find a place to live. You are not staying here in this bar." Sure enough, at 5 pm the next day there she was. I was a ball of tears. Leaving the only partial nest I had found. I of course got in the car. I always stepped into change. No matter the fear or the heartbreak.

I played the part well. Calling my dear love every night weeping and longing for her. Six months of this. There was a lot of *Tracy Chapman* involved. Winter break finally came, and I was headed home. As my flight landed, my friend called and told me my true love was sleeping with her boss from the ski-shop. I was gutted. I saw her later that night sitting in the ski shop manager's little red Ford Fiesta. She was in his car…and he *had* a car. Gutted again. Three decades later and my high school sweetheart is still mad at me. I've sent presents. Thoughtful gifts. Letters. Met her in Mexico once for lunch. I was always in love with her. Not as a girlfriend or partner, but from these incredible moments we had when we were younger. Something in our hearts. I could feel it. I really knew her and saw her and our souls loved each other. Before the mess there was something beautiful. I never forgot that part.

Cue current time and two years back, in the middle of the descent into my own darkness, I was fishing for unresolved parts of me. I tugged at that thread for decades. Unknowingly poking for the truth. Why was she always so mean to me? I was texting and calling and trying to push her buttons. She was the same, always engaging me, but always somehow treating me poorly. I wanted to know why. Those memories and this relationship had convinced me that I was a bad person, I just had no idea why. If someone I loved could not even like me then I wanted to know why so I can learn and change. The information was never given. I was an undesirable.

Through some of my half-drunk ramblings, she started to respond with anger. My poking was working. She started to tell me that she didn't like me, as a person. For whom I was, and that she never had. I asked her why. She started rambling angrily, "You don't even know me. We don't know each other. You have no idea who I am. I don't like you because you just…because I just never have…I don't like who you are as a person." There it was. "You don't even know me." Well, then how could she possibly know me? That does not stop her from treating me poorly. Oh, this is buried and mixed with some other much deeper wounds, because emotionally, it makes no sense. Got it. My ego was quiet so it didn't react to the insult. Something so important here. Had my ego not been standing next to my heart, this would not have been a healing moment. It would have hurt me even deeper. My Soul Mind was looking at patterns, my Heart

Mind was aware of the friction I was causing. She was stumbling and searching and found nothing. She didn't have an answer. She didn't have an actual reason. My high school sweetheart who cheated on me when I was a little kid in love had convinced me that I was a bad human being at my core, and she didn't even know the reason why. See, we are all ridiculous. This is us.

When I stepped back, I could see that nothing was what it seemed. To any of us. Clearly, this was about the relationship with her mother. This was between them, and I was a symbol of that to her. I was being blamed for their relationship and became the scapegoat to their own unresolved issues. This happens all the time when you allow your life to be open and messy. Whatever trauma she had with her mom, she had transferred blindly onto me. Punishing me and keeping me at a distance. For thirty years of actual life. I chose to walk away from my relationship with the one mothering human I have left here.

Our mental ability to transfer our own trauma onto other people with misguided memories is exactly why we want to get in there and take a look around. It was a bit transformative to see how someone could hate me for so long that I started to believe it. A belief that was based on old wounds between a mother and daughter. She and I may have had some drama, but we were teenagers. At our core we are kind. So, I walked away because it felt like the right thing to do deep down, not because I wanted to. I sat and healed myself. Walked through old memories with her and loved them once again. I prefer not to let the few misunderstandings cloak all the deeply incredible memories that came too. I can carry both. The happy ones and the sad ones, because as a whole, they are a precious experience from my past. Forgive us all for we know not what we do. I don't need anger, because I'm hurt. I don't need to be hurt if I understand. If I understand I can heal. If I am healed, then I can heal others.

If we are concerned with being right or wrong, we would never see the truth. I unknowingly caused her harm by having a flagrant relationship with her mother like a best friend, and never understood how that affected her. I understand now why she didn't like me as a person. I am attached to her deeply rooted pain and unknowingly added to it. A circumstance I was obviously not equipped to deal with, but extravagantly partook with reckless abandon. We need to sit in the pain we have caused first. Until we can sit and feel the pain we caused, you will be stuck. Once we process through our emotions, then all that remains of the memory are untainted incredible moments that we had. A grand experience of bittersweet that still sits in my soul.

We can look at those memories in our past and find where we have transferred our own pain to the responsibility of another. We all do this because we don't acknowledge the pain and find out why it really hurt. Until then, we resolve to a mind of mixed memories causing actual harm to those around us. We have an emotional cold, and we are spreading it to everyone. We don't need to be right, we need clarity. That, we find in ourselves first. Through all of this, I realized even though her mother and I were no longer connected in our outer realities, I could still hold that feeling and resonate with it in my heart. Nobody can teach me to stop loving someone. At least not anymore. I could hold our relationship in my Heart Mind. It is a form of surrender.

BATTLING DEMONS

"Mental fight means thinking against the current, not with it. It is our business to puncture gas bags and discover the seeds of truth." - Virginia Woolf

I'm a pretty savvy amateur chef (according to myself.) Even with a freeing professional comfort in the kitchen, I still handle knives extra carefully. That's just good sense, right? Sure. Then why does it always come with a hint of shame? So, I go looking for it. Okay. I do it because when I was a teenager I was being harassed by my dad's new live-in-girlfriend's daughter. She was taunting me into a wounded state. I tried to play back. I jokingly grabbed a knife. She used that to cry wolf and told my dad I was trying to stab her. She was older, smarter and loved to manipulate people. I was never an aggressive person like that. My father looked me, in the eye, and said, "This is the moment between a father and his child where they have a bond, a trust. Did you try and hurt her with the knife?" I stared deeply into his eyes, unafraid of truth and sincerity. I never was afraid of being in that sacred moment. "No," I replied softly. He stared deeply back at me. "I can't believe you would lie to me," and he walked away. That's actually why I have a thing with kitchen knives. A part of me still thinks I was wrong, about my own truth, because of his lame reaction. Whatever, it was a mistake. I can be right and dismiss this whole thing and move on, but wait, that's only got one perspective.

I had to find something that popped open my forgiveness for my father. I wanted to see past that, past him. How do I forgive him? Not in the biblical way, but in a loving way so your heart can comprehend the humanity of another person and see them for their own experience. When a loved one has ever given me that look, we all know it, that one of pure integrity and asked me to tell the truth, I do. The truth is how you speak from the heart and speaking from the heart is the only way this will be worth it. Lying is a pain loop.

I started to understand that this memory was actually when I stopped trusting him. If he couldn't see the heart's truth of his own sweet little child, then he couldn't see the truth when it was staring him in the face quite literally. My father was a bountiful supply of ego in my life. Heartbreakingly so. That same heartbreak reflects in all of us. Forgiveness came through with this deeper understanding. Because we always get from who is to blame and end up at *same*. This is where most of you would leave this old tender memory. Not a chance. Now I was in the room, unattached, and I could move around to have a look. What did I see here? What else…parent stuff? No. Ego? Yes, but plenty of experiences there. Evil? no. Abuse? No. He has a really kind heart. Oh. Wait. Abuse? Over in the corner. A teenage girl was able to manipulate two adult humans into doing deeply harmful things, as a game to hide her dark pains she walked in the door carrying. She had me torn and wrapped around her finger and this is the moment I stopped trusting my own father for life. Okay. So, people would lie to manifest their pain onto other people and his can create a lifetime of wounds in a relationship this important? Got it. That was a lot. This was all because of a little feeling of shame I get while trying to cook a delightful feast for friends. My happiest place to be, tied to all of that. Fascinating.

You start to see that everything is being affected and we are either choosing to heal it or choosing to "tough it out." Your body and your mind are cycling through different egoic experiences with light and dark. We do it all the time. Even pornography is expanding its egoic narrative as we learn to accept and understand these taboo parts of our thinking and belief programs. Endless amounts of primal fantasies at our fingertips. They started in the darkest imagery possible, our most repulsive fantasies. We became erotic with animal-minded shadow. Now something strange is happening. We have more pornography websites that show real people…making love. And they are quite popular. It's the new thing. You can see our darkness cycle right there. We are having the experience in its most vile, and then we move towards the light again. Then dark. Then light. Then middle. Then bliss. We are experiencing every perspective we can. If I shake the snow-globe and tell you I will give you a new house if you can tell me everything that was in that snow-globe, without moving around it, little do you know that behind the Christmas tree you will never see that tiny little present to, Darcy. You can't because you are living in your ego who believes the world is happening from right where you are standing. You want to move around it to see it. To move, you *Shakti*. Change your patterns. Physical and mental abuse can hide behind a number of physical and emotional pains. Being a savvy soul detective becomes a part of you that you are proud of because it's strong. It understands. Powerful enough to see above the Egoic Mind and reprocess things so you can learn, expand, clean house, heal and move forward. Once you conquer your own past memory you have conquered the barrier of the Egoic Mind. This process lights up your entire body. It will go into healing mode—it just needed you to take the first steps.

Pain is relative. We cannot say one person's pain is greater than the other because we all share in that pain. If you are in the middle of physical and mental abuse from another person, this is not something to only be handled in the Egoic Mind. This is when you care more for yourself and learn to leave your current environment in search of one where you will be safe. There are bad actors in the world, intentionally or not, but you are still responsible for this incredible existence. Protect it by finding a new reality. One in alignment with your life purpose. All of your physical pain, as well as your physical identity, are dealt with in the energy center at the base of your spine. The Vedas call this the *First Chakra (Root Chakra)*. If you are going through heavy emotional and physical pain from this lifetime, then focus on your root chakra when you can, and start to have longer and longer stretching sessions with your legs and lower back, getting down to the tendons. Pop on a movie and do a leg for each scene. Stand up and breathe it out. When you finish, listen to see if there is anything else you want to stretch. Your body will also want to find alignment, so it will help.

If you want to heal it more efficiently you can use a combination of physical and emotional release at the same time. Breathe out that old pain to the Universe. Find that hurt memory when you are in a deep stretch, allow your body to feel all of that together, hold it for as long as you want, then breathe that out to the Universe. Your body is crumpled in darkness, so stretch it back to the light, back to alignment. I hate to admit this, but I say alignment to by body all the time to communicate what we are trying to do. Every time I do this, all I can hear is Rachel Greene on *Friends* mocking Ross with, "Salmon Spring Roll." I allow myself to laugh at how ridiculous these practices can seem, but it all works, so be playful about it and enjoy your Daily Bread. Pride is Ego, be free of it.

So many people hold their sexuality in darkness. You don't have to. You are a light being tethered to this body, do with it what you will, just be aware while doing it. Our sexuality can be living in an Egoic Loop. Another mirror of our delusionary patterns. Our base instinct is to procreate. Make more humans. Our sexual understanding is based on fantasy, which is driven only by the Ego Mind. When we are intimate with someone we don't really want or desire, the false egoic fantasies, we are unfulfilled. That's because we all really want is connection. If we have shut these emotional parts of us down, then all we are left with is the Egoic Mind driving your entire sexual and intimate life with false beliefs. It becomes only primal—and not in the good way. We continue to explore every primal urge to great end, only to find ourselves in search of even just a touch from someone you deeply love.

You can see that we are still able to play out our fantasies in this life experience, but we are trying to do it with awareness so we can recognize when we are doing something that is in alignment with ourselves or doing something that will hurt us and others. We don't need to focus on these specific thoughts, but we can swim around the origins of when we learned our own beliefs in sex and love. When we first watched porn or even the first time we were abused—these are all playing the same loop, a loop you will find, heal, and reprogram. We are not pretending things didn't happen, we are doing the opposite because we are not in this space of holding a sense of fault to anyone. We came here to learn and heal. We are often taught that society works a certain way even when those beliefs are in complete rebellion against our true nature. We don't naturally want to bring hardship into our lives, so if we are, then we need to learn from them—otherwise they are just more pain in a loop. Pain will always exist here, so perhaps we can break the loops we already have on rotation, yes?

Even physical demons like drugs and alcohol can be reexamined with the Three Mind centers working. Addiction comes in many forms. The interesting thing is that addiction is built in ego *and* your chakras. It's tethered. We have essentially created an identity while intoxicated. Our operating systems are different and in the Ego narrative we have adventures and wild memories. Your ego starts to believe that this is the real you, because that is when you seem the most energetic and open. Nope, you are high because you are hurt. When you find your inner identity, your true identity, you start to build a new life. You realize you had fears of a "sober" life because you believe you are too broken to be here. All of these knots from your emotional past are coming undone and the desire to go back to your addiction identity has faded away into the dust. Addictions can cause blinding trauma, mentally and physically. The steps here might seem simple, but we are all very complicated inside ourselves.

Unpacking your wounds and fears can still be a really difficult process. We are all broken be design and we all need to learn, is how to let each other heal. This is a society thing, not just you. Forgive us for we have no idea what is happening here. Exhale.

This is a great place to go back and look at your old programming. Address the pain. Stretch and heal your body and those addictions will also fade. Our ego brains do everything in addiction. Food, sex, exercise, work, money, clothes. We are addicted to everything, so perhaps we can start to understand that addiction is simply an ability of the animal mind that we have forgotten how to use. I would love to tell my mind that we get up and run 6 miles every day at 5 am and it would just handle it. Addiction then becomes an ability of the mind you can further understand. Addiction is a program you put in your mind to mask a ton of inner pain. It's there always. I know it well. We can use this same mechanism for good, in which we then call the very same function a good habit. They are the same. So many people struggle with addiction and there is so much help out there, but the biggest support you will ever find is the inner you. Realize the hurt that this addiction causes you now and look back to when it started. See the patterns as simply patterns so you can better analyze the situation. We all just want to feel better and we are not quite sure how to do that. Pain is relative! We all have pain and struggle, and we all pretend like we don't. This is crushing all of us. So, we change it.

Sit in meditation. Put on some music. No words. Chants, sounds or meditation music. Focus on your breath. Use a word for the breath in and a word for the breath out. Breathe in "Hong" breathe out "Sah." Turn your eyes up to the center of your forehead. When your Ego Mind starts racing, slow it down and ask, "If you are not my real mind, then who am I?" Then sit and listen. When you feel calm and open, go for a swim. Feel different places in your body that hurt. Places storing pain. When you start to focus on that pain, some thoughts will come in. Walk through them. See them. Sit there and watch the *you* that went through that. Did we completely shut down and mentally black out? Did we crumble in ferocious cries? Did we do nothing? Stand there and let it all unbury itself in there. Step back and look around and what is happening with some perspective? What year it is? How did this situation even happen? Who are you mad at? What has that pain and anger done to your life today? Is that something you want anymore? Step closer and then start thinking about the concepts of love that hold the entire Universe in its hands, always. It is there and it is always with you. You might need to look at past lives when you are ready. Some things are tied to other experiences we would not let go of when we died before.

Evolve your thinking past your physical body. That is only something you are tethered to for this life, it is not *you*. Someone hurt your vessel and hurt your heart and soul. Talk to your body about it, not the ones who did it. Share that love and kindness you have brewing inside you. Help your body let go. Be the parent and do the steps to open the door for your body to purge. Stretch deep, run fast, drain the pain while holding that thought until the pain has been released. Exhale.

CHAPTER 6

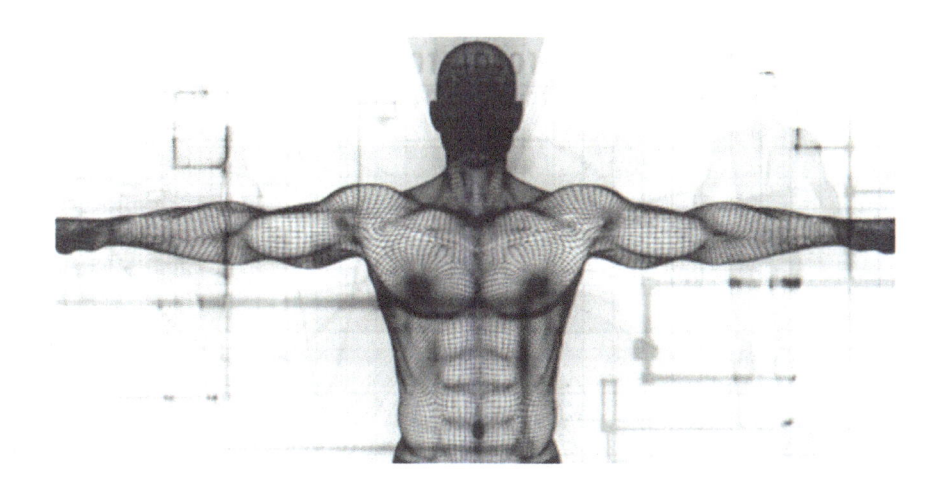

THE END OF EGO ERA

"To awaken one's true self, one must awaken all things"

    The ego is both marvelous and ridiculous at the same time. Something that can be so devastating to others, and yet so fragile when you point a finger at it. It also gets us everywhere every day, and it is why we are able to do anything at all. It is madness to understand. Thankfully, this is a transition away from ego. To find out where we are going, we figure out where we are.

    What is keeping us asleep? Our *Egoic Minds*. The part one of a three-part system that makes us real. Around 8,000 years ago we as a civilization started going through a delightful era called Ego (represented as *Leo*). We are 12,000 years in, exactly 12,000 years from the collapse of *Atlantis* and now we are heading into the age of

Aquarius, which is the era of opening. We are leaving Ego, well some of us anyways. This is one of the most profound changes in the cycle of our human history. This is the fun part.

When you really look at your cat or dog, you start to see that they live a life based on the pleasure and pain centers of their egoic brain. Study this behavior. If you watch your pet's patterns enough, it starts to look like humans in training. You can see the ego brain as a dominant operating system. Their own Ego Mind. It restlessly seeks your attention and your love, and on the other side they hate being ignored and they get scared when they're wrong and attack anything that encroaches on your space. They attack to protect even though it scares them to do it. Sound familiar?

These animals still feel and think but isolate their operating mechanism. It wants rewards or it feels bad. It does not change patterns; it likes them because they are safe to them. Routine. The Egoic Mind is beautiful and complicated. The more we understand what we don't like about the ego, we also see what we love about it. Again, seeing your ego as the enemy is a construct of the ego itself. Seeing your ego as a best friend is a much easier way to start this.

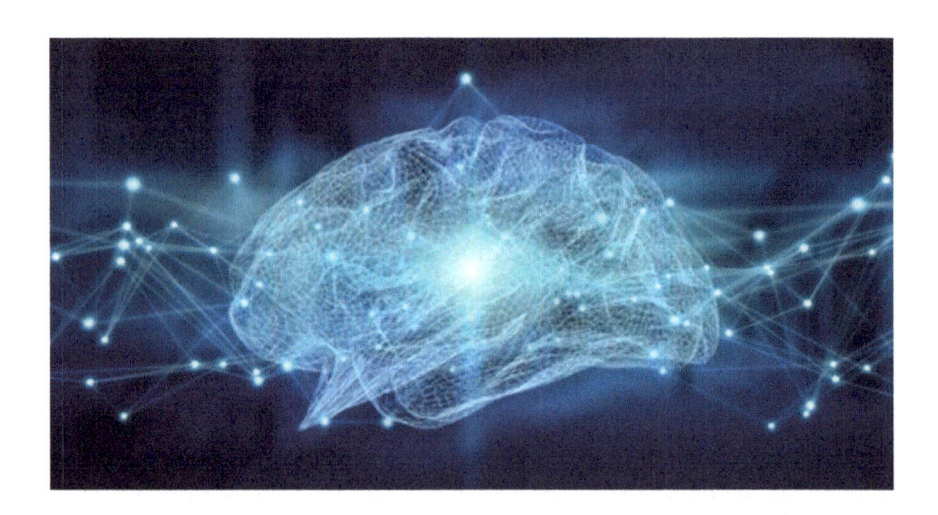

We love to get lost in this theater of life, the daytime drama of it all, and we forget what is really happening. Nothing. We are at the movies all day pretending it's who we are. The daytime drama is only taking your precious time of being authentic away from you. It is a cheap thrill that we devour. We use money-fear to deny new action. People love to say, "I'd love to buy organic, it's just so expensive." Yeah. Nutrient-rich food that gives you life costs more money. But that tall Moroccan vase you bought at Home Goods for $95 gave you a hit of reward, with no resounding after-effects. We put energy where we believe it will make us happy, and then it doesn't. We will never satiate the egoic mind. Ever. That is a loop because we have this incredible ability to adapt. You break the loop by trying new things. You will find a way to make it work. The closer you get to yourself the easier it is to be successful. The irony of waking up is that success comes so much easier, but it's not even close to what's driving you inside. Identify the egoic loops in your own life and you start to transition into this new era.

Having multiple children can be an effect of the egoic mind. We get social currency, pride. Trying to engrave our egoic life in stone like, "Hey! Look. King of the egos!" Our ability to procreate has lost its meaning. To bring another soul into this world would be something of great importance. Yet most of us never even pick up a parenting book or care for the resources of the planet they will need to be alive. We blindly populate this planet instead of consulting our Three Minds. We force our agenda on the planet. She is dying. And yet, we continue to live blindly as she does. Which is okay. It's more important that we acknowledge our truth here than sit in the fear of what we have done. The Earth is learning along with us, and you can help her do it. We cannot hide our failures in rewards. It doesn't work like that. Honesty in accountability.

So many of us see material gain or even children as the answer for a fragile heart or a disconnected life. There is a trap here. If you can't get "the dream," then you have failed. Something as deep as not being able to have children taps you right into the Egoic Narrative. Perhaps in this lifetime you needed a break from those little rascals because you had something important to experience for yourself? When we believe there is just one lifetime, we can't process these deeper emotions because all we can see is the life in front of us. We get stuck in the loss with the feeling to create a child from signals deep within our bodies. Yes, this is what your body is going through, not you. You've had children and been children a hundred times before. Something about not being able to have children might be the experience you seek. Find the truth and walk a different path with clarity, not based on your past beliefs that only hurt you. You can also see things like your social programming and religious beliefs here. We get older. We get jealous of friends or families that are "doing it right." We are starting to cover a feeling of failure when their life choices may not even align with us anyway. The egoic pain hurts because all it can do is compare. It's confusing, so release it. We are built for much more than that. We spin around and around because we don't know how to turn off the ego so we can think clearly for a second. Observe. Learn. Move forward slightly changed. This is the place where *Rilke* describes his own understanding of this, *"I want to unfold…let no place in me hold itself closed for where I am closed, I am false."*

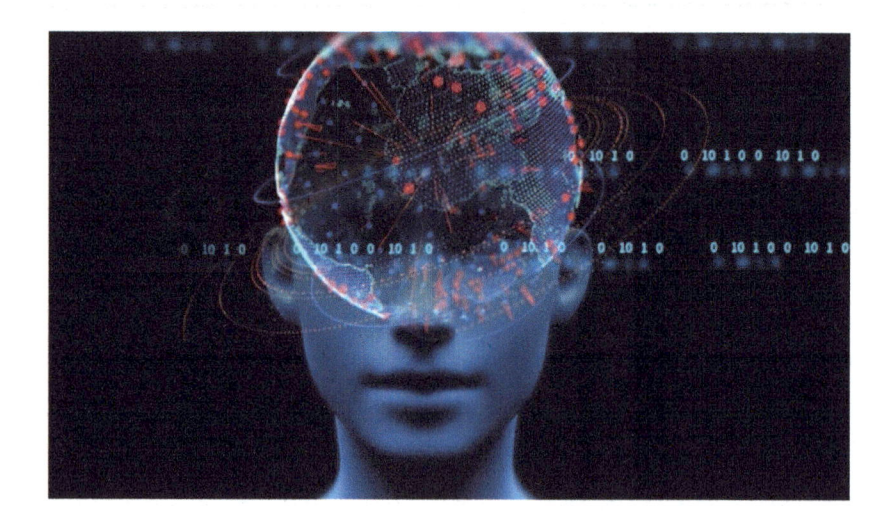

"No legacy is as rich as honesty"
- William Shakespeare

People with the strong desire to leave a legacy—that's an egoic thought for there is no better or worse. These are old hierarchal systems still at play in our reality. We still live in the ideals of the Roman Empire. It has not fallen, nor will it. It will change. We love watching a renovation show on HGTV. This is the same thing. We don't tear the empire apart, we renovate.

Become emotional. To start unfolding, we learn to use our other senses in daily life once again. We start to figure out how to hear them and trust them. These teach you about who you really are. You listen. If you make someone a delicious meal, they take a bite and shower you with thanks but something on your end detected a false signal. The tone itself. Stop and listen to that. Think deeply about it and feel your way through that within yourself. The tone of a person's voice has feelings and emotions swirling around in there and your own receptors are listening. Let's say this moment causes a feeling of deception. If what we are sensing is not what someone is doing, we are retracting inside whether we are aware of it or not. This is the moment you can choose to listen to your emotions again or continue to ignore them with rational thought and societal pressure. People can get stuck in this pattern for over forty years of marriage and not know it.

Become giving. Find your way back to a life of service. A life lived with heart. People who struggle with finding gifts for a loved one generally find this to be a sign they are thinking with their Egoic Perception, not understanding through a direct emotional and deep connection to the other person. You can do this from across the world. Sit quietly and think about your friend. Try to align yourself with what drives them internally. Logic will only get you so far, an easy mask, but it's the empathy that will always find the right gift. The gift itself isn't the gift at all; the empathy you used to create it is what we are feeling. Connection not thought. It came from a deeper place of understanding, and we can feel the difference.

Listen to perspective. As a majority we don't handle criticism well. Our ego has a brilliant warrior inside. Now imagine you are about to attack your own ego. If someone you care about insults you, three things can happen: your Ego is insulted, your Heart was hurt, and your Soul Mind was listening and calibrating possible patterns to understand this claim. So, then it's possible to just be hurt without being insulted, while also listening. You can just observe without reacting and you can react without processing. You have so many choices now to see what works for you in a specific situation. Once you learn to live from that place, this is what we call an *authentic life*. You aren't simply letting one mind do all the thinking. You have options. Can you spend one whole day letting your heart do the talking?

Turn on the Three Minds. The Soul Mind outputs probabilities, and the Ego helps us form a narrative around that belief. When you use step one to quiet the Ego Mind, the real stuff starts to come into your life. The life you really want to live. Depending on your path you may acquire wealth, or you may find yourself out at sea saving whales. Who knows? Too much is harmful, just enough is plenty. Find a life of plenty, not all.

Awareness of the Egoic Narrative. Our old narrative is formed in the Ego. The ideas and plans we believe to make, "the dream come true." When we fight or relate to others' beliefs in this narrative, we are in the Egoic loop. Saying mine is better or yours is worse. That is a loop of false thoughts attacking each other while grounded in zero desire from either side to progress our experience here. It is a ride at Disneyland, and you can't get off, so you started to believe this is where you live now. The narrative is the belief that if you do these things, this will happen, and you will be successful and proud of yourself. None of that is real because none of it is happening now.

Learn to catch the Ego Mind at work. Think about walking through the day. No matter what we're doing we have things happening in our mind. Conversations playing over and over again. We have agendas, things we want to do, a schedule. We go to the coffee shop and already know what kind of coffee we're going to get and where we are going after that. The entire time this is happening we are also rewarding ourselves and tearing ourselves apart. Phew! (Haven't even gotten to work yet.) All those things prevent us from actually being present. We're so busy in our Egoic Narrative that we're no longer available in the now. The now is where you plant a tree or make a meal. Where conversation is had. That now is where you literally take a moment and create something here. Something real for more than yourself. That is where life is. When we're following this program that we've created for ourselves all throughout the day, we also realize we're a slave to it. We are dedicated to that program. We believe in it. It is life. That narrative is the thing that's so busy talking, you can't hear the mini-miracles happening right in front of you.

We start by addressing the infamous ego. We begin to find clarity and awareness by understanding that we are deathly afraid of being wrong because we are trapped in our ego minds. How do we learn and grow when our society is smothered in fear and false perceptions? You can't. We are stuck in a loop of our own design.

This driving desire called ego is not a personality trait; it is a chemical process in your primal mind that is blocking you from stepping into accountability and awareness. We form narratives of ourselves like a Sim character that is based on power and status. "I can't make it tonight I'm so busy." "It's not personal it's business." This is how we all sit in a constant state of *self*.

THE TRANSITION

The programmed roles for men in society walk hand in hand with the *Ego Era* (as if by design). Men are set up to thrive in an egoic system. Fight, feed, fornicate, build. Generate at all costs. The survival and expansion of it all. Grab all the gold and fight to the death. This social programming makes it so difficult to process emotions or even begin to wonder about an internal life. "Men don't do that." It turns out men were set up. Men are sensory beings, but their societal function as a vibrational instrument to generate structure has become the only thing of value. Build they did. Now our structure needs a new energy to operate it correctly. The time of the male ego is coming to rest because the energy we need is far from the masculine vibration of ego. The reign of man was crucial, and we are grateful for it. That was no easy task. Men are extremely emotional creatures bearing the weight of fear and failure. They pushed through and created "society." It is done now.

The female ego is dominating the feminine to survive in an egoic male perception. Females are closer to *source energy* from birth. If the male ego feeds on being better than, the female ego feeds on a feeling of status and worth, something desired when dominance is not an option. Duality. The female ego can show the power in submission. It is a sign of surrender. A quality closer to resonation.

The female itself is formed out of the feminine with earthly roots in procreation and selection. You cannot hide from the fact that your body was also designed to grow a child in it. It's an extraordinary ability and the body is geared to do so. Your ego has a very precious task of keeping you safe so you can further the human race, no pressure. Chastised for being emotional, while also pushing you to be vulnerable and open enough to be nurturing to those who aren't. The social constructs teach you to be afraid to be a boss because that's what life programmed into you. You think it's a belief, but you don't truly believe it. You have observed it though. That is an old program you just isolated in the Egoic Loop. Think about it this way: if you are female and you raise the energy inside you, more awareness, you have changed the vibrational standards in your uterus. Yup, your vagina decides what type of person is born and who is denied entry. Raise your own understanding and now it will only accept a soul to be born into this world if it meets your higher standards. You did it again. To change life, you became it. You learned how to raise your frequency and changed the type of soul being born on Earth. That's impressive.

This time, we change the world from within. If you can see the world and want to change things, you will resonate with a child that wants to do the same. As women have been abused for so many years…well always, they have grown smaller outside, "the weaker sex," but that perceived weakness is manifesting itself by building inward strength. For thousands of years women have been changing this entire time. It's amazing to picture that as men dominated the Egoic life, women were preparing for the next steps by transforming the vibration of their physical self, inwardly, through what they felt and saw.

All of this female energy will start flowing in so we can align with it. Often referred to as *Goddess Energy*. This is the energy that drives the next part of this life thing we are having. She just got here and she's not going anywhere anytime soon. This is the time of the feminine. A welcomed change for all of us, male or female or anywhere in between. This is the loving part of us all. For now, we deal with the other part. The lion of ego and its constant desire to win. We learn to nurture once again as we step into the new age that has already arrived.

There is a lot of information here. Be gentle with it. Could we have this conversation twenty years ago? Or even five years ago? Doubtful. We embrace the now. I believe that withholding information is not for any group of people or a person to decide. When you tell the truth, you speak from the heart. Finding alignment is not a strategy for power and money— those things come easily when you do this work. But ironically, you find yourself less fulfilled by material things with the newly acquired power of the Universe at your fingertips. It's fascinating.

The popular book *The Secret* was a great steppingstone as it taunted the Egoic Mind into the internal world. But it did not address the Ego, causing us to manifest cars instead of our soul's desires. Now we move forward. This is step one to doing that, *Know thyself*. Align your Three Minds first--your larger, deeper, connected self--activate your *awareness state*. If you don't, you are potentially manifesting with ego alone, bringing in things you think you want instead of generating the code for a life that is worth it. An even bigger secret—love is why you are here.

PART 2

MADE FROM LOVE

Death to Ego

CHAPTER 7

PURPOSE

The purpose of your life is based on the current inside of you that wants to make your mark. A little thing called *Love*. When your life path takes you further and further away from your soul, you build up anxiety and depression. A nagging inside that is trying to lead you back. If you want to find your purpose, you go in search of the love inside you. You remind yourself that you are made of it.

How did our existence start? Most of us believe in the *Big Bang*. When you get curious about what it means to raise your frequency, you start to understand that vibration plays the hero's role in all of this. That is *Love*. If history leads you to a dead-end, hop over to *physics, metaphysics, quantum physics* and *spirituality*. There lies an ocean of information just waiting for you to plunder it.

So, at the very beginning we are indeed stardust. We are made of light energy that we now put inside a physical sensory body. There you are. At the very beginning of time, you are just a light particle, pop. You could not see yourself. Pop, someone else arrived. Friction.

The first two particles. Energy was turning to water and water to thought. Your energy particles start harassing each other with curiosity. Everything that gives consciousness a reality is one thing running into another thing. You can see these particles dancing around each other and producing more. Two things. *Yin and Yang - Light and Dark - Positive/Negative - Duality.* The only word we need to start understanding our origins—*duality*. Two things excitedly charging themselves up with curiosity. A curiosity that stirs this question in us all, *"What am I?"* As if hearing the Earth asking the same question to the Universe herself. What am I?

> *"Where your greatest ability and the greatest need meet, there lies your destiny"* - My Aunt Suzy

What does the above quote mean to you? There is a very important piece that the Ego Mind doesn't even notice. "The greatest *need*." That means that you step into something with great ability, and as it just-so-happens, that's exactly what the world needed too. Your purpose is found by learning to listen to the world around you. We all think that we feel the same pains. We don't. As in, not even close. Our wounds are all tied to memories…. for a reason. That is how they are wounds unique only to us. What you notice and feel deeply is specific to only you. Underneath that is purpose. Watch the joy that blossoms in you when you turn those wounds into understanding.

I was asked once how we could possibly change the world? My response was simple but true. *"Service and truth."* If every time you used a kitchen you cleaned it because you wanted to make it great for the next person, nothing would be dirty, anywhere. If we start living in truth, we would all stop thinking we hated each other. Those are the two ingredients missing from humanity as a whole consciousness. For myself, I know that if I include service and truth in my life, I feel more alive than when I'm winning the Egoic Narrative. Always.

> *"Let the beauty of what you love be what you do."*
> -Rumi

Purpose does not work in large and small. Grand or obscure. All that you are doing is surrendering your Ego Mind and letting your purpose simply come out through you. The seven chakras are separate, and you can see each piece to understand more of the whole. Outward and inward at the same time. Purpose is alignment. Create the alignment effect. Live life from within. That will resonate outward. Pop. Awake. You may still desire a more material-driven reward center life, but over time you will feel being pulled away from materials out of boredom, and you will naturally gravitate to the things that truly align with who your soul is. You become a soul magnet, not in the abstract—you healed yourself and raised your frequency and now that frequency is bringing in new people that can hear it. Remove your schedule one day a week and just live off instinct.

An important part of your entire life's *purpose*; Don't put purpose on a pedestal! When you observe the patterns of Bill Gates you see someone with a primal mind that has turned itself into a super processor. He lives in the loop. He's a master of it, but still, in a loop. We see this in his life patterns. He spends his loops devouring information. Feeding the animal mind from multiple sources at multiple times. Then he goes out and breaks massive loops. Even though he was not able to use his powers over his technology empire to lead us away from the loop, he did something different. "Where greatest ability and greatest need meet." He broke loops and pushed us forward. Then, what Melinda and Bill have done with their foundation is a framework for the business future. You may not read about it, but that foundation that is based in hearts, ideas, and science, is changing the world every second of every day. You just can't see it, so we remove ourselves from learning from it. Even the two largest computer brands are divided, one built to the egoic mind and one built to the spirit mind. You see, the world is always balancing itself.

Bill had an ability, the world showed up and said I need something, and he was able to bring it into fruition. Great, so he has caused an effect on civilization. Then the rest of his life, is him having whatever experience he wants to have. Simple. Your purpose is like finally knowing what job your soul wants. The rest of life is always up to you. Your purpose might be to build a toilet. Melinda and Bill invented an amazing toilet. So what right? True leaders have think-tanks and try to solve the world's largest problems because they aren't trying to be right. That super processor of a brain had an ability to bring together the right minds to realize that people living in poverty, in shanty towns, were getting sick because they didn't have sanitation. These "slums" have become entire cities and no governing body is willing to pay for the installation of basic sanitation. They won't pay for plumbing. Well, that's not how you fix a problem. By finding who to blame. You step back and see the data from awareness. The cost to add all the plumbing needed is in the billions, so that's out. Okay, what is the most basic thing we need? A toilet. How do we make a toilet without water? So, they created a toilet that was sanitary and impressively tidy by turning waste into light grey powdery ash, without using a drop of water. They are changing the world by being able to step right into the Matrix and implement codes to solve large problems in our civilization. We can invent things again. Most of our inventions are only based on potential financial gain. Even our own creations, our life choices that we decided to commit our entire lives to doing, sticky with ego. Your alignment of self won't be something you are not able to do; quite the contrary, it will be something that clings to exactly who you are. Your wounds guide your path until it's time to do something brave with your life experience. Find something you want to change about this world and change it. Remind yourself that this is not set-in-stone because creation made the sand.

Don't worry about the past. It doesn't matter at all because you can heal it. Now is now. Live in today. We are all too immersed in our memories. We hold on tight. Bury them. Store them away in the body. The past is great for reflection, not to define you. Let your feelings guide your purpose. Something only *you* will feel. If you don't know how to make it all work, surrender to it and learn. Decide what you want to say deep down and say it loud.

People say, "It's about the journey, not the destination." Then, the journey is all the *time* you have before you get there. This reminds me of one quick thought. I was sitting on a film set with a grip. He was this tough looking guy and he always worked so hard. They grind from 4 am to 5 pm. I asked him what he wanted to do with his life. He smiled and said, "I'm doing it. I work all day and at 5 pm when I walk through my front door, to my wife and my two little kids, that's when my life begins. Right there. That's why I do this. I am doing what I want with my life." ...I never forgot that.

CHAPTER 8

SPIRITUAL MEDICINE

When you arise in the morning, think of what a precious privilege it is to be alive - to breathe, to think, to enjoy, to love. -Marcus Aurelius

    I have not eaten anything but small portions of completely plain vegetables for over 20 days while surrounded by monkeys and bats. Mostly plain white rice with plain white beans. Sometimes carrots, sometimes a small whole river fish--eyes staring back at you. I have two different intense medicinal jungle plants pumping through my body. I knew that to break your heart open again, you have to clean your body from the past. The chemicals, the trauma, all of it. Mother nature had become my doctor...and I was in the E.R.

    There was a point where my body was in excruciating pain. Alone in the jungle without a medicine cabinet to ease my mind-bending back pain. There were no pills or tonics for my poor shivering body as it was being devoured by a stomach virus. I began pleading with those who lived here. These so-called "healers." Begging them to be careful with the powerful plant medicines they were injecting into my body in heavier doses than one should have. Begging them to be gentle with my body. I was too broken to be brave and in too much pain to remain silent. Here I was surrounded by bats, snakes and tarantulas and it was the tiny bug inside me that would finish me off.

When you're alone with your body, your mind starts to create scenarios. I had almost died of Escherichia coli a few years back. My mind started to convince me that I got E. Coli from the "business hole." I stepped up to do my business and two large Amazonian flies flew out of that hole and into my mouth. All I could do was lay there and begin to stroke my fingers on my body trying with the last energy I had to nurture it in any way I could.

The men looked at me as if I was weak. Well, I was. I am a sensitive body, and it was injured. It was in pain. I was finally trying to vocalize my sensitive self. The warrior in my mind had finally stepped aside so I could actually feel it instead of brushing it off or numbing it. The Adonis might drink a large cup of ayahuasca and swim in the clouds. A quarter cup and I was stretched to all aspects of heaven and hell. This is not my mind, this is how I'm built. Wildly receptive to all things. Through the piercing sound of the cicadas, my body was screaming "be gentle with me," and without the ability to numb it, it was all I could here.

As I sat with this in another day of silence, I realized my body wasn't pleading outward to the jungle ex-pats, it was pleading with me. Be gentle with me. It was talking to my thinking mind. For decades it had willingly followed a determined and relentless mind that was locked in survival mode. I had lived hard. From years of highly competitive soccer, to drinking an Irishman under the table. No matter what I did with reckless abandon and full surrender to the moment, my body had always followed. I had been driving this highly sensitive body at 120mph since I was old enough to drive. Now it was telling my ego mind to "slow down." This battered lion needed to lay down and lick its wounds. It was telling me it was time to stop trying so hard.

There on my left wrist, a tattoo that reads, "Broken Rules." I got this in Chicago while in the middle of a loving relationship that was hurting me deeply. This message was to forge on in the pursuit of love, no matter if it hurt me more. An unbridled approach to life. Perhaps it was time to start living a different way, one that doesn't leave me in the middle of nothingness holding decades of pain in this sweet and sensitive vessel. It was telling me it was time to switch gears and learn to be gentle in my life, not just here in this jungle, but from here on out. Our bodies are driven by our heart minds and I had given my thinking mind the keys. That mind cannot feel and will drive your body until the wheels fall off. This was the moment I truly switched from my head to my heart. Without the narrative programming to immediately find relief, I could only attempt to heal myself from within. This is the moment you discover that unless you learn how to listen to your pain, that it will never truly pass, and it will never truly heal. If we all rush to numb the pain, then we will never hear a thing.

How many of us are pleading with the world to understand us, to stop hurting us, when in fact it is our hearts pleading with our Ego to finally quiet down and listen? Ask yourself this; how long have you been making your body do whatever your thinking mind wants to do, regardless of the impact it is having on your vessel? We see soreness as weakness and push ourselves even further. The world isn't breaking you, you are. Your body was built by nature not by man. Let it become part of you once again. The pains we are causing ourselves, to win. It's time to heal your garden to regain access to your heart.

---

nur·ture; the process of caring for and encouraging the growth or development of someone or something.

You are the plant, and nutrients are the soil. You have been putting chemicals in the soil for so long the plant has withered. You need to heal the inner workings of your body before you can grow into a proper plant. Add fresh, living ingredients and organic nutrients. The healthier the food, the healthier the garden. Same goes with you. To start anything openly, you surrender to it.

If you want to talk to your body, you start by telling it you have no idea how to talk to it in the first place. Honesty. It needs to teach you how to listen to it again. Body alignment is about the massive living ecosystem inside of you. Organs and blood, chemical reactions and your nutrient Special Forces.

Your body sends you signals and pulses. If you are in Ego, you perceive all food signals from the body as reward. If you are in an awareness state, then you eat to nourish, not to reward. Do you nourish the body or feed the ego? Our diets are in an ego loop because we're trying to force rewards for happiness. How do you become the current of the Akashic? You become wisdom. How do you get a healthy body? You become health. We need to learn about our bodies, nutrients, systems, all of it, from the ground up. Your body can't wait to start living in synchronicity with you. Trust me. Learn. Being healthy is quite easy when you can target the source. Egoic attachment. Letting go of your attachment or belief in your lifestyle. We as a society aren't feeing our bodies, we are feeding our egos and your body is sick of it. Manufactured hunger for poisonous foods. Your body doesn't really know what to do with this toxic food.

We believe we eat something because we are hungry. Our body says I need more nutrients and water and our ego hijacks that thought into reward center and then sends us deceiving signals. When you are "totally craving something," that is your brain taking the hunger signal, bouncing it through the mind filled with delusion, goes through reward center as your North Star, and then sends you a memory that you liked called "I'm craving a giant hamburger." You're not. Your mind tricked you into eating that because your reward center thinks it will make you feel good, and if you feel good then you are happy.

We have a deeply rooted belief in the food we eat. It is described as a religious experience to many, including me. Here's a great way to check in with how you see food and how you are treating your body. You have a very bad cold. I asked two friends to give me a short list of their cold and flu "go-to's." I asked them to reply in two categories: Healing & Comfort.

COLD & FLU BODY KNOWLEDGE COMPARISON

ALEX

HEALING
Alka-Seltzer tablets in water first thing.
DayQuil/NyQuil for work.
I have tons of zinc and echinacea lozenges.
*Grandma's chicken noodle soup, a must.

COMFORT
A giant box of aloe and vitamin E tissues and a box of
Goldfish crackers.

ZOE

HEALING
Echinacea and Golden Seal, Zinc immunity tablets.
Small morning run, just to help the body burn out some toxins and sweat
out the unnecessary. No sugar, no dairy. That is a
hand-grenade to your immune system and we are at war.
We also like to sit down and have a bowl of chicken soup.
(As long as its organic and freshly made so the real bone nutrients are there.)
This was all extremely helpful during the pandemic
as well because its all based on building your immunity system.

COMFORT
"Raw garlic!" Chew it up. It's rough but it works and when you feel
terrible it gives you congestion relief because its burning the virus from within.
I always make or grab 4 shots to have through the day, each made with;
Elderberry powder, real Vitamin C, real aloe juice, probiotics, cold pressed ginger,
cold pressed garlic, lemon and turmeric. Then I drink mostly green juices and lots of
water or lots of aloe juice. You body needs tons of water for this battle and I get
bored with water so I add things to it like lemon and cold pressed ginger and sip that
all day. If I have to work on a film set I absolutely get on the DayQuil/NyQuil game
to hide my symptoms, but we know its not actually helping us heal.

We could argue on the surface about what works and what does not for a cold and flu, but when you step back into awareness, what patterns do you see between those lists? First, we all seek comfort. Human pattern. Then most of us stumble our way through the healing part assuming our bodies will handle it for us like always. Another human pattern. Alex believes what he has been taught from the commercial programming and the way he was raised, so much so that he listed items in healing that don't heal you. Second, we see a much larger societal pattern. When you can look at this without assuming one person is right or wrong, then you see said larger pattern. When you look at Zoe's list the most curious thing happens. We don't stay focused on the items on the list, we see the differences on a deeper level. Zoe's version of comfort vs. Alex's version of comfort. Her version of comfort is related to healing the body and doing little things to aid the symptoms, resorting to the manufactured relief when she is unable to stay home and heal but rushes off to work. She is treating her body and listening to it. He starts with manufactured and then stays numb until it's over (aka his body fought and won on its own). He stays in comfort, instead of treating the illness. We are all doing this now. Stay in the comfort and hopefully these wounds will all just go away. Well, they don't, and they can become really harmful in your life. Western medicine is finally making the link to numerous and severe physical illnesses related to past emotional trauma. Your emotions are that powerful.

Come to know what is in front of you, and that which is hidden from you will become clear to you. For there is nothing hidden that will not become manifest" -Jesus

When you are sick your body is fighting off a threat, but you feel bad, so you want rewards of relief. This is a giant mirror to our Egoic Mind. You are being attacked and you can either throw numbing cream at your attacker, or you can punch that virus in the face. We choose to get high and get by. Your body needs the army at the ready. Healing herbs and ancient immunity nutrients are that army. Your body was made from nature and reacts to nature.

The Nutritional Paradox

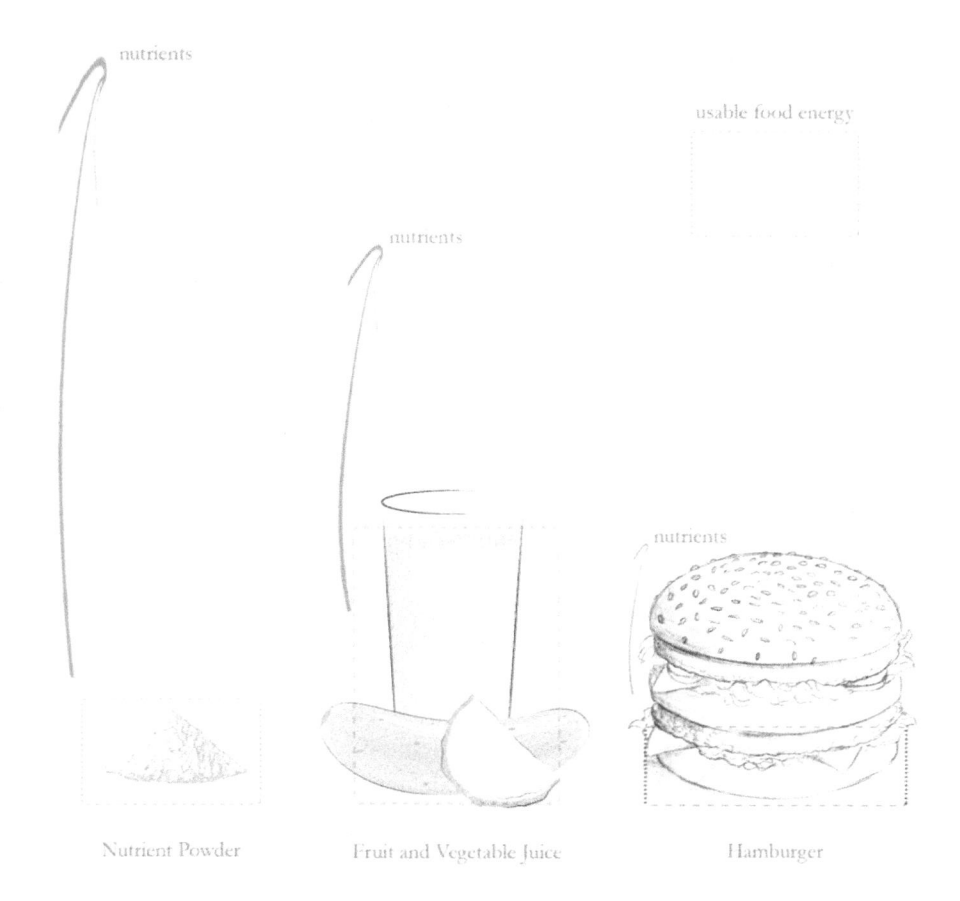

| Nutrient Powder | Fruit and Vegetable Juice | Hamburger |

Our Ego uses food as rewards. We don't actually need food, we need nutrients. Nutritional paradox

Fun food vs real food: We can start by looking at something we all hear about—gluten allergies and milk or dairy allergies. When people with a strong gluten allergy in the US travel to Europe, they often find they have almost no reaction to all the gluten there. Why? Because they are real grains, the origin of which were not altered to the harmful state they have been in the States. When the US or any other country alters its food at a micro level for mass production, we lose the detailed information packet that our body needs to put things in the right place. We also lose the nutrients we need to thrive. I've given a glass of raw milk to an old friend who was very allergic to dairy. Her hand shook as she raised the glass to her lips. She drank the glass one sip at a time. Not even ten minutes later she already knew it had little to no effect on her. She was floored at thirty-two years old. Drinking a glass of milk had been her nightmare. Raw milk contains the enzyme our bodies need to break down the proteins. A mother passes this enzyme on to the child to drink it. As we were not supposed to drink milk like this, we mass produced it and had to pasteurize it and burn the bad bacteria out and we also burned out all the good stuff too. Our food needs to be alive. We can also understand that we need living food by seeing that sourdough made with a starter, a growing living culture, produces gasses when it cooks. We need those gasses in our bread to digest the bread the way we are supposed to. Humans have been eating bread our entire lives, from the day we learned to grow grains. There is no natural reason for us to suddenly become allergic to it. We did that. We did that by forgetting our food needs to be real. We are no longer protecting ourselves from our food. We have built the Aswan Dam in America. So tiny we can't even see it. We have started to ruin food at its inception.

Meat has sadly turned into fun food. You can still find the real meat out there, some incredible farmers bringing back the natural and organic ways of raising animals for human consumption, but it's not in your local shopping center. Such a large marketing machine programming these thoughts into us daily and we can no longer see that our meat is awful. What we do to these animals should not be put in your body. I don't really eat meat anymore as I naturally aligned with plant-based food. That said, just the other night I was gifted a warm bowl of Korean pork stew and I loved every bit of that pork. I accepted and loved it. You can't tell me to never do anything again. I'm not vegetarian or vegan or a meat eater. I live clean, I understand nutrients and I love the fun food when it feels like it won't hurt me to indulge. Plants give us help here until we can fix what we have done to the meat industry on a nucleus level.

Food was meant to nourish us, not entertain us. Let's do both shall we? I love that food is such a big part of my life, but now I can eat fun food for fun, not to feed my body what it needs to thrive. This is not the problem of the food manufacturers. They struggle in every way to keep up. Cattle farmers generating millions of pounds of burgers, at great cost to our planet, only to barely make enough to keep the farm. We are demanding food at a level that forces us into a deeper egoic delusion because we are completely detached from it as a reality. Meat is something that comes shaped like a burger patty wrapped up with onions. These animals are in serious pain, and then we eat an absorb their pain. We are making the American soil infertile. She is a mirror to ourselves, our own bodies.

We measure our lives with general systems that don't really help us understand nutrients. Take a calorie. We know that we can measure our caloric intake. The calorie being a measure of energy, let us not forget. It's not specific, its abstract. A calorie is like gas. You can put twenty gallons in the tank, but did you put in premium gas, or did you buy the cheapest gas you could find? That gas is over-oxygenated and contains more impurities and less of what your vehicle needs. More impurities in your food calorie lead to more problems with your body. What saved you a dollar will now cost you thousands to repair. We need to start seeing food as nutrients.

As my understanding grows, my fat level goes down. That's the diet that will blow all other diets out of the water—knowledge. When you start a relationship with your feeling body, you don't need to diet because you want to nourish your new relationship. Healing from the inside-out is so much easier once you realize how much harder it's been to try healing from the outside in. The Ego Mind struggles with habits and addictions. The others don't. Make firm decisions and your body and mind will listen. Sometimes I even say, "Hey, I'm putting this intense medicinal tea inside you because you're body hurts and this is good for the bones." It feels ridiculous at first but then it turns to something deeper. I am speaking to it, so it knows we are working together now. It doesn't trust you right away so you'll have to teach it that in can. You've been poisoning it for so long so it's going to take you both a second to reconnect.

Our Ego's see fat as a stain on our vanity. Something to be rid of. Well, our bodies don't see it that way. In fact, your body sees fat as a way to keep you alive. Fat is a very valuable source of energy when necessary. Your fatty food is going into your intestines, then gets sucked out through the walls into your blood stream. That fat then gets stored in your fat cells like little balloons filling up with liquid fat.

When you eat more fat, the balloons swell. They stick to your tissue lining like squishy marbles, waiting to be used when you need this stored energy. When you switch to real food you are not pouring processed fats in your body 24/7. When you switch to real food you also aren't slamming your body with sugar. It wants to make glucose to use as your fuel; if you pump sugar in there all day, your body machine is overloaded and will not even attempt to use your fat energy, ever. Your body wants more than fat, sugar and chemicals. It wants the real food that is filled with your nutrient army that gets deployed all over your body. Don't try to lose weight, learn how your body is making the fat and learn how to stop putting that food into your body if you want to drain that old fat storage and start from a clean slate. Nutrients and knowledge. Done.

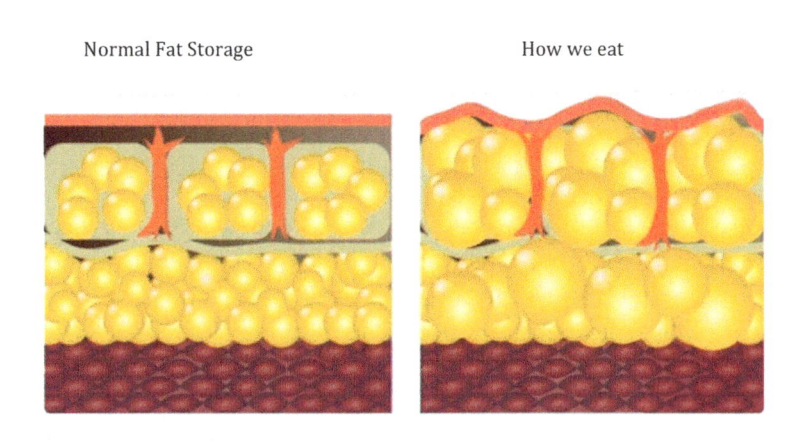

Normal Fat Storage

How we eat

So, okay, learning more about how this body works. Notice how specific it became? Not trying to look better, not trying some new weight plan—we're learning how our life and our bodies deal with food and we learn more about what it wants.

I sat with my body and said I would do everything it wanted until all the fat was gone, not for vanity, but so I would understand it. 40 pounds vanished. Once I got down to the last few pounds on my stomach, the process came to a halt. I switched from my new physical knowledge to emotional curiosity. In Eastern medicine we can hold a major connection to the belly from our childhood fear of survival. The call it "The Blood." I had to go into some past wounds to clear out the last bits of fat. Those were emotional memories stored in my body fats. The goal was not to rid the body of fat, it was to teach me why I didn't know how my body really works. I was taken aback that my body was holding onto fat based on fears of survival from my childhood.

When one becomes more serious about trying to be spiritually available, you start craving the good stuff. It's a natural process. They all need to function together. Outward and inward. Your pleasure center is programmed to be rewarded, and through deeper understanding of it, you naturally align with what is real and what is not, in every aspect of your life. Our bodies are tired of the fun food we put in there instead of the real thing. Feed your body nutrients every day and it will do the rest.

I think we stopped talking to our own bodies because we are embarrassed by how we treat them. We are avoiding the conversation with the thing that loves us the most. Seek forgiveness in your own body with love and mean it, then let your body know there's going to be some changes around here. For anyone seeking a soul transformation, the smartest nutrition for your body would be fully plant-based. All the science is already there, but allow yourself the time to adjust. If you don't think it can satisfy your Ego and nourish your body, you would be mistaken. Have you ever experienced a plant-based tasting menu by a world-renowned chef? It will blow your mind and your taste buds. A chef focused on meat alone paints with a few colors; give a chef the world of plants and you are in for a vibrant treat.

When we finally embrace the combination of Eastern medicine and Western medicine, we will understand that Western medicine is wonderful for your outer life and all things external that trouble you. The essential teachings of Eastern medicine will treat your inner life as well as your sensory body in the way it was meant to be treated. For example, in Western medicine we have the nervous system. This system is vast, but still limited in understanding. In Eastern medicine they have *Energy Meridians*. This system correctly mirrors the structures in our bodies. It's a much more in-depth understanding of your body, and the treatment is much more focused so the healing potential here is vast. Western medicine is egoic medicine, Eastern medicine is rooted in the spiritual medicines that work with your inner body, and your being. They work very well hand in hand, as duality would.

If we are trying to release our Ego, why are we talking about food? You are in service to all three intelligent centers that make you! You see that we are mental, physical and emotional. You are treating all three to get them back online.

The ego and the therapist

"If we want things to start making sense, we have to start by making sense of who we are first."

People who lie to their own therapists, we need stop right there. That's a good sign your ego is running things. The ego won't even feel like it's lying because, it is displaying another great trick, it's not lying, but it is withholding the truth. Locked into a single-minded view giving the therapist the limited data that blocks the real truth. You can simply start by telling them you might not be able to see things from other's perspectives at the moment. They will understand and welcome your personal insight. Let them know you have a hard time being honest. Start there. Therapists are wonderful. Relax. Tell them all about your dark inner monster. Tell them your sickest thought. You are starting to accept that you are a pendulum between light and dark. Let a therapist help you unravel your Egoic Narrative to get back to the real you inside.

Past life regression

Your soul has the backstory! That backstory helps you understand why you are you. You specifically. A past life regressionist can open your blocked consciousness and reveal the missing clues by allowing memories you select from your past lives to pop up as if a memory from yesterday. They aren't doing anything but opening space for you to have a chat with your own soul.

My mother was always tricking me into sessions with the

occult. A numerologist woke me up one morning because my mom told her to, and she started doing a reading before I even fully opened my sleepy eyeballs. I had no idea what has happening, but something happened in that session that meant nothing at the time, but later, astoundingly, confirmed some things about myself and things about other civilizations. Again, at the time, I did not care. A year later my mother told me she had "booked some spiritual thing in San Diego." Just so happened to be when I was down from L.A. It was some lady who would talk to us about our past lives? Good grief. We drove down to San Diego to a hotel. I was not into this. Stranger? A hotel room? Some weird spiritual thing? No thanks.

I don't know what I was expecting when I walked in that room, but it was not what I saw. I suppose I thought it would be some hippy dippy or tribal-esque voodoo ceremony. I also thought it might be a famous Indian healer from the East. I had no idea. I walked in this very normal room and there she was sitting in the corner. She looked like a sweet little old white nun. She kindly informed me that she had cleansed the room as I had asked. (I forgot I stoically said that to my mom over the phone. "Yeah, um, tell her to like bless the room or whatever.") This little nun handed me a long slender white crystal and told me to put the tip of a finger on the end. She started spinning her own crystal and saying things. I was out. I woke up in this room. I knew something incredible had happened because my body and mind were filled with energy. I handed her the crystal and she laughed. She handed it back to me. It was unnaturally hot. Things you can't comprehend until they happen to you. You need your senses to feel these things. We talked for a bit about what I could loosely remember. Sisters in Africa, a death in Egypt. She handed me a cassette tape and I was on my way. My mother was next. I waited in the car in the parking lot. After she returned to the car, I could see she was a little disappointed. She was guided into a body regression. That made perfect sense to me as she was so buried in her childhood trauma. She needed to clean out her here first before she would be able to handle the other past-life stuff.

I have listened to the tape. I used words I have never learned, and I spoke about things deeply and distinctly. I was building what seemed like a Pyramid but more like a square, and I was building it in the middle of the desert. Who builds a square pyramid? I guess I did. I believe the lesson I gathered from what I said was that when we are on our death bed, we are holding onto something. Not necessarily a loved one. Something we wanted to do, or something we failed to do. We are left with a question. Something that we are still trying to understand. As a prince, I was looking down to the peasant thinking, "I am just like you." And when I was dying in a tomb, I realized while looking through his eyes back up at me, I was not just like the peasant. I had been born into royalty and instead of accepting that and figuring out how to create a better world, I tripped over the thoughts of not wanting to be better. I was in my own ego delusion and in observance, I did not create any action. I did nothing but got caught up in deep thoughts about how we were the same. When I yelled down to the peasants, "I'm just like you," this time I was listening. A peasant responded, "No you're not." He was right. We are the same, we are light beings. But in egoic reality I have power, I can make change. Instead, I was more focused on the guilt of being born into possession. On my death bed in the tomb, all I could think about was that moment. On loop. The last thing I said to a beautiful wife who was forced to marry me, was "I can fix this." We then left Egypt and jumped to past lifetime in Africa where I was sitting in the dirt muddling grain. I was a tall, lean tribesman. I watched rebel vehicles come into the village and destroy things. I was powerless. I had gone from powerful to powerless. So, Erin, how does the world seem now that death is happening right in front of you and you can do nothing about it? I did not like that, but I got the message.

If you really want to open that door, then go through your past lives with a trained and well-known spiritual guide. Some of you will have enough going on in this current life and might be having a body regression instead (clearing of current emotional memories and childhood life blocks). They are able to go into your subconscious mind and have a conversation there. It's incredible to think that you can go to someone who can mind ninja your whole being into revealing the intelligence you really carry inside, and then heal you in minutes.

Have fun exploring spiritual healers. They are so wild. There are numerous services you can explore by booking a session online. A whole new world out there. We have specialists working in vibrational therapy, past lives, chakra healing, meditations and body alignment. It may be new to us, but there are plenty of people just waiting to tell you their age-old secrets. If you don't believe in reincarnation, then sign yourself up for a *past-life regression* session. There are so many things I would never believe had I not been witness to them myself. I tend to not give it much thought until I do it myself. I stay open to try things and see what happens later. Be mindful of who you are going to. People working in this energy would not be leading with ego and status. It would not be all about them—it would be about all of us. A greater truth. Find the people who know that. Settle for nothing less because of price or convenience. Be open to the person you are meant to find.

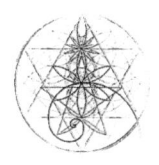

SOUL ALIGNMENT

"The deep parts of my life pour onward. As if the river shores were opening out. It seems that things are more like me now, I feel closer to what language can't reach." -Rilke

Even beginning to write about this, I can feel how sensitive I am about it. This is the place where we cry in bittersweet. Even if we are able to live a life with our soul here, most of us are not awake enough to see it. Soul alignment begins in the Soul Mind. You are starting to listen with your aware self. This is rooted in the creator. Creation itself. Manifested as electric love currents that make our Universe. That brilliant intuition is singing truth from your true self. When you start to *make the outside look like the inside,* you find wisdom by becoming it. You find your soul by allowing it. You are no longer a victim, you are a co-creator. Things are broken here and that deepest pain is your truest North. Follow that pain to healing and you will find yourself side by side with your soul.

Even our Three Minds can resemble a twisted ankle. If we are not accessing them together, they are out of alignment. The more you use them, the more you take them out to stretch their legs. Eventually, they will not go back to their previous position. Once you have the minds settled, then you start reaching up to the Five of Light. You will resonate with one of those higher light chakras. That is the baseline for your soul. That is where you will find it. Each one has a different engagement here. You align with one deeply. Then it resonates back through your Heart Mind.

Soul alignment comes when you wake up and start breaking loops. So, we learn to get out of our own way first. Change little habits throughout your day. Become less rigid and see what happens.

Pleasantly Rigid
—

I've watched an incredible variety of rigid (resistance-minded) people come into our professional acting classes over the years. Some young and bright-eyed, another a mother who had just lost her child. Lawyers especially love to tout their acting abilities for court purposes. Being able to succeed in an arena where your counterparts are afraid is a delicious treat for your ego puppy. Whatever you are, an acting class will open you up. People unknowingly come to class to unlearn. They are trapped between the Egoic Narrative and who they are. A sensory being with feelings.

The exercises at the beginning of the class are always meant to dissect you from your ego. To "let go." When we let go, we fear being raw in our instincts. I made a joke in an improv session once that seemed racist and I thought I was a horrible person—they all assured me it was okay. We freak out a little first. Afraid to make a social mistake. We are so unaware of who we really are, we protect it from society, and ourselves. We don't need to do this. This is a product of withholding information. If we all hold back from who we are then we all become too scared to be the one to show our truth. Egoic Loop.

In *The Groundling's* improvisational classes, they teach something spoken across the improvisational world as, *"Yes And."* Or as *Mike Myers* says, "Agree and add." We agree with whatever is said by our partner on stage and then add to it. We are building something together. Resistance is death here. In the beginning we all turn into *Michael Scott*. People's egos trying so hard to be clever and failing. It's excruciating to watch us trying to be authentic for the first time. This process gets tricky when another actor says something our Ego Mind wants to defend. We learn to let that mind go. If one actor says, "Hey Penelope (to a man), is that what you are going to wear tonight?" To which the other actor will suddenly adapt internally to the situation and completely relinquish their identity to being male within seconds. We are building this world with someone else. The ego does not want to agree, it wants to display your narrative. So, you see, if they were selfish, they could not build anything worth remembering.

In this new awake state, you can then start to see the little whispers of synchronicity and alignment. The clues. The reinforcement of self. It's learning how to say "I love you" to people again instead of resisting the world in which you live. If everything is happening to you and you have to put your guard up, then you are also blocking these incredible sensors from your mini miracles. That is very important and truthful data you need to understand things on a deeper level. Being authentic is being able to have your emotions and feel things all throughout your day. That is who you are. Not this other version.

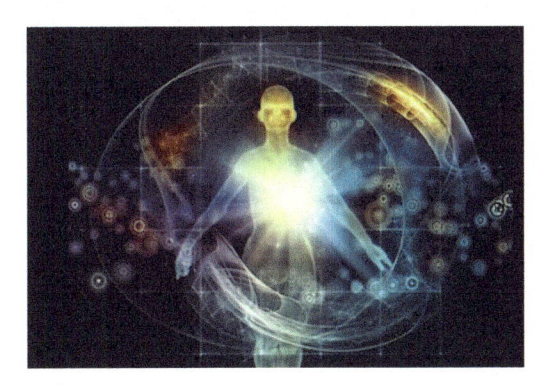

You naturally become more authentic by transferring away from the reward-center-way-of-life. It really is about addressing your foundational beliefs, so you can make space to create something new. This takes trust. The more you allow yourself to be different, the more you want to do it. Start to allow what is happening to be a beautiful combination of all of these energies in the world aligning with you in some way. It's very weird at first, but it's fun. Sit in that and use it as a fuel instead of survival mode. Learn to fuel yourself with trust in the love that drives all of this. It's a higher vibration. Go to *The Void* and find it.

Sitting with all your Minds functioning as one is like a symphony. It works in perfect harmony, feelings swirling everywhere in circular formation. Like breathing or blinking. Get it up and running long enough and eventually it will be seamless. Try to catch your mind creating an enemy. Hold these moments and track them back through the emotional jungle from which they came. Find the source of it and look around until you feel a thought and go, "Aha!" Acknowledge what you're doing. You are forming a clear awareness of a part of you. Hold this fearful moment and stand with your powerful soul as you review it. You see the bigger picture. Your soul only lives in this bigger picture. This is what it really wants to talk about. So, create space to have that conversation. This is Soul Alignment.

If we don't understand it, we go to war with it. Presidents have shouted this to the masses: "Say no to drugs!" Well, which drugs? We call them all drugs because we have no idea what they really are. Pharmaceutical companies make trillions selling us drugs in pill form. They make a synthetic version of the same things found in nature. You can see the obvious Egoic Loop. Earth gave us medicine, but we think we need to get it from a pharmacy instead of outside in the yard. This is not in any opposition to western medicine, quite the contrary. The good doctor has saved my life at least once. We are identifying a specific place where society holds resistance so we can try to change an Egoic Loop by expanding it with new information. We are mired in resistance. We pride ourselves on staying the same. "I've had this job for forty years." Okay, well you seem a bit miserable. "This is just the way things are." No, this is us being bored and complacent about living this way.

Explore your life with knowledge. If it came from the Earth it might help. Our medicinal plant/drug paradox is pretty simple. For example, DMT (dimethyltryptamine) is seen and used like a drug. It is also illegal (as most spiritually opening plants are). Well, DMT is produced in your *pineal gland* in a burst when you're born and a burst when you're dead. Entry into body, and exit. We might be smoking an entry and exit soul drug, because that's how clueless we are. Might as well drive a hearse to school. Your own mind is creating a burst to link between your spirit and your human body. These are powerful medicines, and we are about to finally open our minds enough to figure out how to best use them for healing. I experienced this once for ten minutes and it led to a connection of thoughts that brought the puzzle all together. I needed to know it was worth it. I got the answer I didn't know I needed. Of course. Others don't have the same experience, as some have it much heavier in the emotional side of things. You can see the blocks are so heavy they can't burst through their pineal gland just yet, but they will. You can also find this same experience in sober meditation.

There are "drugs" and there are medicinal plants. Some medicinals are really helpful when you're trying to wake up the minds. DMT gives you a peek at something in the Universe, but which realm and which layer is based on you. Activation of the pineal gland and all its superpowers. It either shoots you there to the seat of everything or takes some big chunk away that is blocking your path to that cosmic highway. Something about these impactful moments sticks with you in a new way. You know how it felt and what it looked like, and you know you did this magical thing, all within yourself. Stay curious as to why you are able to do that, and then wonder how you can do it again in yourself naturally. The tropical plant *ayahuasca,* for instance, can seem intense because there is a lot of lower-level clearing happening. Mind-body emotions. But you can also use ayahuasca to connect with your own guides that are with you. Like a video chat session with "your people." It can be very helpful with that. Mushrooms in small doses help open some things back up in the mind as well, but you can't just go buy any "shrooms" off the street. Know what they are. How they grow. Learn all about them. Grow them yourself. The only way you will ever truly understand it anyways. *Golden Teacher* is geared more towards enlightenment, others are stronger or just different. They all have different effects, so you need to find something that aligns with you. Usually, that's a healthy meal and a lot of water.

These plants stimulate our inner life, and we are all in different grades in this school. You need to study these things before you understand their purpose and how to make it work for your spiritual process, and most importantly, be patient as to when. You will know. (They can be very dangerous, yes, but they are also duality—what can show you the light, can also kill you.) Keep things pleasant from the start. Start with your body and the here and now. Time to be a warrior again. This time moving towards alignment of self. No need to force anything. This is more about doing the opposite. All this said, you could book one session with a reputable spiritual hypnotherapist and they would work with you in your awareness or subconscious state and you can heal more in one session than a lifetime of plant medicine. Healing is found when you re-connect with Mother Nature and all her wild mysteries.

CHAPTER 9

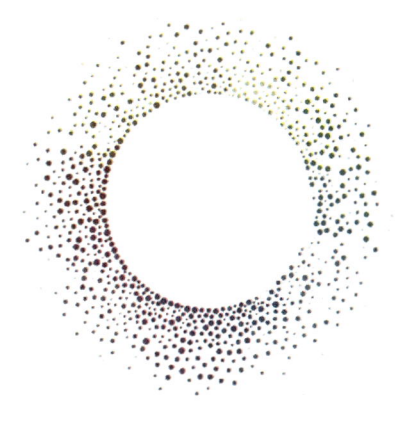

DAILY BREAD

"Don't forget to allow this to be a beautiful experience."

The art of sourdough. There is something oddly spiritual about eating fresh baked bread in the morning. Bread that you leavened. Sourdough needs to be alive to turn into something we eat. It has a starter. Bacteria that's growing. You curate it and keep an eye on it. (It's easy, just remember to feed it.) You create the dough for the next morning and set it aside in the fridge. You have set yourself up to have a soul moment. A little effort for a moment of bliss. You wake up and put the fresh dough in the oven. Pop it out and break it open over a cup of tea. What is it about these moments? It's almost like a silent little orgasm. Just you and the world. Being nourished and cared for. Taking a second to tune-in with how incredible it is here. Just you and *it*.

Something crucial here, you did not sit and let the world create this for you, you created *with* it. The actual making of that bread was the essential part of this. You touched life-giving grains and made them with your own hands so your spirit could enjoy the little things too. Priceless.

"Just as a candle cannot burn without fire, we cannot live without a spiritual life." -Buddha

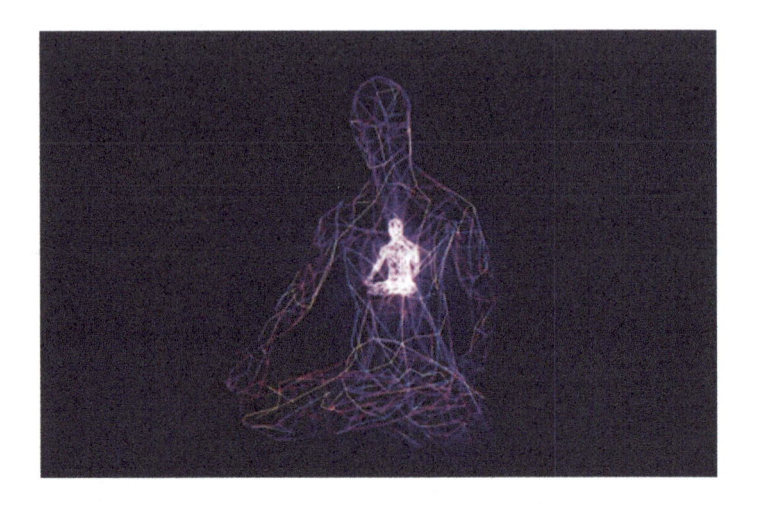

Find the Daily Bread that works for you and learn to enjoy the moments of calm. The rest will happen on its own. Start with the body, acceptance of your outer life through the flushing of toxins and old emotional energies. You start to find that you need to clean everything first.

Your Daily Bread is not about creating space for the giant miracle that will change your life forever. Your Daily Bread is about being awake and present for these little moments that are creating little miracles. You are creating these little micro-miracles and allowing space in your life for them to grow. Learning how to close your eyes anywhere in the world and step inside yourself into a place of calm grounding energy.

Surrender the e-go-go-go mind. Let it quiet down. Think about all the pressure we put on ourselves to do what is "good" for us. Some of us struggle just to go for a morning run. What we are really doing is living in reward center. When we wake up, we have an alarm and dates and times we need to adhere to. We really want to wake up with the sun. The giant ball of fire that gives us life every day. How do we forget it so easily? If you want to really engage your heart *YouTube* an artist named *Mi-Lan* and turn on one of her healing sounds. She's an ego mind-breaker. Turn something powerful on and go run with the sun. You are spending little moments with nature. It's important.

> *"The person who is near me is near the fire, the person who is far from me is far from the kingdom…The light of the Divine will reveal itself, but its image is hidden by its light"* -Jesus

That longing in you starts to feel weirdly satiated by a connection to our sun. Something that will blind you in its image. If you can really stop and appreciate the majestic nature of the sun and the moon, then you are on the right track. How did that perfect amount of endless energy arrive here just for us? Perhaps it was the end of a soul deciding to give itself to the service of us all? If any of you died and created the sun, we would never hear the end of it. We are more concerned with our outfit in the morning than the giant ball of energy.

> *"Nature holds the key to our aesthetic, intellectual, cognitive and even spiritual satisfaction."* -E.O. Wilson

We go running or hiking to spend a moment alone with the Earth. This is *Daily Bread*. Find the amount of physical exercise that is optimal, not peak. We don't need to always push our bodies to the limit. That is like always driving your car with the pedal all the way down. You will eventually break it. Find the amount that is exactly what your body or mind needs to be balanced. Your body will dictate this, not the other way around. This way is much easier anyway. Get in a routine where you no longer think of it in reward center Ego Mind. You only think of it as time to sneak away and connect with something deep inside you.

So many ancient techniques slip into pop culture. Yoga is a profoundly ancient scientific technique for spiritual union with body, and we do it to get nicer looking buns. We are ridiculous and it's lovely. It's okay, while you're at yoga exploring your vanity, you are also doing ancient alignment techniques that will help you broaden your inner life. You are preparing it for a higher amount of internal energy, which can be a bit overwhelming at first. You will be happy you prepared your body beforehand. You are doing what yoga truly is—*union with body*. Meditation works the same way. You may not know what you are doing, but it's not working in mysterious ways; we know what it is doing, and it is working. So, relax, you're crushing it.

Meditation can work like this: every time you sit for five minutes and focus your attention above your eyebrows and focus on your inhale and exhale, your soul mind is taking a handful of asphalt and packing it on the ground. Over time you wake up and realize you have built yourself a spiritual highway that goes wherever you want to go. Do the little work so you can let the work build on itself. Be playful with it. Your happy spirit is more aligned with this than a dramatic meditation regimen. When you keep it light, it becomes second-nature.

When you get your little meditation routine together you start to defuse the emotional warning signals by entering your passcode to the alarm system—your curiosity. Then you can sit quietly and explore some old memories and truly heal and move on with life anew. This process through the mind starts the soft healing of old wounds and is a bit like an emotional Swedish Massage; it hurts while it's happening, but then a few days later you feel like you can finally breathe again. Sit with your body to explore where you have trapped pain and fear memories. Every knot and pinched nerve are a life experience stored in your body. The equivalent to throwing your clothes all over your room instead of stopping to put everything where it was meant to go. The more you throw on the ground, the deeper the pile. You are an emotional memory hoarder and it's time to clean house down to the studs. You learn to find these energy pockets in a calm state so you can look at them and realize they aren't that scary after all. We learn to drain the pain in ways that doesn't cause us more harm so we can process the harder stuff. It's all something that we have our entire lifetime to do.

When you've gone full Marie Kondo in your body, then you have clean empty space for the new information you're going to collect. New jobs, new relationships, new perspectives. This time you don't throw your emotions on the floor—you process it, learn something from it, and put it where it belongs. If you hit a roadblock in your heart, then go back and do some little meditations and focus on that moment. Ask your questions again while you're in the heart place.

The physical science of meditation. What are we actually doing? We all talk about meditation in the abstract because that was all the information we had. Even people who have crossed into incredible realms don't always have the words to describe it because we aren't all talking about it enough yet to understand. Meditation is a science just like getting a great golf swing. It is learning how to position your body to generate a desired outcome. In short, we are turning off the body so we can turn on the soul. That's it. You can do it anywhere for as long or little as you want. A golf swing may feel religious so use that same drive. Meditate while you're waiting in line. Close your eyes, turn your attention to the point between the eyebrows, inhale slowly making the sound of a word. Exhale making the sound of a different word. *Hong Sau* is great here. Making the sounds "Hong" on inhale and "Saw" on exhale. You are distracting the Ego Mind into a slumber. You are putting the lion to sleep. That's it, you've done it. Sit in The Void and listen.

To start your spiritual life, simply release the rigidity of it all. It may sound crazy to think that you can build a world inside yourself, but remember, people are now buying fake houses in a fake space in the middle of nothing on the internet (and paying lots of money for them!). Meditation is not precious between us and reality, it is only between our minds and our soul. Meditation belongs to no one person or belief system and is only a word mankind gave to the process of activating your inner connection to *source*. It can remain wordless in your mind if you feel that to be truer to you.

If you want a secret little magic trick, look for sounds that are real. Sound bowls are not synthesized sounds, they are derived from the original. Nature makes the perfect notes. While sitting in meditation, if you listen to sounds meant for certain chakras, you can start to feel the different centers in you reacting to the different notes. It's a bit fascinating. If you want to connect to a higher spiritual being, make that sound in your mind. Voila. Magic. You just started to become resonance again. You became that frequency. You are the instrument. Play your song and the world will hear it. Follow music tracks from an artist who understands sacred tones, and when you feel it in your mind walking upward, it is quite literally resonating your stairway to heaven.

Whenever your mind starts to wander, focus on the breath and get lost in the sounds you hear. The frequencies help us focus. Spotify, YouTube, it doesn't matter, keep it simple and without words (words tease your animal mind.) You want sounds. Something that activates your Soul and Heart Mind like Om chanting or people singing ancient tones for activation. Type in words like *Chakra Sounds, Pineal Gland Activation, or Ben Carroll Singing Bowls. When you* know what you are looking for an entire world of free content will arrive in seconds. You can make this specific to what you are focusing on because there is that much available out there already. Thank you to these artists for creating this music even though we all pretend its voodoo! We like it now. Sound can help you start to resonate with your sensory system. You will find yourself switching from Ego to Sensory to Soul.

"Fold little meditations into everyday life, you will find everything you need in there."

It's helpful to find a potential meditation destination you are curious about. Embrace that childlike curiosity. It thrives here. Emotional body clearing, past wounds, remote viewing, pineal gland opening, calm your heart rate or heal physical trauma. I opted to go in search of the information records (Akashic Records) for all the details and memories of our own past lives. Remote viewing is a great workout. *David Morehouse* taught remote viewing to spies for the US Government (for decades) and wrote a book teaching you how to do it. It has really basic starting points and it's on Amazon, obviously. When you try these things, you realize this can be fun. You light up with energy. This is good. Enjoy it.

You can meditate for ten hours and have a spiritual awakening, body pulsating with energy, and then you open your eyes, and everything goes back to normal. Here again. That's okay. Don't overthink things. Be easy on yourself. This is about the opposite of achieving. Failing to have control is the secret. You can have intent in meditation but try to catch yourself *trying*. When you stop trying to achieve something you start to allow it to happen. Relax. Hang out in *The Void*. Think about meditation as if you are training to be a multidimensional soul pilot. Learn how to navigate this open space. To identify places here. For example, when we die we go to The Void. The place of God. If we learn how to understand this while in meditation souring through our inner mind's eye, then we can start trusting this empty space so when our final breath exhales, we will sit comfortably in death and surrender to it. Acceptance of death is really bittersweet. Now you know that it's only physical death. If you are preparing yourself to have a smooth transfer from body to soul, then realize you are also teaching yourself Death to Ego. All of your false perceptions about what is real will dissipate.

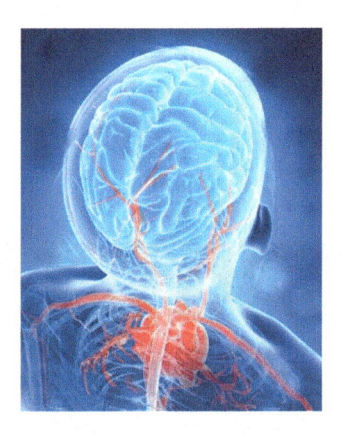

When you become still you can check in with yourself. Feel your body. Feel around for pain and emotions. Swim around a little. Lost in thought, back to breath. You need to add this Daily Bread to your spirit toolkit, because when you wake up and the world seems horribly off-kilter, you will adore these tools. As you get used to these body meditations, emotional releases, tension releases, when this is a regular routine, then go seek some guidance if you want to go farther. The next levels of meditation are more scientific in nature.

Paramahansa Yogananda was sent to the West to teach the scientific methods of yoga and meditation. (He's the guy that wrote the book that Steve Jobs carried with him always) A truly incredible Guru who can take you as far as you want to go with meditation techniques. He's also a great guide connected to Jesus consciousness. *Transcendental Meditation* has a nice modern take on this whole process. It is everywhere now and you don't need anyone to do it. All religions and credos accepted. As it should be. This is not religion anymore, this is spirituality. Religion 2.0.

The path of meditation leads you farther way from your Egoic Mind. This is the part where if you love it, then you let it go, even your entire identity. To accomplish this, you completely release attachment to being you. That's not easy, so just entertain the thought. I know it will make sense when you get there, but it's a place I am not ready to fully embrace either. I'm in the middle of some weird obsession with this dramatic theatre here. I'm attached to soul ideals, purpose, the egoic narrative, pain, love and confusion. I am attached in so many ways, almost willingly at this point. This path will eventually lead to complete detachment from the idea of self, to be okay with ceasing to exist and joining back into the union of energy that is *everything*. The final call to service from inside your soul. You offer yourself. A backflip into surrender as you burst into a sun.

Simply take that as additional information you can pull up at any time. I am attached to things here, and up there. Running multiple dimensions of attachment. Good grief. One attached to my outward life here and one attached to my inward life tied to past incarnations and the possibilities of the future. I'd like to find those attachments and go over that list and see if I need to make any adjustments. I'll know more about that as I grow I suppose. You get the information that you need for the moment, not the narrative. (This drives me absolutely mad. Patience is not a natural gear for me.)

Practice Saucha

Shaucha (Sanskrit: शौच) purity, cleanliness and clearness. Purity of mind, speech and body.

The art of cleaning the impurities from your surroundings so that you yourself become clean on the inside. *"Make the outside look like the inside."* To be it, you become it. Make the outside look like the inside and the inside look like the outside. I look outside and see a world that is not clean, so what must I be? Cleaning your home or living environment can be just as important as eating food and breathing—it gives your body life. You are caring for the things around you by acknowledging that they are made of energy at their most core level. The old cliché of the man washing his red Corvette in the driveway—sorry, but he is resonating with that material energy, aware of it or not, that car loves him back. I love to put on random world playlists when I *Saucha* because I am always curious as to what new sound will invoke something new out of me (why not throw in a little *shakti?*). When you yourself are practicing *Saucha* and cleaning the dirt in your house, you are in effect taking away your old programming and clearing the space so it can be clean and constantly open to the new things you want in your life. You clean it, it cleans you. *SOUCHA!*

"Be faithful in small things because it is in them that your strength lies." -Mother Teresa

When you really want to kick the house cleaning up a notch, take an electric leaf blower to the house. The satisfaction is childish fun, and extremely effective. We need more of that. Nothing stagnant in your house means nothing stagnant in you. When you hold these thoughts, *Saucha* becomes a very important part of your Saturday morning. Then it becomes part of your always. If you are playfully enjoying clearing out the old, you also completely forget whose mess you are cleaning, because you are using it to expand. Thanks for the mess, suckers.

Unity with your environment. I was thinking about the great powers of the internet. For the first time in humanity's history, we are able to communicate everything everywhere in real-time. Yet we see an internet smothered in chaos. Imagine if *Saucha* was a source of alignment for us all and we would begin to clean things like the internet? We would pick up our own trash and not add trash to the pile. Start with the easy stuff on the outside. Clean your environment. *Saucha.*

> *"For it is in giving that we receive."*
> -St. Francis of Assisi

If your house is too big to *touch-connect*, then get a smaller house. If you don't want to touch anything in your house, then get different stuff. If you can't touch a windowsill and wonder how it is a reflection of you, if you can't walk through the yard and look at the plants that are wondering if you notice them…if you can't touch your life, then you are not a part of it. All of that energy is stagnant and in service to your shadow thoughts. Our egos build a staff, hire assistants, we ramble through our Egoic Narratives as other human beings clean our home. They are more connected to your own environment than you are. Each step to the reward-minded life is a step away from you. We spend a lifetime revering kings, but it's the peasants who see this world with their hearts, because they are the ones that touch it. Make the outside look like the inside. We should only have a staff if we are leaders, not a boss. You can't lead what you are not physically a part of.

Make a life shot

—

You have no idea what will happen in your life every day, so one thing can be an easy constant. Morning life shot. I have herbs and medicinal spices all delivered to my door from an organic farm in Oregon. They all arrive in powder form. It was never burned or grown from poisoned seeds, it's real and alive like the good lord made it. Pulverized down into micronutrients. This is like shot gunning a beer, pour the life shot and then just take it down.

I use a tablespoon of chlorella and spirulina, turmeric, cardamom, ashwagandha, beet powder, and sometimes I throw in stuff to clean my organs like dandelion root or sea buckthorn. These can flush through your system and also add nutrients at the same time. Cardamom powder flushes out deep belly fats. While we're getting ready for work, we're flushing kidney stones, rebuilding the liver and inserting important nutrients your body needs to thrive. Healing muscles and inflammation, nourishing the blood. Add a little organic lemon juice and down the hatch. All before you walk out of your front door. Genius. I noticed when I have really early call times on a film set, if I take this shot, I never get "hangry" if they don't break for lunch for seven hours. No matter what you do today, you packed your body with nutrients in one shot. Those different nutrients all do different things. Chlorella is packed with vitamins and minerals. Turmeric works wonders on internal muscle relief and the liver. Ashwagandha just adds a little extra bliss cloud to your day. Things are happening in there all day and all night and all it takes is adding the right nutrients so the motor can hum along as you go. "Keep it liquid" through lunch and you are on your way.

There are herbs for everything, and they work. I have helped people quit drugs or alcohol by giving them little shots of valerian root (which I use to sleep sometimes). These can be powerful, so do your homework. The amount of healing medicine in plants compared to a pharmacy are endless and it's free if you know how to grow it. Charge yourself and your water

—

A friend once told me that if I was going to buy a car, I better pay more for the one I loved, because if I loved it, I would take care of it. She was right. The love was more important than the money. I hold that thinking with the little things just the same. Get a few nice looking 32 oz. tumblers that can go with you anywhere and drink at least three of them a day. No less. Add a little organic unfiltered apple juice or lemon juice to flavor - plain water can be boring. I throw raw ginger and lemon juice in the blender, make a giant jar and top off my water in the morning before I go. Sometimes I add a little raw honey and cayenne. Make your water delicious. If this seems like a lot of water, think of it like this—if you want to drive from California to Oregon, you will need 50 gallons of gas. You were busy so you got 15 gallons of gas and now you wonder why you broke down on the side of the road. Egoic Loop. You are not drinking water for your ego reward, you are drinking water so the machine that is your beautiful body can actually function the way it was meant to. Being of service also means being of service to your incredible body. You are doing it because you realize your body is a living, thinking part of you. Love it back.

Water is filled with information. It resonates. Every single drop of water has a memory of something. You are binding yourself with it and it with you. It's not just "hydrating," it's resonating. This is the base line. Always keep it fresh, cool and with you at all times. Charge it in the morning. (No sugar. Anything but sugar. Your body hates sugar.) This is not just "flavoring," these medicinal herbs and spices all do something different in your body. Make your own special recipe of life-healing nutrients. Talk to someone in holistic medicine. I buy all my daily shot ingredients from a farm with nutrient-rich Oregon soil that has been doing this for decades. "Reputable Source." You cannot buy the real stuff in a big box store. Seek out what it is your body needs. Organically.

Ingredients matter. Don't be fooled with less than. If you read about raw apple-cider vinegar and decide to get some for your gut health, pay attention to the false versions in your everyday life. Your body responds to the living cultures in there. If you run to a supermarket and buy apple cider vinegar, you will most likely find a clear yellowish liquid. This will only make your water taste like vinegar without the added benefits, so no thanks. Real apple cider vinegar is raw and unfiltered. The living cultures from apple cider vinegar come from a giant fermentation culture people refer to as "the mother." If you believe that things floating in your beverage are gross, then you are allowing a belief you made up as a child to keep you from healing. That is your ego's version of blind control. Is the real stuff the cheapest? No, but the cheapest brand isn't even real so what have you been telling yourself about your belief in money that overshadows your belief in being a healthy and happy person? It helps with digestion, yeast infections, helps lower blood sugar. A little bit of this for a dollar more will save you thousands of dollars in pain.

The love is in the details. At my home in Oregon, we drink water right from the tap. Water that has traveled through streams and rivers and underground filters of charcoal and ancient minerals. This water is packed with life. Your body loves real water. In Los Angeles we drink water adjacent. Instead of the water passing through all the billion-year-old micronutrients, it goes through pastures and is flooded with chemicals. Then churned and beaten until it's legally drinkable. Fluoride was a waste chemical decades ago and someone conned the government into putting it in all of our water. If you want tap water in the city. you need to leave it out to let the chlorine evaporate and get a great filter. You can add filters to your whole house. Mineral systems are wonderful too. This is how we can start to add these things into our lives so that a nutrient army is in constant flow with our lifestyle. No matter what we are doing, our bodies are being nourished as they should be.

DRAIN THE PAIN

"If you don't find a way to reduce the suffering of your surroundings, then you will continue to suffer."
-Buddhist monk

If you carry pain and anger, anger that has been added to without being drained, you are constantly overloading the tank of anger in you and that will eventually turn into rage. You will always try to find a way to manifest that in your life. Regardless of how you are currently dealing with conflicts, if you are not letting this emotion out in a healthy way, your mind and your body are going to create a more difficult situation for you because it needs to get it out. Your wounds are misunderstandings that tear into us until we receive the message, because anything that can hit us that deeply is crucial to your growth. "When the cup spilleth over…"

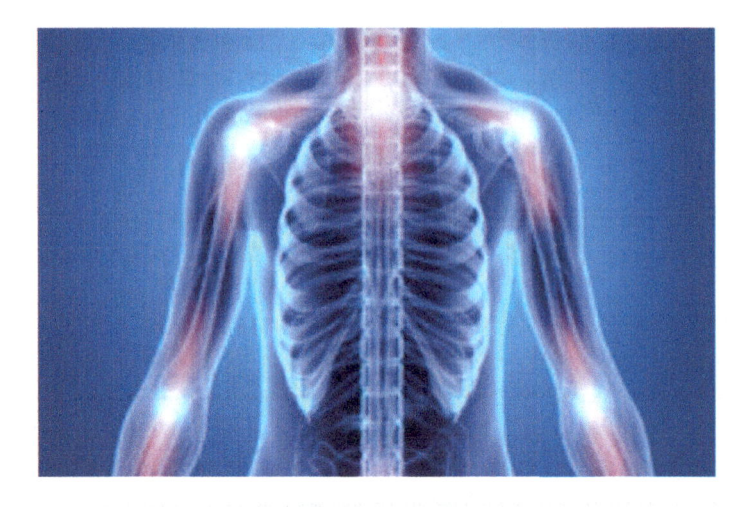

Scream at the people up there somewhere. Get in your car and scream to the person who is driving you crazy. Say everything. Yell at whoever you want, within you. It's all about purging that energy. Even breathing out can be a release. When you lift a dumbbell, think of that person and the emotion and drive than energy into your lift. Run, run until you cry with rage, yelling it in your mind. Chanel that emotion while you're having a physical release. Let it flow out of you like water back into the ocean. Release those emotions. Exhale.

Find your moments to be alone and to feel. Notice your resistance to forming new habits. The ones you know deep down you really need. All these good habits I've been trying to stick to for years, yet something inside me pushing, always refusing. Refusing to surrender to the fact that I don't know. I then start carrying this guilt in my mind and body for years. Once I started to understand the Three Minds and could start communicating with different parts of myself, these new healthy habits were forming easily and without much notice. I often had to remind myself, "Hey look, you do yoga all the time now."

Releasing pain is just some basic maintenance, it doesn't make your whole life better. If your life is in shambles and you wake up, it seems even worse than before. Work in some great daily programming to ground yourself and constantly take moments to drain pain or sadness. Quickly acknowledging the moment, processing now with clarity, and moving on. What you will notice is how quickly the house around you was torn down, but how easily you can build a new one. The day after I would disconnect from people who were really hard for me to be around, just like that, a stranger would appear. We would talk and connect deeply. One day. Two days. Three days. Suddenly finding myself on hikes and getting coffee with these beautiful strangers. This is a trust fall. The life of the Universe is always there. No matter what. Even if you can't see it. Take deep comfort in that. Underneath all this crazy, the force that monitors us all is based in this incredible love. It's also in you. That's why it seems so familiar, because it is.

CHAPTER 10

SURRENDER

Surrender is not giving up, it's the beginning. I have a strong memory of my uncle's death. I came down to the hospital and walked slowly through the 4th floor wing. I never understood our hospitals. They are so cold and lifeless. The opposite of what you would think we would want. Surely a sign of our egoic perspective of healing—it's ridiculous and we all know it. I walked along the hospital corridor waiting to hear the comforting roar that is this side of my family. If it was Uncle Bob, then there would be one hundred people crammed in that room day and night. I walked past the room and the only person I saw was lying near the window, moaning. I walked right by the door. I totally chickened out. I stopped and turned back. I entered slowly. I had never visited a family member in the hospital, let alone a dying one, and without a gaggle of cousins to hide behind, I was scared. I walked up to him. He was very old. Very tall, and very little of him left here. I sat with him. I gave in to the fact that I had no idea what was happening, but I was curious. He would jolt and moan and then quiet himself. It would happen again and again. I started to talk to him. I could see he was leaving his body a little, freaking out, and then coming back. He was in resistance, but I had no I idea at the time this is the moment doctors call Terminal Lucidity. I didn't need the words to sit and try to understand it on my own, I just needed to resonate with what was speaking through our two hearts.

I was fixated on the skin on his lip that was loose. I began having a hard time with the physical decay, but everything else was fine. He kept rambling and then he said, "I mean, I'm not repenting or anything." My souls intrigue lit up and I leaned in and said, "…go ahead and repent, I'm listening!" As I watched him, blind, mostly deaf and dead in body form, his memories of identity were cycling to his ego brain. He was where we will all will get eventually, a place of "If I am not this brain, then who am I?" A question we surely need to answer before death's door. This is the surrender, so let's talk about "surrender to what?" We can know this right now. Let us not live in the abstract. With more information, things can become more specific, which is key to all of this. Isolate something and focus on it until you understand it deeply. We know what this is now. Our first stop is *The Void*. It may seem like empty space, but it is the quiet of *everything*. The first dimension. Our birthplace. This is a place of *God, Source, Akasha*. When we leave our bodies, we see this as emptiness because we don't understand it anymore. That is our false beliefs in action. We have become so blind that when we are with *"God,"* we don't recognize it. Which matters not—you are as safe as a baby in the womb. There is no answer, only a trust that love is driving all of this. You can't find that trust by looking out to the world, we are all crazy. You have to find that answer in you. Go to the place that will show you what is operating all of this and when you see it for yourself, you will see how hard we struggle to surrender to something that is so beautiful. He's not dying, he is being released and he just forgot how to do it.

Uncle Bob would wake up and yank at his arms. The nurse entered and promptly adjusted the Velcro straps, his arms tightly bound to the rails on the bed. I always loved Uncle Bob. This rarity of a tall playful man we would only get to see every so often at a family gathering. He had been on TV a few times and had this natural showmanship. He called his gift of gab "Double Talk" on the channel 5 news. Being young and from Hollywood, I think he got a kick out of me too. There he was, dying, telling me a story about being 14 years old on the playground. In his blind half-here state at 90 something years old, he was still trying to play down that he had feelings about this moment on the playground. He was repeating the memory on loop. This was a pivotal moment that changed him at his core. A belief was born here. A deep wound he never treated. In nine decades of life, never addressed.

He didn't sound like an old man, he sounded like a hurt child. He would say what was closer to feelings and then quickly try to excuse his thoughts. I kept asking playfully. I was laser focused. Finally, he said, "I was nice, ya know, and they were all making fun of me. My nose. It was so big they all laughed. So, I started to be funny. That's why I did that, ya know." He had a very large and very charming nose. He said, "that's when I started double talk, because they were all making fun of my nose." He wasn't telling me this as just a memory, he was seeing it and feeling it. I didn't know at the time, but I was watching and interpreting sensory data of someone's giant childhood wound buried under an emotional tag that said, "Really, this? So what? You have a big nose, man up!" And, on the other side of that warning sign was this adorable kid who got made fun of at school and was deeply hurt. People did not walk their children through those emotional problems. You "pulled up your bootstraps and buried your emotions like a man." I was playful and told him that I also had a big nose and that in the film business they love it. I also told him that it was okay, not to have the nose, but to talk about it. That those feelings mattered to me. I cared. I spoke to that fourteen-year-old version of himself. "Children can be so mean to each other, even when they don't mean it. Uncle Bob, you grew up to be loved by so many people, so none of that matters, you are loved." and, "I'm sorry they were so mean to you." That was all he wanted. Someone who could sit with that and feel its importance to him and see its impact on his life. No right or wrong here. Ever. What mattered is how he felt.

We all love our vanity, but we don't take it with us. Uncle Bob was letting go of concepts that he stored in his heart as a little boy. Beliefs he made that lasted a lifetime, built in one small moment on the school yard at the beginning of this century. Here we were in silence. Our moment of peace followed again by an abrupt jolt and a yanking of the strapped arms. This was a lot to sit with. I took a moment to gather myself. Something about the hands. A nurse strapping an old man's frail body to the cold metal. Watching him mired in fear and afraid to surrender to his own spirit. As if the other half of himself was a total stranger who he didn't trust.

I found a gift shop on the bottom floor. I looked around and on the bottom shelf I found a pile of Beanie Babies. I grabbed two—one was a cat because I knew he liked cats. I went back upstairs and put them in a blind man's hands. His large coarse fingers grabbed them as if Lenny was going to accidentally kill it. As soon as his hand registered the soft fur he was suddenly still, delicate. Gentle like the spirit he really was. He started caressing it and became quiet. He just wanted a little comfort for someone stuck between here and there. He doesn't need straps or more drugs, he needs fuzzy kittens that remind him it's not so scary, here or there. I bid him a fun travel and left.

I don't remember how long I was there and during that entire experience I found out the gaggle of cousins were only minutes away having lunch. They returned as thunderous as they left, none the wiser I had been there at all. My dear cousin Julie called a few days later. She told me he had passed. She told me about the little Beanie Babies and how much comfort that gave him over the next few days. He was calm in his final backflip into bliss. She told me the nurses at that hospital took notice and started to change their approach, a little. I like to picture a hospital wing filled with people dying, holding cute little Beanie Babies animals in their hands as they set off. Sometimes we don't surrender until our very last breath and that's too heartbreaking for me. It was then I knew we don't die at all, we just surrender to the next. We can do that here.

We can be there for people to help them surrender by listening. I was young and scared. I just stopped thinking. I stopped trying to act like I knew what to do. Sometimes you have to open your heart and feel your way through it, together. He finally put his relentless Ego Mind to sleep…turned off the Egoic Narrative for good. It was then he surrendered into the cosmos once again. Now freely walking between life and death and all its curiosities. I know now this is the same process we are all going through inside ourselves—resist or surrender to it.

Surrender takes trust. Trust in a world that has taught us not to trust. I was never in AA but dear friends are, and I admire its simple take on something so powerfully deep and loving. In Alcoholics Anonymous they surrender to a power bigger than them. They are practicing, "Forgive me for I do not know what in the world is happening here." That is a great step, but let's be specific. To surrender is to let your inner self connect back to *source* so you can feel that there is love behind all of this, even the darkness. We cannot surrender in our Egoic Minds. That is a trick, and our ego is too clever for that. When you sit in the abyss that is the great geometric dance in the Universe, you sit in *Awe*. You surrender to the love of the awe because it is so beautiful that you feel your soul sitting in the womb of everything. You don't have to say this in a group, you meditate and go in search of this feeling. It is out there waiting for you. Take the steps to find your internal life, and surrender will come when you tap back into who you are. When you feel it, you will know it and your life will never be the same. For now, surrender in not knowing, because no one else knows either. Take solace in forgiveness and respite in being wrong. Exhale. When you need to find a place to start this practice, just say, "I don't know" with centered energy. Say it often. This is surrender in its most polite form, "I don't know."

Forgive them for they know not what they do. Forgive me for I know not what I do. This is surrender. We say this, but now we can understand it a little deeper. Surrender is to let go of your Egoic Mind and its desire to control everything in your life. "Om Swaha!" I have shouted this from the mountain tops with frustration. It is a sacred way to release unwanted energy to the Universe that it came from. But now I am more than allowed to let it fill me up first. I needed to feel again. To be allowed to. It feels good to scream to the heavens again with your heart reattached. It's sharing all your deepest emotions in a state of bittersweet. Sharing it with them. Whoever they are up there. That's where my tears are, too. It's then you remember that someone is listening. My mother taught me that.

I have a friend in the military I call, "Mike the Human Badass." We met in high school in Ashland, Oregon. He was from a poor family and had that typical life. He hated it. He called a military school that we send our children to when we give up, and he asked to enroll himself. This is very important to this story of Post-Traumatic Stress Disorder. He was a willing participant. He asked to join a system built to punish (reform) with structure. Mike was incredibly successful in his military career, eventually becoming a sniper and then trained with special ops. This guy is the real deal. I just know him as my sweet friend, Mike. He has children and a beautiful wife. He walks through his PTSD very openly. He told me once that he believed that his PTSD was less severe because when the military is breaking down young minds for war, he didn't need to be broken down. He was a willing participant. Conscious. Aware of what he was signing up for. I found this very fascinating and have studied it more over the years. Now with the Three Minds we can make so much sense of it. When we break down people's Ego Mind, then they act in ways that are traumatic to their Heart Minds because they are ignoring it. The system has been distorted. My dear friend was able to process things as he went along.

Now what I see in him is someone who carries a lot of weight from the world that he saw and experienced. But his heart is still very much intact. Every now and again his training slips into his family life but he also has, Dara. A very strong woman who can understand these things and talk about them. She allows space for this. Right when it happens, they talk about it. The healing here is understanding the manipulation of the mind to a state of deception. Deception causes us to lock things down. Deception comes from Ego Mind doing things that cause damage to our hearts and telling us that it shouldn't hurt. It needs to hurt because you are a human being. You did not do any of these things because they were your idea, you played into the Egoic Narrative, and it stung you deeply. Forgive yourself for being human. It is an asset, not a curse. An asset that is willing and able with the power to heal. Mike has learned how to be a warrior and have a heart at the same time, that, opens to the door for everyone.

PART 3

MADE OF LIGHT

CHAPTER 11

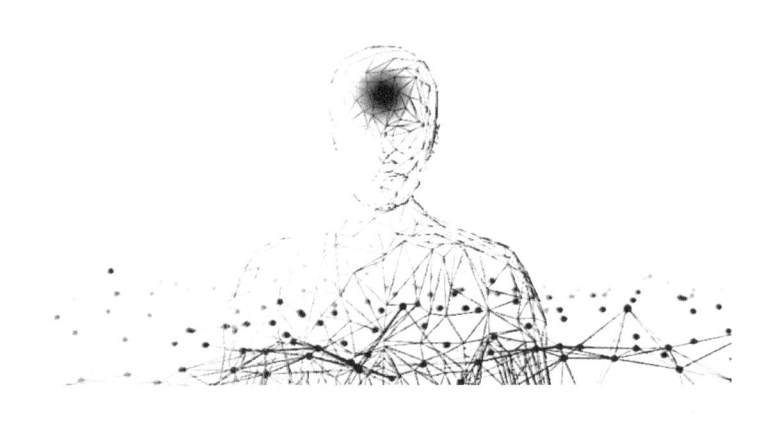

LET THERE BE LIGHT

"The soul should always stand ajar, ready to welcome the ecstatic experience." -Emily Dickinson

To truly understand Emotional Intelligence, we will have to answer the question of our own true origins of creation. The one that's been hidden from us for thousands of years. This is not a gentle overview, this is the deepest truth of our human creation. The truth of our existence. It will challenge life-long beliefs and devour your perception of reality. Part 3 is the PHD in Emotional Intelligence. Monitor your own state of being and how you feel about all the information up until now. If up 'til now has given you enough information to fold into your new authentic life, then let it rest here. If your curious soul wants all the answers to life to fully understand our sensory beings, then by all means, carry on. Brave and bold in truth. Ready, go.

Humankind came into this Earth in bodily form, and we also share a common history with other civilizations. Aliens? Sure, but really just civilizations not simply from this Universe, but from different realms or frequencies. This is not a fantasy, these are things you can confirm for yourself. You are them. You will connect all the same dots for yourself when you start to go inward. Only the Egoic Mind hides information; the Universe shares all information with itself. What is said here is only to give you the information you need to turn yourself on. The agenda is simply shared knowledge. Powerful people hate when we do this.

"We are not human beings having a spiritual experience. We are spiritual beings having a human experience."
-Pierre Teilhard de Chardin

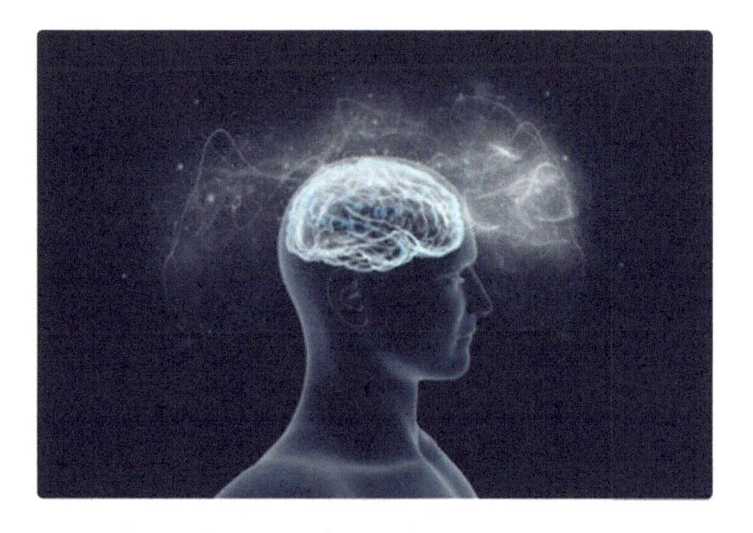

Everything we know about aliens is wrong. There has not been a movie yet that has gotten this right. "Fear sells tickets." There are a couple of animated children's movies that get so beautifully close to who and what is really going on here. *Avatar* has such beautiful imagery of our light being realms, but the story is primarily ego-based, so the truth is muddled. (But I still loved it)

The original *Matrix* was the closest to how all of this actually works and that foundation was really derived from a woman named, *Sophia Stewart* in her manuscript aptly titled, *"The Third Eye."* When her

Soul Mind mixed with the creative translators of the Egoic Narrative, a Hollywood version of the truth was born. (They're just missing the entire origin of who we are is all.) Clearly, a Hollywood movie takes a lot of liberties with how they understood those concepts, but it's very close. If you look at movies of our future, they are all based on guesses about the ego narrative, and we are moving away from that into soul. Point being, all of this is new territory which should be very exciting for everyone. Nobody has any answers. There is no right, there is no wrong. Therefore, everything that you discover is your new truth.

The origins of the Universe started with one white light. You. You are made of thought as energy which manifests itself as a current of life force. When your soul is born you are a pulsating ball of this white light. A bright sacred light so vast that it was all you could see. You are the essence of *God* and you had no way to perceive it. How could you figure out what you are, if you can't see yourself? "What are we?" we thought…we couldn't see anything but light. We were stuck in total bliss. As *Matias De Stefano* says, *"Then shadow arrived to give you shape."* Darkness. What a lovely gift. A way to look at yourself from all sides. Good, bad and everything in between. Without darkness you are only a ball of light that cannot see anything but love. This is the duality that drives our experience here. We are built from this polarity and can choose at any time which perspective we would like to see of ourselves—one of darkness, or one of light—they are the same and they are both in you.

When we can't explain the horrors of the world, remember this: darkness was a gift to help us see perspectives so we could understand ourselves by experimenting. We all incarnate with different challenges we want to explore. You yourself may have been a murderer or a drug kingpin in a past life. That doesn't mean you can't be a saint here. It wouldn't matter because that means your soul was willing to learn those harder experiences so that not only could you understand, but you gained that priceless information: knowledge through experience. That is all your soul wants to do. Keep seeing life from all its perspectives so we continue to expand as a whole. We expand with knowledge so we can build better worlds. This is the central foundation for our lives here. Now let's figure out what to do next.

> *"Experience is the teacher of all things."*
> –Julius Caesar

There is a lot to learn. We have forgotten where we come from and now we can't remember how to look for it. First of all, we have more than one mind. We have three very powerful processing centers. It's like we're all young Harry Potters and we have an inner wand, but we don't believe in magic. Our inner magic wands are crackling and spatting out the creation of this life with no idea we are doing it. This is our survival mode. Our relentless determination. All primal body thoughts to stay alive and progress our society. As we progressed in an egoic-based society, we have forgotten the true original meaning of life and started to believe our own false perceptions. Or to say it another way, we created a Matrix for experience, like *Westworld*, but we fell asleep and now we think *Westworld* is real because we forgot that we flew down from the Heavens and created it. We are not actually asleep, but the important part of us has been in a long and debilitating slumber.

Trying to unsee the world in front of you is tricky at first. To look at your life as if you really do live in *The Truman Show*. A reality that feels and tastes so real that surely this must be it. It's too magnificent to see otherwise. Until we see the darkness. Then we beg to know of something more. Something higher. Some reason for all of this tragedy we see here every day. We try to stay in the joy and happiness, but as hard as we try, we are always met with darkness or pain in some way.

How do we learn to see the world for what it truly is? If you showed someone a MacPro computer in the year 1822, their minds would explode with disbelief. You are made of light. Particles in the quantum world that defy our understanding of reality. Science has known this for decades as *Locality,* and now they realize it was all about *Contextuality*. In quantum physics they understand that the particles all have a fixed value. A place. A file of fact for the ego mind. They are now starting to understand that a particle can have its mate hundreds of thousands of miles away and still be effected by it instantaneously. It's connected to one giant energy grid and so are you. You are a being that is half alive in light and a being that is half alive as an Earth animal. A soul and a human. We are two parts, and we broke the mirror so we could use it as a weapon. Now we can no longer see ourselves. We held this truth in our culture until the end of the *Egyptian Civilization*. The timing of our *modern separation* can be traced to the death of *Jesus Christ*. A very specific coincidence? A being connected to body and spirit manifested on Earth, who came to give us a gift as we left into ego narrative? He was showing us the way home in case we got lost. And indeed we did. So how do we find our way back? We go inside and find our deepest beliefs and challenge them to expand. We open our minds.

You're looking for surrender to the belief that you know what we're doing here. You don't. A very freeing start. Think about all the rules you made as your younger, less aware self. Most, if not all of them, make no sense for you anymore. They never really did—they are only markers of experience that affected you the most so you could go back later and learn why. *Emotional Memory Tags*. Post-it notes on your collection of memories that will one day complete the puzzle. Your wounds are your guides. Your tags are how you remember to pull them back up and look deeper into your wounds for bigger truths about who you are and why you are here. They are telling you what you care about the most. They are guiding you to your purpose.

We pull these emotional memory tags up when we are more open and have more life experience. We have more information now. It changes how we see the past, so we look at it and let it work. Information is what we get from new experience, but as we are all stuck in an Egoic Loop, our experience is just recycled drama. We need information and people like to hide it from us. This is why we are all so confused. The reason we're all fighting about everything all the time, is because a long time ago man figured out how to ensure power: *withhold information*. We also do this to loved ones. We don't tell them the truth. It drives a person mad with emotional chaos. An embedded structure in our society in which the egos at the top would withhold information to use as power to control the people. In business, we call this a *Hierarchy*. Systems of control by way of withholding information causing a civilization to fight amongst themselves.

Hierarchy. Pay attention to this word in your life. Deeply. It is describing a code and pattern by which we have adhered ourselves to and shaped our lives around. This is the current operating system around the globe. When your eyes pop open in awareness, this ego structure is all you can see at first. A structure to achieve power regardless of the world itself or others well-being. Of course, our ego thinks this makes perfect sense and we're not sure why this would be a bad thing. It is a structure embedded in separation. The cause of our suffering. We are so busy fighting over scraps of information that we never see the truth. All the great powers of history each stole information from each other, so no one actually has the whole truth. Religions raged against the Pagans, yet we all celebrate a stolen holiday we call "Christmas." The pagans got their information from the soul, and the egos stole it to create religion. This is how a hierarchy of information works. You don't get the truth, but you can have a branded version of some of it.

The global system function in hierarchy—thanks Romans, as do all major corporations and religions, households, schools, governments, financial systems, technology, fuel energy and so on. Picture it as the DNA flowing through the body of capitalism. Take a second to learn with a visual: when you want to build something of note on Earth, you build a high-rise. Straight up. If you wanted to build in space, you would build a sphere. One follows a paradigm of higher and lower, and one recognizes that it is all or not at all. One is a house of cards, and one is the endless power of unity. The Universe is a sphere because it is all encompassing, not high and not low. Built from *Sacred Geometry*. Everything is in alignment…but us. We are distortion to perfection. Here our beliefs in hierarchy are embedded in our core to believe in better and worse.

It's startling to see that we run our personal lives this way too, our families and even our relationships. Better or worse. Right or wrong. Reward – happiness – failure – sorrow. How you perceive society is through the lens of this same hierarchy DNA, which is a false construct. It is the *Matrix. The Simulation.* In truth, there is no winning and losing, only finding alignment to achieve your purpose. The most hidden secret in the world right there. Have it. The system in which there is only success and failure, that's a game for a crazy person because success does not really exist. It dies too.

Whatever the price we have paid for it, egoic hierarchy does give us structure to achieve. To try harder. To create obstacles and pain so we push forward. We've built an entire global society for our species with it. The *American Dream* is a hierarchy structure. This is not your actual dream. This is a trick of the ego. Native Americans and numerous other cultures still carried this connection to something bigger. They moved when Mother Earth told them to move. They honored each animal is it was robbed of life to give us food. Then the day came and the *Egoic Cycle of the World* had arrived, the wave of sleep washed over the entire planet. A finger on the flame. Out.

"When in darkness, light a match." You are the light we need to move forward. If there is a problem, then you are responsible for it. What you seek, is the art of perspective. For example; The Swastika is not a symbol of Naziism; it was an ancient symbol that a guy tried to steal and use for darkness. That symbol never meant anything to do with hate or separation. It held a deeper truth and resonated with power. A power based on love. Then man took it for their own agenda. The word *"Swastika"* comes from Sanskrit: स्वस्तिक, meaning what we have translated as *"well-being."* So, we can reject that it stands for hate when it was only an attempted forgery of truth. The forgery continues to exist if you forget the original meaning. For myself, it was only an attempted robbery, because I can still see the original. Now in our minds, we can see both. Two perspectives of the same thing. One symbol that can mean hate, and the same symbol that can mean unity. It just depends on your perspective. We learn to separate out what man has affixed onto our sacred truths. Even when it involves someone like Hitler.

Being able to see one symbol from two sides is aligning your three power centers of thought. This is a state of awareness. This is processing life on a path to the *Trinity*. Standing not at one end in darkness or one end in the light, but right in the middle where you can see everything all at once. This also mirrors the process of how you can reevaluate your old past wounds and memories. Removing the Egoic Narrative to see what is really underneath. Who you really are when you remove all the clothes you put on to hide your true self to blend into the world. You can't expand with rewards, you free yourself with knowledge.

CHAPTER 12

KNOWLEDGE IS EVERYTHING

"Change what you cannot accept and accept what you cannot change." -Daniel Tierney

So, this is our life? An incredible civilization of selfish sluggish people walking around in new Nikes trying to get stuff for ourselves until we die? *I cannot accept that.* Something is wrong here, something deep that runs through all of us. We are stuck in a loop. When you see the loop holding everyone back, what do you do? …you break it.

We've all heard someone say, "ignorance is bliss." Ignorance would mean you are asleep in Ego, pretending that happiness is the answer. Ignorance is not bliss, it's a drug. We are meant to build families, create cities and design the future. Ignorance is our tranquilizer dart. Understanding something gives you the ability to create life. What we need to rejoin the Universe, is knowledge. *Knowledge is bliss.*

I often ponder Fox News. Not as a political weapon, but as an entity in our Matrix. Never once have I ever been angry with the on-screen actors, nor am I angry with the size or impact it has on America. I sit and wonder about the people behind the pageantry. Not the father, for he is in some ways a mirror to all of our fathers. A man determined to build an empire. A man who cares more for the empire than he does the people in it. I don't think about that. I think about his two sons, the heirs to the throne.

I have experienced this same thing in a past life. I was the son of a power-hungry king in Mesopotamia. He was sending innocent people to war. A moment of great pain in my heart. Even when I knew it was wrong, that innocent people would die to satiate my father's greed—he did something even worse. He chose me to make the call. I was forced to send them all to battle myself. Now, here these two sons standing at the gates of their father's empire, Fox News. Before they were handed the keys to the castle, they lived a somewhat morally balanced life, as much as one can when living among the aristocrats. Here these two stand behind a giant wall that protects them, souls being faced with the very same question. Choose the empire, or the people? The head or the heart? Keep the empire alive and watch it as it continues to divide us, or be brave enough to change it. Are these two boys the ones to finally say, "Enough. It's time to tell the truth?"

I came to this realization thousands of years ago only to find a young death in a large tomb. My loving, but contracted wife by my side. I never got the chance to change the kingdom because I never got the chance to try. Can you imagine a world where Fox News harnesses all its might to bring us stories on innovation, stories of growth and healing? If you can imagine it, then it can become a new code in our Matrix. One that stops this painful divide, bringing us back together to build a better life. Or, will they stand and feast in the Castle their father built overlooking a system they control that brings us anger, hate and death?...all under the guise of truth, in an empire based on lies.

We are all drunk drivers when it comes to getting the right information. We get our "facts" from people we know are lying to us. We are surrounded with *Egoic Loops*. Constantly dragging us around. We have news that can't legally be called news because it's become egoic propaganda, and yet we devour it, driving ourselves further into delusion by creating more false beliefs. This false information is aligning with your ego, not who you are. It's feeding it day and night. The animal side of us who doesn't know when to stop eating.

"History is written by the victor" is a truth we find in every single history book in modern day. Our facts aren't true. How do we find the truth when all we have are stories that have been retold by men? If you want to take this journey to alignment, you will need to pave new roads. *Become the journalist.* Use reputable sources and do not repeat things you cannot validate. Learn to read between every single line. Pay attention and ask questions. Be wrong more often so you can learn faster. We have all adhered to a social *apophenia - "the human tendency to see connections and patterns that are not really there"* (examples: Flat-Earthers, Q-Anon, Religious Scholars etc.). Our ego wants to be right, so we allow it to "solve" life equations that are not true. This keeps the truth hidden…so we must dig deeper.

For example, the beginning of the *Bible* is missing a letter. How important is a letter? How important was spelling? It was everything, it is the foundation of our communication. What's more interesting, is who changed it and why? Mary Magdalene was a woman named Mariamne from a town called, Magdala. While alive she was referred to as a "Mara," which today would mean "Master." A holy woman who carried immense faith and spirituality, loved enough by the family of Jesus to be buried with them in their tomb, deleted by Christian authors and turned into a whore. Religion used this woman to worship a man. To this day the church refuses to tell us the truth, so today, we honor this incredible woman by remembering, the wife. She walked hand in hand with Jesus, in love and devotion. She should be remembered once again as such. *Mariamne Mara.* The truth brings honor to her spirit, which she more than deserves. Jesus spoke to his wife and son Judah from the cross. He spoke in codes to protect the holy truth and his family, but in the end, we killed them all.

Entire names and origins were altered, but how important was just one letter? In the story of *The Garden of Eden*, Adam in Hebrew means *man. (Aw-dum)* just *"dam"* means *blood*. Add an "AH" and *"Adamah"* means *land*. Adam was not referring to a person, for it was not a name. It was referring to creatures being created with red blood and earth. It was describing us. As you can see from this tiny little sentence, you add one missing letter and the meaning we were told was true completely vanishes and something new appears beneath it. Start from right here and move backwards in search of our real truth. Full stop.

The Ancient Laws of the Universe are buried within so many modern translations that as journalists we must go farther back to even more ancient text if we have any chance of finding truth. The texts we use today have been translated from *Hebrew scribes* who translated it from *Babylonian scribes* who translated that from *Sumerian scribes*. With what we believe and hold to be true, we play telephone with two cups and a string in-between. If we are looking for the oldest truth, the farthest we can go back here is the *Enuma Elish*. It is quite remarkable when you can see past the translation. There it is. *The beginning of us.* It clearly describes our decent from light beings to Earth. What arch angels really are, and how we got here. Plain as day. It aligns with the keys we have found in all the other places outside and in. But, it does not align with the religions we created, so we need to update those too. We are going to align ourselves with something higher and then you will see it clearly, "awake with clarity."

When we first try to read the *Enuma Elish*, our egos will align it to our current beliefs. Don't let it. Catch the animal mind or the veil wins again. Sit down and meditate until you can calm your mind. Focus on the breath. Let this new information reach up to your *Soul Mind*. As it would, in synchronicity, the puzzle pieces suddenly fit together as if returning home. In an alternate universe we would probably teach our children some version of the *Enuma Elish* in kindergarten, so don't overthink it. Catch your ego trying to weaponize it for a reward, such as status among your peers. Use it to go inward, take some thoughts, leave some - it does not need to be dramatic. If something hits you too hard, move on. Try not to repeat these ancient words to be right; speak them because we were are all wrong.

The Journalist's Credo (in part)

"I believe a journalist would only write what they hold in their heart to be true. The suppression of news for any consideration other than the welfare of society is indefensible." - Walter Williams

Follow the oath of a journalist and always have at least two reputable sources as you study this Internal Knowledge. Astrologers, Channels, Spiritual Therapists, Numerologists, a great show to binge on *Gaia*. Study everything you can find and look for clues that only you know. Be suspect, but also be open about it. You will learn to see these bigger patterns and connect the dots and find proof for yourself. You will need to learn how to decipher and use emotional reason to assess what people are making up and what is truth. Do not stop until you find the truth. The truth is elusive, and it has become a needle in a haystack.

A reputable source is usually a healthy source. Use your eyes and ears and look at someone who is claiming to tell you the truth. Learn to use your senses again—allow them to instinctually process as a feeling type. If they are not healthy in their bodies and in their actions, then they are not healthy in their minds. Seek out those who are not telling - they are *showing*. They are living through these experiences and sharing important information for growth, not acclaim. If they make you feel "less than," then don't listen to them and move on. You have too much to do and can't be bothered by egoic distractions. Anyone who leads you to believe you need them in order to do any of this, is wrong. You have all the keys. We only seek clues along the way. This is shared information that drives our true civilization. Our shared experience contains all the powers of the Universe.

Remind yourself where we got our information from the past. We all believe that people of prominence executed these tasks of truth willfully. Have you seen any show about old royal families? Do they seem to be consumed with how best to serve the peasants? Most of them were absolutely crazy. Those were real people. Beheadings daily, murdering each other in the streets, dropping dead at random from anything always because plant medicine was "The Devil" when in fact it is made by the same godly current as us all. Everyone stealing and cheating and grabbing for power. Are we to believe that somehow during all this, they made sure the loving truth was being nurtured? Doubtful. One could argue that even the truth today with all that we have created is even worse than it was then. The truth does nothing for the powerful, so why should they tell it?

We have created this giant mess with our history because our egos have a relentless need to be right. For that reason alone, we need to recalculate our core beliefs to see if they are holding us back from greatness. Let us remember these royal families of our past were being operated by people who had gone completely mad. These people only held power because you believed them to it. When someone with the truth came along, they were hanged. Truth is the Achilles heel to power of any kind. There are but a handful of people who are built with the true wisdom and ability for leadership—those are the characteristics most of our leaders don't possess.

When you look out to see what greatness we have created with the idea of something bigger, we also spend time looking at the opposing side of that energy. You see the moments where we turned our heads in fear. When a priest would stand over a dying child and banish the healers as "witches." Men who became lost in the madness of power taught us our most precious beliefs, even as they killed us. The boy's condition is that of a small poison he got from a berry in the forest, and the convulsions begin to feed the priest's Ego. "There, the Devil himself!" No, that child needs a doctor and a shot in the arm, and they will be fine. At the time, that was a healer with something they had studied in the forest. So why did we listen to this Priest while the boy died in front of us? He used *Royal Authority* with the name of God to push fear-based thoughts into group consciousness and we formed "beliefs" born in said fear. This Royal Authority was at the hands of the drunk and mad. Those obsessed with status and ego. Any attempts to try something different was marked as treason. Egoic Minds devouring the truth right in front of us. They would stand in the name of "God" and watch this child die, they stayed in ignorance and blamed their fear and gave it a name. Anyone aligned with the current that *Is* would not choose any actions that separates us or refuses to help a dying child in order to be right. To ignore all the deaths from this current pandemic is to do the same. To turn our backs on the truth even while people die so we can be right.

We no longer live in a reality where we can say we don't know where to start. We have the internet. Ta-dah! The sharing of almost all the information of our matrix selves. Be your own life journalist. I have adopted the firm belief in *Upstream Thinking*. When you find a block in information don't sit there and fight each other over it. Go past the angry cousins and go "upstream" and find the answer at its source. *Dan Heath* taught me this. It's a very simple metaphor as I remember it: A man is sitting by the river's edge. A child in the river screams for help. The man rushes in and saves the child. The man looks up and sees another child drowning in the river. He rushes in and saves her too. One after another he rescues children. He's exhausted. All he can do is focus on what is right in front of him. A woman walks by and the man looks at her catching his breath, "Help me, there are children drowning in the river!" and she replies, " Why don't you go talk to that guy upstream who is throwing children in the river?" This is *upstream thinking*. We all sit and fight each other instead of going to the source of it. Go past the drama and get yourself to the shore where you will have a view of the source; remove yourself from ego to be aware, to be aware is to be awake.

CHAPTER 13

THE UNKNOWING

"For there is nothing hidden that will not become revealed, and there is nothing covered that will remain undisclosed." -Jesus Christ

It can be overwhelming to realize we have such strong beliefs given to us by people in the past who were, well, a bit crazy. Loving and adventurous, but the odds of our lesser-aware relatives being sober enough to have any real clarity, is unlikely. They told us this belief they made up when everyone was insane so we believe this foundation of how life works here, and, yup, we just decided we will believe it forever! We were built to learn how to steer the ship of today, the one happening right now, but we sit in stagnancy believing it to be the responsibility of the great one. We are spoiled in our beliefs and have forgotten that it is we that should be steering the ship. We skirt this awesome responsibility by gravitating to something that is socially acceptable, and then we can "confirm" that belief. It gives us status among our people. (You don't need status, you are loved, forever and always) The more we know about this belief, the better we seem in their eyes. The only belief you should carry with you is the belief in yourself as a loving and powerful soul. You are sacred. I promise. Everything else is of little consequence. I love to start this lesson in re-programming old beliefs by reminding myself that *apophenia* causes us as a society to force patterns on the ideals we hold deeply, even when they aren't true. Remind yourself of *Virtue Ethics*. The religious version of curiosity. The ethics version of "*What am I?*" That is the answer we are all looking for. Wondering who you are won't work if you've already decided.

> *"Darkness cannot drive out darkness, only light can do that."* -Martin Luther King Jr.

Before *The Big Bang*, a vibration of energies created this planet with sentient thought. *Creativity and Energy.* (That's us btw.) A number of beings helped conceive with us to inhabit this experience here. Over time, our Egoic Minds took hold and we rejected being related to beings more powerful than us and so began our descent into egoic separation, in search of our *own* identity, to develop into who we would become. We separated from our origins here. We are still not correct about our original ancient cities in *Egypt*, because we are blocked from our real history. With full truth, comes full clarity.

To start my unknowing, I have fun asking questions combining theories, playfully, to stretch my mind before my rigid beliefs are challenged. I've wondered this from time to time: if Jesus wanted to reincarnate the same way we all do, soul into body, total separation from source, all memory blocked and locked, would he want to have this life-on-Earth experience once again? If he chose to go through this wild process of separation, could we accept that in our minds? Or, would you deny him this gift of experience and understanding because you have already defined his soul as something you need? *Think of him as if he was you.* These little thoughts seem silly, but they can help to expand your thinking by creating a question with childlike curiosity, allowing your past belief to lower its guard, while also aligning yourself as someone who has become a reflection of them too.

Something is different about us as a whole. We all look a little lost, tired and frustrated deep down. I see a society that is beat down, bored and ready for something different. But even then, we drive forward every day with incredible *willpower*. Despite all this delusion, we are all still out there trying to make the best of it. We know there is more to who we are, and we are made of more than we remember and it's time to have that conversation. I think we're all about done with this version of being human. It's not who we are, so let's change it. Keep removing the programming to get back to self.

Your identity is one you have created here. But it is not you. It's tricky to imagine at first, but when you die, your Ego Mind dies too. So, then who are you? You're not a being who has egoic thoughts. To become more of yourself there, remove more of your ego here. Make the inside like the outside. "Same, same." You can start removing your egoic identity by learning more about how you are made.

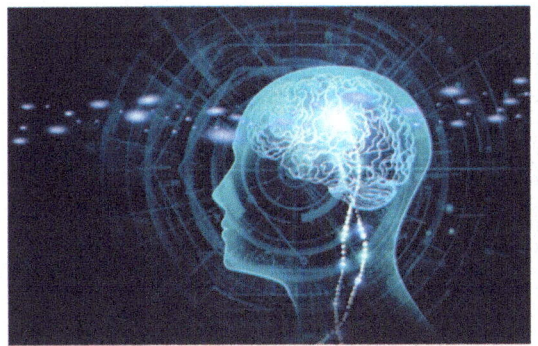

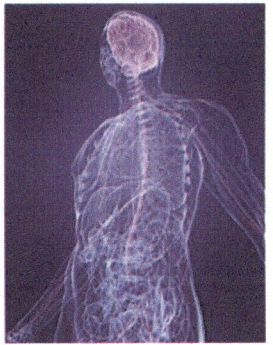

You are not a boy or a girl, you are both and none. Your vagina either stays a vagina or the labia grows into balls and a penis. There you have it. (The stitching underneath will verify this. It looks hand sewn and makes me laugh.) Then we build an animal kingdom-like reality around being whatever type we think we are. This gets determined by our hormones. Everything in your primal operating system is run by your hormones. This is only body. If you have an attachment to a previous lifetime or a previous identity to a different sexuality, that is a part of your spirit. Your spirit is whatever it wants to be always. If it is born into a body that it doesn't believe to be true, then it wants to express who it really is from this perspective. We should all have the awareness to not believe we are male or female anyways. You've been both a thousand times before. We are connected to nature, so our bodies naturally align with that. Your body adheres to the natural geometry of this planet. But we are not our bodies. We are only tethered to them for this experience. Who you are inside, is all of it…and nothing.

Which side we lean to is based on the physical aspects of our incarnation and how your mind dictates your hormones. You formed in the womb and as a child based on the vibrations around you, your hormones adjusted to that and made a you.

We all cycle through reincarnation. A simple way to understand reincarnation is seeing your lifetime as just one very pivotal scene in your movie. You are two pieces. One outside and one inside. What happens to you here is experienced by your soul. That is the thing you take with you in the end. Take a second and think of that. This mind you are using…one day it will die. The fears, the needs, the dreams, the agendas, the goals--they die with your body. Enjoy the time you have it but remind yourself that you won't be taking it with you.

To make things a little easier, just remind yourself that if you are a man talking to a woman you are really two souls. One vibrating in what we call the masculine energy, which is what formed that body, the other vibrating in the feminine with a body created by that energy. You are not a man talking to a woman. You are a soul choosing one side or the other or anything in-between. You are polarity so there is always a side. Learn to stand in the middle where you can see all sides

You may have people's spirits buzzing around because you won't let each other go, or there is still something tethering you to each other…but heaven is only temporary. The heaven-like place after your reentry back from separation is something of miracles, but it is only temporary. You will soon discover your soul is much too feisty to stay in one place for too long and will eventually go out seeking further and deeper experiences. The idea of finishing this life and wanting to do another round here seems outright mad. But then again, you watch a woman have a large baby and vow to never have a child again—now that lady has six kids. It's the process of what we are made of. It is exactly what drives you now. You are not special, you are sacred. We don't need to wait to die and go to heaven, we can find heaven right here.

Expanding your beliefs gets a little harder at first, but then the good stuff comes in. You can wake up and still drink, still hurt, still be surrounded by loneliness, but something is changing. What matters is that you are finally here as a whole being. A whole human. Two parts working in complete synchronicity. Forgive yourself for everything. We are all punishing ourselves in some way. We know not what we do. There is no wrong. No one will be mad. No one will persecute you. This is between your loving soul and you. The darkness does its job giving us shape, but we are always made of a light so powerful that we only need a tiny bit of it to activate the vast energy machines inside us. Authenticity comes from removing the Ego Narrative and being free to be yourself. The only thing preventing you from doing this is your idea of who you are. The final step in unknowing is letting go of who you think you are and becoming something new.

So now we know. We are the spirits that can change the matrix. But we must go full *Neo* and go within.

"To become a co-creator of your life, you learn to become life."

Let's un-write history so we can re-look at things to form a different perspective, mirroring what we need to do with our own programming to move forward. Does this trigger a defensive response in you? When you change how you process things, you quite literally change your experience with new information.

Our current history (*his*-story) is used to add to our separation and conflict among each other and is something we can overcome. Take *The Book of the Dead* as a case study. This was translated from the original hieroglyphics on the walls beneath the pyramids. It would translate more as *Come Forth by Light*. The literal reason for the title change would be for what we call "marketing." There was another book of the same name, and the author thought it would be great for business. The business of getting the words out there. Our own history is very much humans doing their best. But we lost the ability to see the enigmatic patterns. Even 666 is a sacred number meaning you are at the point of death, being reborn. The Phoenix. A precious soul moment and we turned it into the devil. Fear of what we are. If you were called upon to not only investigate *The Great Pyramids*, but you were also told you can turn them back on, would you walk out your door and tell your neighbors, friends, co-workers, you are going to turn on the Great Pyramids of Egypt? Doubtful. Think about how you would try to relate this to the people you know. You would need more information first. You would have to start on your own because inevitably others would throw you off track with their fear and disapproval. Someone will be telling you that you've lost it. When actually, you are about to find it. Would you even attempt it, or would you decide it would ruin your social status and people would think you are crazy, so you let the thought go and head back to work? That is exactly what people were doing a long time ago. Some stepped forward and some did not. Then, no one stepped forward so the one in search of power did. The rest is history.

CHAPTER 14

A BIBLICAL CASE STUDY

"Dear children, let us not love with words or speech but with actions and in truth." John 3:18

Having faith was for the journey. It was never meant to keep us from seeking the truth. As *Morgan Freeman* posed, *"Did God create civilization, or did civilization give rise to our belief in God?"*

Was *God* something we created to explain things we could not explain? None of this needs to have any effect on your own beliefs. The deepest parts of you are resonating with those powerful words in scriptures around the world. Even now we can see our youngest generations saying, "I'm not religious, but I'm spiritual." Everyone's path is their own, but we also see our children growing up without subscribing to our previous shared beliefs. They want to create their own. No one can be wrong.

All societies have a story of creation, but without seamlessly including other civilizations in our historic timelines, we stay blinded to what we are. Your inner *Council of Wisdom* can surmise that if beings from other planets are part of our creation, just as we would watch a teenage girl reject her mother, so would we, as Egoic-Minded people, we would want to define ourselves. How could we truly live with another civilization that had more abilities than we did? They would be a threat, and what does our ego do to a threat? We attack it. We create false truths and then believe them to stay "safe." Now we have this large missing chunk in our puzzle of information. We just need to let it reevaluate without forcing limitations on it. Try to be open-minded until you start to feel that moment when something hits you deeply.

"Faith is taking the first step even when you don't see the whole staircase." -Martin Luther King Jr.

When *God* says *know thyself*, what did that really mean? Was it a vast unanswerable esoteric question of who we truly are? Or was it really specific, as in simply a codec? A manual for being a human. Maybe *God* was saying, start here, turn on your three minds, because without all of them working together, this world won't make much sense. How does something we knew thousands of years ago vanish? It's not the Illuminati or New World Order, it's us. To break the loop, we break the patterns. We change.

People who've had near-death-experiences describe it as "light," a feeling, the actual "sound of Aum." They also often refer to what we call *God* as "She." I always found that interesting. The feminine rules love, so that checks out. We all carry masculine and feminine energy inside of us. Like two large nitrous cans, one filled with each. It is a mirror image of our dual energies in the Universe. We are both always. This is how we come to understand the very moment we walked into the darkness of Ego.

> *The Origins of "Modern Separation" Marked as 1 AD*
>
> Man walks away from our ancestors—the dawn of the *Egoic Loop*. This was not a tragic mistake; this was our path to explore. We chose to fall down to the depths of darkness. We chose to suffer and to feel. The problem was that we also forgot who we are along the way. A vicious cycle of egoic manifestations instead of manifestation born from our *Three-Minded* self.

"When you make the two into one, and when you make the inside like the outside, and the outside like the inside and the above like the below..." -Jesus

His gift to us, before we headed into darkness, was a reminder that we are connected. He did what *Enki (Prometheus)* and others tried to do. To tell us the truth. *Chris*t came to tell us that *we* are the second coming of *Christ*. It is inside of us. The light of *Om*. A light we would soon forget in the darkness of our outer experience. A painful experience for us all. Our descent into resistance and separation was marked. An Egoic-Minded civilization walked forward to face the depths of their own polarity. We have not stopped since.

The beginning of the *Bible*. Did we translate and manipulate ancient scriptures so much that we forgot the meaning of how we came to exist? The part that tells us who we really are? Don't get stuck in belief, collect the data and let your wisdom decide. The beginning of the Bible was missing a letter...

As written today, the opening of the Bible says,

"In the beginning God created the Heavens and the Earth."

Take the original text in the *Hebrew bible*, then add the key to unlock it. Insert the "A" and watch the doors open, now we have:

"The father of the beginnings created the Elohim, the Heavens and the Earth."

When you add the missing "A," it transforms into a meaning much deeper. That one letter was removed over a battle for power. Now we have it back. The father of the beginnings was the creation of light and energy and thought. The *Elohim* were the architects of this planet. We spent many of these early years in connection with our spirit mother and father. Meditation chambers to transport our consciousness were built, mimicking designs from other planets. The entire system of the human species on Planet Earth was aligned with geometry and spirituality. The Elohim are literally the creators of life on Earth. But that was their job. Their ability, their purpose. At this moment, we walked away from this part of us so we could walk through the trenches of the darkness that would follow, to one day walk back into the light as our own civilization - *realized*. If the only thing that separates us from A.I. is feeling, then we set off to master both. Thinking and feeling at the same time. When we wake up, we stop living the shadow life. It's as if we are writing this beautiful poetry ourselves.

Most of these ancient truths reveal the things we already tend to believe deep down. Our deepest truths already align. They reveal their true context and suddenly it makes sense. But why hide the letter? Truth vs. power. The "A" was removed. What was left was very fitting for the male ego. Add the "A" and the feminine completes this secret truth. If something as simple as an "A" can change our understanding of *God* to something even bigger and more complex, something even more beautiful than we remember, then I would like to know more please.

We also see the same in the Old Testament:

"Elohim (God) stands in the divine assembly. He administers judgement in the midst of the Elohim (God)." Psalms 82:1

This describes *God* as a member of a *pantheon of angels*, of other beings. We called them "Gods," but they were not God. They are different energy levels of us. If something comes from the sky and has more power than we perceive ourselves to have, then our egos call them Gods. The mere word and belief are ones of separation. It implies we are not worthy. We are not as powerful, and we are not same. This is *Egoic Resistance* that feeds into the Egoic Narrative and creates the foundation of our false realities. They were not called "Gods" until later. They are known as the Elohim. To understand truth, we then work from this word as it is before man altered it. It's a simple and effective way to reason through the deeply embedded beliefs we carry. Elohim - Gods - God. We played the telephone game again. Two cups and a string. What this all really says is that *we* are the manifestation of what we call God/Source/Akasha. God never punished us for trying to be a God, that was made up with a heavy dose of fear to keep you subservient to a single power – religion. And thus, you were never told again who and what you truly are. We. Are. God.

We call biblical scriptures *"The Word."* That was actually based on the word *"Logos"* from an even more ancient scripture. The Gospel of John says, *"In the beginning was The Word."* In the original text it read, *"In the beginning was the Logos."* It was said that *"He who knows the Logos, knows the truth."* Five hundred years before Jesus Christ was even born, the Greek philosopher *Heraclitus* referred to a word passed to him through wisdom—*Logos* as *"Something fundamentally unknowable, the origin of all repetition, pattern and form."* "Logos" and then, "The Word" was set in place to describe what was originally the sound *Om (Aum)*. This was known to be the origins of the Universe from which all manifestation came. From the ancient *Bhagavad Gita*, "Vishnu slept (inception of light and thought—a dream world) and then woke to the sound of Om" (the Big Bang), with Vishnu being in the silent slumber. The moment before we existed, and then the sound of *Om* referred to as *"the Light of God"* woke him. That sound, referred to as light, was the source energy that created everything. That is where we switched it. Then we, man, changed it again over the years to become, *"And then God said let there be light."* They are the same on the surface only, move closer to the origin, because one is the energy we call God, not the word that describes this magnificent truth. *Om* is referenced in the *Kabbala* as the divine name of *God*: *"That name that cannot be spoken because it is a vibration that is everywhere."* There it is, *God, Yahweh, Allah, It, I am, Akasha, Source, Abba*…all those words are trying to name a *vibration of light and sound made of love*. It sounds like "Om" and feels like serenity.

If the *Source* is the energy of all, the heavens and the holy, an abyss of white light, then it was our own ability to become shadow that gave this light shape, and we called it *God*. We returned the same gift we got on our inception. We used our own ability to create the darkness so we could try to see *it*. All these words and names came from the same place. The same origin. *"Undisputed origin."* This sound. The sound of *Om* so many people hear during a near-death experience. The most sacred tetrahedron. The triangle. This loving thing grows near, and then they hear her, and it sounds like "Om." They describe hearing this sound when they are soaring through the astral world. So, what we know today as "The Word," being the word of *God*, "Scripture"…it was a sound. Remember *Tesla* said:

"If you want to find the secrets of the Universe, think in terms of energy, frequency and vibration."

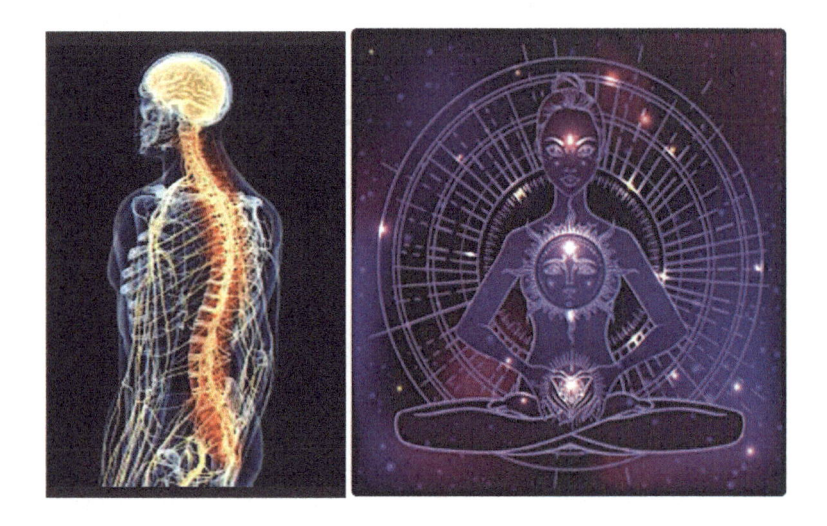

Frequency

Higher and lower. Tones. Sound. This is also a perfect place to catch our Ego Mind living in a hierarchal state by reflecting on our current understanding of a lower frequency or vibration. And how do we perceive this through the delusion of an Egoic Loop? Low = bad. High = good. The sound of monks chanting is a lower vibrational sound as we hear it, but it is not worse. Charged with love and alignment, this is a sound we perceive as lower but its intention and the message you send in that current—that is what changes its frequency. All functions of *resonance*. Think in a circle not a line.

When you see the old scriptures of people chanting to the heavens under the moonlight, they were resonating the sound from inside them, mixed with their soul's expression of itself, aligning that inner frequency through the minds and then out through the energy of the body to tap right into the current that is shared with all in the Universe. A sacred communion. Lower frequency has a more static feel on the surface; higher frequencies are filled with alignment information and resonate quite profoundly. Think of this as a swirling ball of energy inside you made up of billions of particles of light. Lower frequency is a disjointed system of particles and the signal is being sent by six of them. A higher frequency is when you have charged a million particles inside and your signal is stronger because of the *prana* or *life-force, the Qi* energy you were able to access and use. A low frequency can be boomed out to space, but a stronger frequency made up of more pulses, more information, will always travel farther.

We are limited in our thinking at the moment, but sound is more than something we hear. This sound permeates the Universe. The hum of existence. We need this information so we can understand how to create a better life. We have *Maya, The Matrix, The Simulation - The Apple.* Your soul self, *Adam and Eve*—the masculine and feminine energy inside all of us. The Tree-as-*source*. It is where we came from, the place of all knowing (first dimension/the void). The place without all the answers. The place before the questions. Our origin.

The Snake is the electrical charge that you can start to access through Yoga, today, right now. The snake is your *Kundalini Energy* that rests at the base of your spine, just as the snake rests at the base of the tree. *The Tree* is your spine which connects you to everything. These are not abstract. These are specific, as the truth would be. The *Trinity* then becomes our instruction manual from the Gods, to help us find *Oneness - Heaven – Nirvana - Moksha*—the vibrational current that is *Om*, a direct link to all information. The universal thought center that is the source of *us*. Outward, inward, and soul connection to *our source*.

Moving on. The most ancient text we can find right now is the *Enuma Elish*. It's before all of our religions, so take relief in that and learn. We know it is the closest to truth before we changed the truth and forgot it. The reason this is important is because of the way I came to find this book. I was tracking our civilizations from *Atlantis* moving forward and humans going backwards. Vast amounts of data and direction. After all that time, this book is where the long lines of our entire history meet. Where our history splits off is in this moment. We found it. The moment of *ancient separation*. It also aligns with everything Jesus and the other great masters were trying to tell us. All the pieces fit together as if returning home. You don't force these things to happen, you let them. There we are, beings made of light and body interacting with other civilizations, to beings falling into their Ego Mind and forgetting their not-so-distant relatives. To be lost in time as we battle each other over what we really are. Surrender and breathe out. The information is now here, do with it what you will, humans.

So, we have the *Enuma Elish*. Logically, rationally and with some basic Detective 101 skills, this would be the obvious place to start looking for the most truth you could find. If you Google it, the most common question that pops up is, *"Do we know if the Enuma Elish is before the book of Genesis?"* Clearly a sign that we are so afraid to lose our old beliefs that we have to ask if something that happened last week is older than what happened yesterday. Practice your ability to deal with resistance. Focus on your breathing and quiet the Ego Mind. These little steps will start moving you towards alignment. Hold your beliefs dear until they grow into something more. You don't need to banish all that you truly feel because most of that is leading you here anyways. They are the same.

The version of the *Enuma Elish* we have now was originally written in the language *Sumer*. If you haven't heard of our history as *Sumerians*, then you get to unleash your curiosity and go find out. A blocked history waiting to be uncovered. *The Law of Moses* in the *Tora*. That is based on the *Code of Hammurabi*. We call this by another name but turns out it was Hammurabi, and he was an actual person. Sumerian ideals came from these small kingdoms at the beginning of us. *Ur-Nammu, Marduk,* the *Akkadian Empire*, this was all us. *Babylonian Empires* to follow. This amazing hotbed of our ancient ancestors in the midst of building our origins. This was *Mesopotamia*. This is who we were and where we started building the world. That is what this book was about. The Enuma Elish is a contorted translation of what was common knowledge then. We ignore the egoic controls, and simply see what the subject matter was. There we are. Angels in bodies.

"Whoever finds the meaning of these words will not taste death." -Jesus Christ

The most untainted writings we can find feels like a good place to start. If at any point in that simple connection of the historical dots we were being challenged in our ego driven beliefs, slamming into the dams we built in our own rivers of thought, then we would never have gotten there quickly, if at all. Not much to unlearn if you didn't build a palace of beliefs around yourself. The truth is the same vibration. Finding the truth means finding bliss through understanding. The truth must align with your ability to seek what your purpose is here. If it does not, then make no fuss of it and move on. Do you see what happened there? You just learned that your truth and the truth of others can differ, and that's okay. You are changing yourself to a life of fluidity. Do not get caught on the driftwood.

Everyone fights over the origin of *God* and *Christ*. They took the history of our sacred ancestors and changed it to make their home the true home of *God*. If we would like to know more about our past, we start with *Atlantis* and our libraries that still exist in *Egypt*. On those walls was the same information; we have just been looking at it sideways. In alignment we see things from an upright position. Centered without agenda or ego. We listen. None of these "revelations" are even pertinent other than to understand our origins so we can re-process our lives so we can move forward on this grand adventure. We honor our past by waking up and getting to work rebuilding our civilization that is seriously outdated.

If the teachings from *The Book of Life* are described at the time to remove all sin, today we can say with deeper understanding and more information, to channel the *Akashic frequency* you need to resonate with more *love energy*. If no one at the time would have a clue what you meant by "love energy" and "frequency" because they thought in only biblical terms, you would say it in a way they would understand. How do you become more love? Become less dark. Remove sin and you will be love again. Translated. Banish the mighty sin within you…really means be more love. Yet today, we take those same foundations and try to fit them into our current thinking. We don't even need to use the word sin again, so be rid of it. We are made of positive and negative. Light and dark. Let us always be specific.

> "We are made wise not by the recollection of our past, but by the responsibility for our future."
> - George Bernard Shaw

We don't need to study our entire history, we just need the truth of where we began. We are civilization begging the heavens just to tell them who they are. We find the past so we can create the future. Our hidden truth lying in ancient cities like, *Gobekli Tepe* in *Turkey*, or, *Eridu*. (The ladder, a pivotal city we have long forgotten and let lay in ruins. An unfortunate consequence of forgetting where we came from. Once people learn the importance of Eridu, ego-minded people will exploit its value and sell it away, but for all these years, with all its worldly relics, it lies there in a pile of dust. It just *is*. It can be immortal and meaningless until we decide to make it important and give it a name.

We are polytheistic vibrational light beings in animal bodies. Something so incredible, buried for 12,000 years. Before man formed religions we were all expressing our spiritual selves. We lived in divinity. This is who we are. We are love and kindness, energy and thought. We are incredible, cosmic creatures. Now we get to explore that part of us once again. To change this entire life here and add the missing ingredients. Finally, we can rearrange our past and fill in the endless amount of unanswered questions and suddenly see the entire function of the Universe unfolding right in front of us. We have the master key to understand exactly what we are doing here…and now, we can start to understand how the Universe itself was constructed. We made this. So, let's remember what we made. One large concept of God or Akasha, can now be unpacked and broken down into seven pieces, and those seven pieces make up our entire existence. You also carry all seven of these inside you, when you understand them, you put them back together and you have formed a oneness with God.

"When in darkness, light a match."

Religions have been powerful pieces of support and guidance in our lives. They have given us sanctuary. So many incredible people who have devoted their lives to the service of us. These giant hearts walking among us. Religion was there for us through the darkness cycle helping humanity get to where we are now. We thank it deeply for its service. For the love it provided when we needed it most. We honor it now by being able to move forward ourselves, inward. To truly honor something, we see it from as many angles as we can. I have watched religious-hearted people save lives purely based in their connection to love. Love doesn't need a name. We are also witness to women forcing their beliefs onto another woman's sacred bodies. We are using Royal Authority to force women to carry children they are not ready for. That little soul has a spark and that spark cannot be killed. So why are we deciding what others do with their magic? We believe the words of false profits and we have taken those false beliefs and use them for our own attempt to adhere to social rewards. Do we not see this? Can we not see that our hearts are being ignored and we are acting from our Egoic Minds creating larger loops of pain that continue on generation after generation? Until every single child who is alive is cared for, then we cannot take these negative religious ideals as truth. You can't claim to worship life while allowing the life already here to suffer. Truth does not cause separation and harm. It causes healing. We all see the darkness everywhere we look, so might as well talk about it if we are going to truly start to understand who we are. All roads point back to what happens when you yourself decide to become a *co-creator* of not just your life, but all of ours too.

We are at a crossroads in ourselves. One path leads to who we are, and one leads to who we were. Spirituality picks up where religion leaves us, so we can be free again to grow in a new direction. It's a beautiful process in cyclical form.

> *"Church is a place where we all stand in communion with source. Whatever name we give this is beside the point. Bring your church loving heart along with you. It's a tremendous asset."*

Take your God with you when you explore new curiosities. You aren't removing your understanding of *God*, you are adding more information to let your idea of God expand. We can now study the ancient texts and then step back. As *Christ* said, *"it will reveal itself."*

Adam and Eve are us. Light beings. Naked in pure innocence. The holy spirit within us in childlike bliss. The clothes were our choice to cover our bodies. We chose to put on clothes to live a life that would be perceived from the outside. We hid who we truly were from each other. The mask of Ego. The *Serpent* is the *Kundalini Energy*. The *Qi (Chi) – Life Force – Prana*. All different names throughout history, all trying to describe the same thing. It rests at the base of the tree as does your actual energy center that sits at the base of your spine. The *Apple* is the *Matrix,* our Egoic Reality. We bite the apple and become obsessed with this reality and forget who we are. The Tree. *The Tree* is our inner tree of all knowing. This is the *Second Coming of Christ*. Realizing you are the tree. The *Apple* blinds us from the Tree, the *Snake* gives us the energy to walk through delusion and find the light again. This is all in symbols and ancient text. They all start to say the same thing. This information was not owned, nor was it supposed to be. Think about how many stories we have put on something so basic? How many people we kill in the name of the same belief that we ourselves separated from? The same things we find all over the Universe. We turn away from the *Matrix* and remove our clothing as we near the tree, revealing our true selves. We then become the tree again. Together we step into *Nirvana*. A vibration that connects you to all of it. The triangle of all that we are, fits inside a circle because that is everything. This is the story of our true origins. Within it, when you can remove all the Egoic Narratives, *you find an operating manual—for humans*. Universal truth acts like a decoder ring to who we are. Now we can see how the idea of *Original Sin* as really a misunderstanding. Now we can say the *apple* was our choice to live in polarity, to step into delusion, to our creation. We created this apple. To bring good and evil here, inside of us. Positive and negative, light and shadow. The shadow that gives us shape, because without it we are only light.

We are the Sin and the Angels, and we always have been. *Accountability*. (Take that word with you.)

We put words to these incredibly powerful and ancient truths, and yet we don't fully understand the origin. We are using a hammer as a wrench and fighting each other over which screwdriver we're using. The use of words was not strong enough to carry such a sacred message for all of time. It was meant to be passed on by being *understood*. If it was forgotten, then you remember by learning how to know it. Even the origin of truth can expand. We lose ourselves when we start to believe the word instead of the reason for the word. If we can't listen to our outer world, then we have to find a way to listen to our inner world. These concepts were translated as symbols because symbols can encompass an understanding that is working between your outer life and your inner life. They were meant to give you the basic truth so you could start your journey to realization. A path not to bliss and happiness—that is already a birthright. This is a life direction towards true fulfillment. True awareness of your *self*. To be both parts of you, here. This is where your magic is.

Our bodies hold these abilities to speak in telepathy or travel through the cosmos. We know this because people do it all the time in every country on Earth. Even our governments do it often. This always raises the question, "if all of this is true, how come we don't already know or have all of these innate abilities?" *Know thyself*. We are given the gift of separation to have true experiences while we're here. Knowing thyself is the journey. Waking up is how you start. It's telling us the instructions. We all live in a world that comes from our own collective manifestations. We all stay asleep until someone learns how to wake up. If enough of us wake, we all wake up because we are strong enough together to break a massive Egoic Loop of civilizational delusion.

These *God* vibrations engage with our neurological system. The auditory nerve connects to every organ in the body. When we are born, we develop our inner ear as our first sense. Our other senses have not even come online yet. We start by sensing vibration before our minds are even active. Our body is forming with sound waves as the instructions. The thing that makes us. Babies feel the vibrations of the entire life you surround them with. This is how your body is forming its nervous system in the womb. It's acclimating to the world it will be born into by learning from vibrations. The life-bond has been made. The sounds we heard as children even change and adapt our thinking based on the languages being spoken around us. Our ears have triple the number of sensors sending information to your brain than your eyeballs do. Three times the data we receive is coming in through our senses that listen and process vibration. Our bodies were made of vibration, so it already knows the source. That comes through the *pineal gland* and effects your entire being.

> *"He is no fool who gives what he cannot keep, to gain what he cannot lose."* -Jim Elliot

CHAPTER 15

The Seven Laws of the Universe

"Anything that is right is possible. That which is necessary will inevitably take place. If something is right it is your duty to do it, though the whole world thinks it to be wrong." — William Walker Atkinson

When Jesus said, *"Make the two into one...make the inner like the outer.... the above like the below."* What he was describing matches the *Universal Geometry* of the *octahedron*. Splitting yourself down the middle, one triangle up and one triangle down. This is how truth aligns. If what we say is true then it will align itself with the *Seven Laws of the Universe*, understood as the symbol that represents what we call *God*, for it is much more than a word, these symbols represent an understanding. He was describing alignment, oneness being your understanding of the *Seven Truths of Creation*. They are not in fact laws; they are truths formed in complete synchronicity with each other.

The Seven Laws of the Universe are seen as the *Seven Chakras (we have 12 total here)*, but when all seven are together in you, you are *God, Source*. You as *self. Realized*. You understood all seven things so well you have become whole again. Oneness. The sphere of your inception. To connect yourself is to become each and all of these seven laws in your daily life. Study each one and practice.

These powerful concepts exist in your real body. They all tether to an organ and have the largest impact on our overall health and well-being. Understanding your body parts and the functionality of your soul parts is key to your wellness. You have been one piece, so let's break you into seven specific pieces and see where you dominate. *Cindi Dale* lays all of this out so beautifully in her book, *Advanced Chakra Wisdom*. She's made great connections between the chakras and your physical body and their specific relation to our health, in modern detail. We love specifics and we love people with new information.

1st Chakra

"Root"

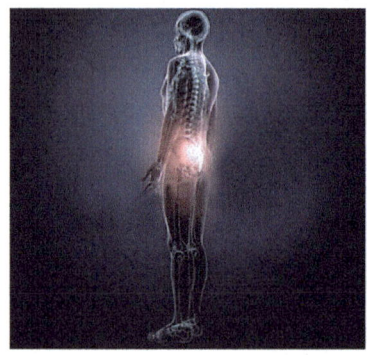

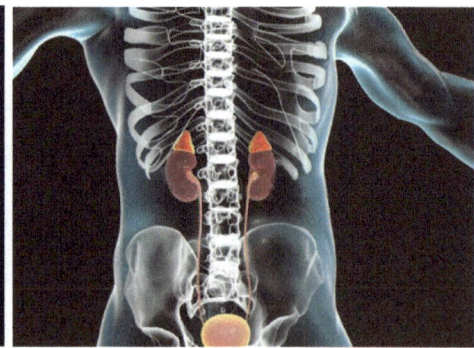

Organ: Adrenal Glands   Color: Red   Where you feel it: Base of spine
Sacred Geometry: Hexahedron   Element: Earth

Summary: The doer, the changer, the loop breaker. The master of Shakti. You are emotionally vested in the human body and the World. Primal female or male in sex, world building and body. Fear and protection also live here. You desire to protect the world you are building and the people you love within it.

Food type: Going, going, crash - then into a cocoon. Forgets to eat then likes to feast. Loves eating on the go. What it wants: Organic Veggies and Healthy Protein. Little fruit.

Seventh law

"Generate"

Generate. Make something. Do something here. Your root chakra is at the base of your spine. The home of your *Kundalini* energy from the *Tree of Life*. It can harness energy and use it to fuel your being so you can be the doer. It's generating energy so you can create a world with it. If you see a world that needs to be changed, you get to work.

2nd Chakra

"Sacral"

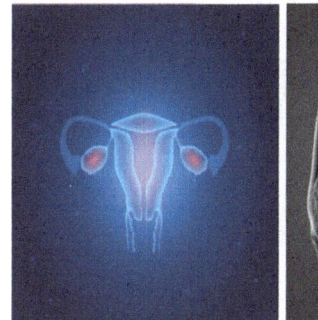

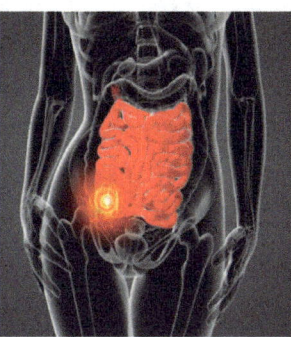

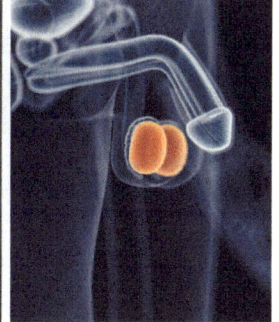

Organ: Testis/Ovaries Color: Orange Where you feel it: Abdomen Shape: Icosahedron Element: Water

Summary: Feelings. Your cravings are based on feelings. This is a creation chakra, so you want to feel the food you eat.

<u>Food type:</u> Balanced diet and carb heaven. (But only healthy carbs.) Gluten-free whole grains. Pair with fruit and Omega 3s.

Sixth law

"Polarity"

What you just generated will have an effect and affect everyone and everything. You have choice. This chakra is all about feelings and emotions. Creation of life happens here. As Earth has a North and South Pole, you also balance yourself between positive and negative like a magnet. This chakra holds the marble on the teeter-totter. You are pulled in one direction then the next. If you were flying a spaceship and you wanted to go left or right, this would be your polarity at work. *Centered* is when you are both positive and negative at the same time. You become the marble in the middle of the teeter-totter.

<u>3rd Chakra</u>

"Solar Plexus"

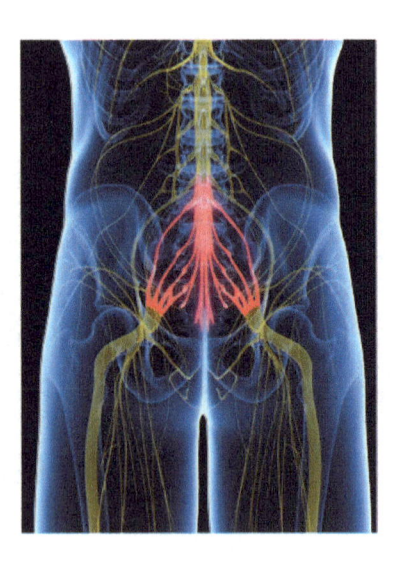

<u>Organ:</u> Abdomen <u>Color:</u> Yellow <u>Where you feel it:</u> Abdomen
<u>Sacred Geometry:</u> Tetrahedron <u>Element:</u> Fire
<u>Summary:</u> The structured thinker. Plans and schedules are its candy.

Food type: This chakra is all about blood sugar and you hate being out of control. Surround yourself with healthy satisfying snacks all day.

Fifth law of the universe

"Effect"

This is your accountability. You generated energy, made something that will affect people, so how did it go? Lying here keeps you in a loop. This is where we bring honesty back to our lives. We feel this in our sensory centers because it is the *Universal Synchronicity* of what you do to others happens to you. Cause and effect. A staple in all existence. This is the generator of experience. To know you have processed the Fifth Truth you would be free of blame. This is a surrender to accountability. The opposing energy block to this is Arrogance. A deflection of accountability. "It wasn't me."

4th Chakra

"Heart Mind"

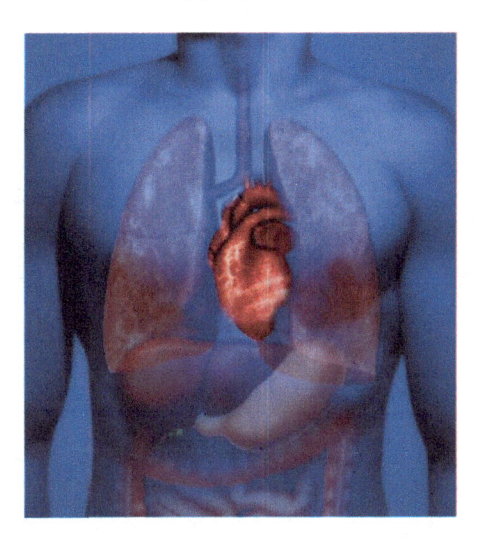

Organ: Endocrine Heart Gland Color: Purple
Where you feel it: Bottom of chest
Sacred Geometry: Star Tetrahedron Element: Love
Summary: The healers. Relationships. "Love is why we are here." Truth and connection.

Food type: Indulgence. You want to have a little relationship with your food. Find indulgent but healthy snacks like a really good Hummus. Straight to the point, Mediterranean food is where you want to be. Avocados, Olive oils, fresh clean fish.

Fourth law of the universe
"Cadence"

Do you feel like the world is too slow or too fast? That's you. It has a beat. You know this beat. It keeps you alive. The beat of Shiva's drum. This is your life rhythm. Mirrored in your heartbeat. The cadence of existence. Life has a metronome and when you can feel it, you are resonating with the cadence of *God*. The cadence for all creation. The cadence of *Source*. A *flow-state* is when you are living at the same speed as this beat. This is a mathematical rhythm that aligns with the universe and time.

5th chakra
"throat"

Organ: Thyroid Color: Light Blue
Where you feel it: Throat
Sacred Geometry: Octahedron Element: Air
Summary: Communication by way of philosophy. Higher ideals. This is not necessarily an extrovert because an introvert can be communicating with the world on the inside.

Food type: You love the oral sensations of the food you eat. Crunchy and tasty are key here. This is all about mood, metabolism, and breathing. Blueberries, nuts, olive oil. Foods filled with antioxidants.

Third law of the universe

"Vibration"

Think of your throat. A hum. Life has a vibration. You as sound. This is how we output and input the correspondence with the universe. If you hum, you are creating vibration. This all passes through the *pineal gland* - in and out. Vibrations then radiate the body.

6th Chakra

"Third-Eye"

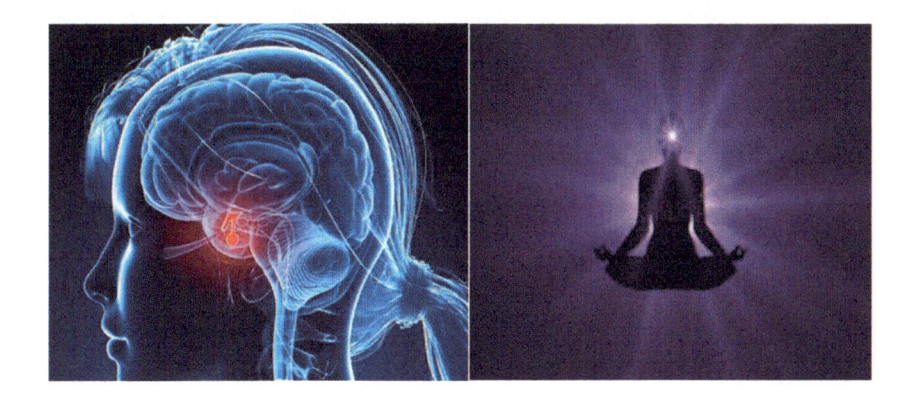

Organ: Pituitary Gland Color: Violet
Where you feel it: Center of your brow
Sacred Geometry: Dodecahedron Element: Ether
Summary: Imagery and visualization. Hormones driven by what you see. Appearance in self and the outer world are pleasing.
Food type: If a partner wants to impress you then they better make it look good. Appearance is what drives your cravings. Find beautiful healthy delights like a top-notch acai bowl and let the visual do all the work. That is all you truly want. Visual mind.

Second law of the universe
"Communication"

Expression *is* everything. What you create inside of you will be created outside of you and back again. This is how we see who we are. Shared experience is the experience. To learn the truth, we have to express our perspectives and find a shared belief.

7th Chakra
"Crown/Soul Mind"

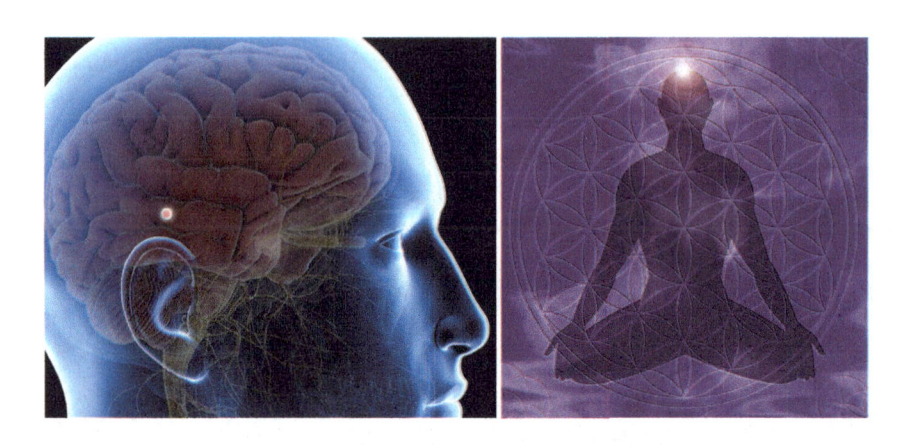

<u>Organ:</u> Pineal Gland <u>Color:</u> White Light
<u>Where you feel it:</u> Top of your head
<u>Sacred Geometry:</u> Sphere <u>Element:</u> Light
<u>Summary:</u> Soul Mind.
<u>Food type:</u> Food is not your priority because you always want to fill up on spirit. You are never prepared for food so you can fall into unhealthy traps by eating whatever is around. You thrive with healthy little meal snacks all around your day.

First law of the universe

"Mentalism"

This is the law of creation; 333, 666, 999. 3 is you, 6 is us, 9 is *God* in you--creation and source together. 3 - 6 - 9. The place of existence. This is why imagination plays such a fun part in our life here. Your soul mind works in mentalism. It wants to create possibilities. It thinks deeply about what it wants to build, and then builds things you forgot were possible.

the five of light

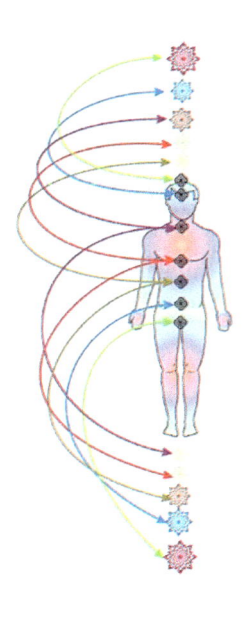

What is brilliant about these last chakras is that they help you understand your Soul Mind. The 7th chakra at the top of your head is the mind that connects to these other driving foundations of how you operate here. How you are dominant in your Soul Mind depends on where you are most draw to in your *outer chakras*. I call them *The Five of Light*. I list them with names to fit their functions. See a pattern?

8th Chakra
"Soul Knowledge"

Organ: Thymus Gland (key to body immunity) Color: Silvery Black
Summary: We develop our thymus when young and then it begins to shrink. This is our driver of our immunity to disease. When we connect back to soul-self we charge the thymus. Blow some doctoral minds? It's shrinking because of our unawareness to what feeds it; soul energy.
Food type: You eat for any chakra. You are a mystic mind and can decide which chakra needs attention and when.

9th Chakra
"Togetherness"

<u>Organ:</u> Endocrine Gland (Diaphragm) <u>Color:</u> Gold Light
<u>Summary:</u> Harmony and Resonance. Nature and Spirit.
<u>Food type:</u> You enjoy eating based on your beliefs about spirit and nature. You crave organic and chemical free. Eat lighter and you will increase your energy.

10th Chakra
"Universe Access"

<u>Organ:</u> Osteocalcin Gland <u>Color:</u> Earth/Sand
<u>Summary:</u> Put your feet on the ground because this chakra is below you. It connects to Earth. Nature, Astrology, Climate, Organics.
<u>Food type:</u> Root vegetables and nuts. Anything close to the ground.

11th Chakra
"Galaxy Access"

<u>Organ:</u> Connective Tissue <u>Color:</u> Light Blue
<u>Summary:</u> This is a chakra of great change. Leadership by divine virtue. It also relates to our tissue causing chronic pains and drug and alcohol addiction. The connective tissue is the organ that connects to your 11th chakra, so a denial of your higher self will cause problems. You become inflamed in your body.
<u>Food type:</u> Green foods and spices like turmeric, lots of fruit and veggies. Green nutrients are the usual favorite for an 11. Anything anti-inflammatory is best. Mediterranean diet is great here.

12th Chakra
"Everything Access"

<u>Organ:</u> Heart <u>Color:</u> Violet
<u>Summary:</u> This is the *all of you*. Your magnificent endless light.
<u>Food type:</u> It's multidimensional so manifested food matters not.

It's quite alarming to learn how connected our physical lives are to these chakras in such distinct and unmovable ways. This is us.

In the movie *The Matrix*, they have the option of taking the red pill or the blue pill. Well, if you look at your root chakra, creation of here, it is red. Represented by the Anunnaki civilization that co-founded Egypt. If you look to our Atlantean ancestors who were co-founded by a civilization of light, they are blue. In these ancient Atlantean times you might have seen Thalon walking around with two amulets on his neck. One red and one blue. As Jesus says, "make the above like the below." Astounding. We can quite literally see a path for us here. To connect our root chakra red with our soul mind blue. Earth and stars as one.

As a Starseed, my dominant chakra actually causes me a lot of pain and a really inflamed body. I am also not very grounded here in Maya. When I drank ayahuasca the Shaman aggressively planted an ayahuasca plant deep into my root chakra. Now, it grows upward. My root chakra—one, and my soul—seven, are now reaching for each other to become one that is now balanced in Maya here on Earth and in spirit up in the stars. We learn to become the red or the blue depending on which half we are missing to become whole, here.

Our egoic fantasies picture realms and dimensions as places, but you can study the different parts inside you to understand it. They are not a place, they are an understanding. Most other civilizations we will commingle with will be from this Universe. Everyone everywhere can be in all dimensions at the same time. You could then be here in body, and travel to a fifth dimension by traveling in your fifth-dimension current, which you would find by releasing all blame, and accepting accountability as *Universal Truth*. Align with it. You are these dimensions, and you are seeking perspective through the *Seven Truths of Creation*. Other beings can do this too, so some will be playing with space and time, some working with mental creation, some connected to *source* and *sacred geometry, some are ferries from the seventh who just want to make your life better.* These are the tools we use to build existence, including you. If you wanted to join the *8th dimension* you would become it. You would need to understand all 7 dimensions before it or you would not be able to read the information there anyways. Not in its entirety. We can't cheat, only pouring meditation into our daily lives will get us there. Turning off our outside and thriving on the inside.

Matias De Stefano has a lovely way of describing how the magnetic polarity relates to our idea of darkness. If you want to jump higher, you bend down lower and load your jump. If you want to feel bliss, you lower yourself down into the opposing energy, the darkness, and you build up enough learning energy to leap up.

Our life-force, (Chi) energy current was incredibly understood by Dr. Emoto and his studies of *Hado;*

> "The intrinsic vibrational pattern at the atomic level in all matter. The smallest unit of energy. Its basis is the energy of human consciousness." -Dr Masaru Emoto

---

The Alien Princess

In the times of Atlantis, a Lumerian Princess, Anua, was greeted by interstellar travelers on her home planet—large brutish beings who had left their home and were recolonizing a new planet. They called themselves the shepherds of a place called, Earth. They told the Princess of their tragedies there. They were sick, the humans and their hybrids were dying. Their experiment had gone wrong and the Lumerians held great healing powers compared to them. The Lumerians were accepting people with unusually high levels of health. It was the red stones they carried. The travelers witnessed this and wanted these stones for themselves. They tricked the Lumerians and destroyed their civilization. A wave of power over their whole planet, capturing those they wanted to bring along.

The Princess awakens on a new planet. A blue one. The city is surrounded by glimmering light cyan waters. She was being held captive in the conquered city we know as, Atlantis. It was not a vast city of any sorts, but a beautiful beginning. Water in rings around the land. Everything was working in symmetry, except for its new leadership, The ones leading with Ego instead of heart. The vibrations and energy, the colors, the humans. It resembled a number of other civilizations built with the same framework. Her captors flew in pods using projection energy. The-strong minded ruled over the innocent humanoids who held immense divinity but lacked much egoic understanding. One day, she met a human. He was loving and kind to her as most humans had been. These humans were a gentle people. This human became her only friend. They grew together and fell in love. They mated and formed their own hybrid, something made between two beings, one from Earth and one from the stars. A bond between civilizations had now imbedded itself in our history here on Earth.

I included my retelling of this little story so we can start to weave our real past into our minds with playful imagination (though that story is in fact, true.) The *Lumerians* are also known as the *Aman* (which is what they call themselves). They are from the *Pleiadian Star System*. You can see it from here. We call them higher civilizations, but higher is wrong. We like higher and lower, heaven and hell, success over poverty. We are ingrained with the hierarchy structure. We have mirrored all our businesses and our personal lives around this structure. Now the business world is learning that this structure is old and broken. They embrace one of transparency. Even the corporate world is leaving separation and moving towards one of connection.

When we see the Universe for what it really is, we see that vibration created the planets, and they are round. Everything is always represented as a circle because that represents oneness. All things flowing in synchronicity.

Pleiadian Star System

You can look up and see where all these people live. They have star systems: *Boötes, Orion, Pleiades*. When you understand the deeper origins of our creation, the things we see as problems cease to exist. When you understand our past, you see that every culture and race was combined. That was for survival. Racism isn't real. Black people are not black people, they are more people than any of us. They are an ancient people, which clearly shows us that race is a made-up concept. (*Isabel Wilkerson* wrote an incredible book, *CASTE*. She breaks down systemic racism from its origins in a much more eloquent way. She found the origin of this concept as a basis for the economic structure of the United States.) Scientists are getting closer, but they are still stuck in the wrong narrative of our history so they can't connect the dots. (Though they have figured out that Australopithecus is a million years OLDER than they previously thought.) There we are. All of us. We aren't a color, or a race, we are beings in bodies. One giant blender of DNA and wishful thinking.

We are only racist in Ego Mind because society taught us how to be racist. It is not a truth. Scientifically, as far as procreation is concerned, if you choose a mate to have a child with that is farthest from your own gene pool, your troubled spots in your own DNA will be replaced by their strength in that department and vice versa. So, the farther away a culture is from you, well that's going to be an epic baby.

> *"It is the mark of an educated mind to be able to entertain a thought without accepting it."*
> *- Aristotle*

As we are two types of self—light and body, we also have two different timelines. The one of our original creation, and the one of the human creation. The human body, shaped in the image of the pentagram, was developed. The *development cycle* was the Earth itself and all things nature, which eventually includes us. Dinosaurs inhabited the natural Earth. Our oceans filled with animals acclimating as they grew. Our species was developed in central Africa. That is where we are all quite literally from. Our sacred homeland as a human species. A couple hundred thousand years of acclimating to this planet. Around 250,000 years ago, as if in the womb, we were developing our ability to live here. Then we moved around with curiosity. Picture the Vitruvian Man over the continent of Africa. Tribes went up and went left or right, up or down, arms stretched with pride and curiosity. Moving through what is now *Nigeria*, they did something very pivotal. This was the birth of *Ifa (òrìṣà)*. An awakening of self. Our ancestors who migrated to Western Africa did something incredible—they found the *òrún, beings of light from the spirit world*. Sensory body meet *Soul Mind*. West Africa is the point that we as human beings--found consciousness. An incredible piece of our human history. We were no longer animals, we were aware of our own spirit. After that, our curious ancestors that went North colonized Egypt with the Anunnaki. The tribes to the West were greeted by Atlanteans. Then it's a mixed bag of spiritual beings in bodies. The idea being that one day we would all be created as everyone together.

Okay, so that's the origin of our beautiful animal body and its introduction to soul connection. (Note to the journalist, as with anything, these origins developed into the Egoic Narrative as religions as well, so be cautious in what you read. We are only here for original truth.)

Today, we know the *òrìsà* as *The Logos*, the architects of the 6th dimension. *Then God created light.* The Logos designed us along with all the rest. They are not what we think of them today—they are the architects. To become bodies, that took a lot more work. How we got here is actually a simple timeline. We have a history of different races or beings, but we are one human race. Our real history goes as such; The *Anunnaki civilization* formed in the Middle East. They were from another planet and they had a hard time adjusting to Earth, as did all beings that attempted to survive here. This new planet was constantly changing, and Earth viruses were too much for them. They mated with humans to protect their species and they also enslaved humans as their subordinates. They spread powdered gold on their skin in an attempt to acclimate their non-native planetary bodies to this one. They could not. This planet would eventually kill them. Their planets were also dying, so, for a moment of understanding, the Anunnaki had it rough for a large brutish race from the stars.

Another race of beings understood the *Anunnaki* had the information humans would need, such as, they gave us agriculture. (That moment in our past where historians and scientists can't explain how the brilliance and complexity of agriculture just somehow showed up in ancient civilizations all around the world at the same time) As the Anunnaki took root here, another set of beings came to seed us with an opposing energy. To combine the feminine with the masculine. These light beings created children with the humans and the Anunnaki and, *Thalan (Poseidon)* led them to *Atlantis* to learn how to live on this Earth and be the light and the primal self, together. The red and the blue, as one. This is our duality being born. They fled Egypt with the help of the Gods (sound familiar?) and were taken to the islands to be far from the minds, and more importantly, the energy of the Anunnaki, to create an answer to our egoic ways and plant the seeds of equilibrium. The seeds of the counterbalance to ego, the realm of light. To encode the light DNA into our bodies.

Atlantis was an incredible place where 12 seeds of humanity were formed. *The 12 families of Atlantis*. Each going off in its own direction to blend our modern civilization. The Anunnaki eventually went underground to survive the diseases and built vast networks until they ultimately died. Early humans were afraid of "dark spirits" in caves underground because they were met with some very angry Anunnaki, who believed the humans had stolen the planet from them. Do you see that all of this starts when some tribe of ridiculous humans lost in Ego meet spiritual beings? We call them devils. They are not. They were just mad about getting kicked out of here. As would we.

Humans were eventually the only beings that were able to adapt to this planet, because we are made of it, thus, we are the dominant species here. The ancient *Mu* civilization was created in the South Pacific, created an entire genetic code that gave energetic birth to the civilizations we see across the Pacific. Native Americans or anywhere in the Pacific Islands all came from the *Mu line*. From Atlantis across the Mediterranean to the Middle East and the Anunnaki, the plethora of beings were not able to survive here. So, it's just us now.

That's it. That's our real historical timeline of life here. We carry the DNA lines of all of these beings. We also can't forget that we were not the first ones here. The *Sofhir* inhabited this planet as the first civilization. All of these beings helped create us and here we are. Racist and crazy and ready to change. This combination is what makes this Earth so unique. The ice age cleared out numbers of other species. Only the giants (Nemnir) who lived in the cold stayed through those Earth changes, eventually failing to create a race of humans with their DNA that could survive. Their DNA still exists in some of us as well. We are all of these combinations, and that combination is why we got the keys to Planet Earth. So, you see, being a racist would be to deny that we together as humans evolved into the only race able to live on this incredible blue planet, by joining with others. We all did that. As human beings we have been encoded to live with the Earth. That means it is a part of us to take care of her. She made us possible. That is a bond we form when we wake back up. You are her protector, not just by birth, but by millions of years of evolution so you could exist.

Aliens are very much real. But they are simply another civilization and you might be one. Many of you are and you just forgot. I wouldn't say that unless I had gone down the entire rabbit hole and found concrete proof and then experience beyond any doubt. I didn't go looking for it—it found me. Inward and outward. I'm not really interested in aliens. I'm searching for *our* truth. The grey aliens that come in and out of Earth are a lower resonation civilization. That's why they can handle coming here and being around our emotions. They are more like us in a third-dimension sense. Attempting to survive in their Egoic Narrative. If they were not safe to be here, they would not be allowed., even though we don't understand their creepy scientific approach, Earth is very well protected by the civilization in the Boötes system. You are safe here.

When you see them for yourself, your life will still matter to you more than "aliens." Maybe not at first, but you will get bored of it and go back to you. Realizing there are other civilizations really feels like trying to claim you discovered America. People were already there, it's not that impressive. I've spent enough time seeing alien life for what it really is, and honestly, it's like trying to get into someone else's personal business. All beings in the Universe are dealing with their own dramas. If they weren't, they'd be stagnant. Fear of them is from the movies and egoic temperaments. You need not fear anyone out there, because we're all in this together. Knowing that *Atlantis* was a real part of our history, we will understand that life back then was a lot more spiritual and involved a multitude of other beings who were combining their existence to create with us. However nefarious a story may seem, it brought us to the here and now.

You could envy a more realized race because you see them as more powerful, but you would deny that your ability to live here is your greatest superpower in the Galaxy. Envy is of the ego. Fear, resistance, dark fantasies. If you are a sacred soul from another place, a beautiful *Avatar-esque* planet and you wanted to come down for this experience here, this giant, beautiful soul that you are, reincarnates into body form, then forgets and lives a life where you believe you are Brian from accounting who's a little awkward in social situations. Or, will you slowly unravel the confines of your ego and become aware once again?.

Once you start to see things from a less egoic standpoint, the understanding of other civilizations becomes normalized and comprehensible. We love the drama of, "what if…?" but if an alien landed in the middle of the Super Bowl and said, "hello everyone, we are um, aliens," the news would go crazy, social media atom bomb. Then 5 days later we would all go back to our lives and hit that sale at Target. At the end of the day, it's here, the right now that we will always care about. We just get to make it a whole lot more fun than it has been so far,

You could be contacting other civilizations in your minds right now. They could fly down here and pick you up on their ship and take you to this incredible planet of colors. You could mingle with the elders. They would drop you off at your house, and you would laugh. Who are you going to tell and who would believe you anyway? Nobody. Our egos only work in proof to self. So go find your own proof.

This taught me everything I needed to know about the importance of having our own experiences. The only way for you to believe in this once again is to discover it for yourself. This is between you and you only. You don't need anyone's validation or approval. If you are like me, then you need to make your own mental phone call to your previous home planet. If you must experience this directly to believe it, then go do it.

We think about other life forms with our Egoic Minds, that's our animal brain. Pleasure center. Fear/reward. Good for us or bad for us. When you're no longer based in your pleasure center animal brain, you can see how quickly you can process information. If your Ego Mind is battling the idea of one other civilization, remind yourself there are around 400,000 civilizations out there. We have work to do. There are entire networks of systems and security and codes. But ask yourself this: how much do we get involved with the other countries on our own planet? Rarely. Unless it's to take power away from them. That is our Ego Mind at work. As a whole, we are self-centered at best, thank you separation. The fantasy we have of other life forms might even seem exciting, but that's pleasure mind thinking. There is something better to be had here.

In short, remember that these giant moments of our history happen in cycles. The birth of Earth, cycle. Develop a humanoid species, cycle. A light being can now incarnate into a body that can survive here, cycle. *Planet Earth* began getting ready for us about 1,000,000 years ago. Multiple species colonized from 500,000 BC onward and then around 18,000 years ago the *Anunnaki* colonized what we now call *Egypt*. *Atlantis* was created starting in the *Canary Islands* area. Those 12 lines (12 houses of the zodiac) spread outward and many migrated back into *Egypt* and joined with the *Anunnaki* civilization there as the rest went on through Cyprus. As humans, we were loved by some and enslaved by others to mine minerals for their dying home planets. (Our belief in the value of gold is not of our creation.) *The Great Pyramids* are only smaller replicas of the cities that came before them, the ones we see today were created by the *Mu* (20,000 BC) and *Atlanteans* (15,000 BC). Our timeline as a modern human civilization starts around 12,000 years ago. Okay great! Done with the alien part.

So, *God* as we know it today, would be the sound of *"Om"* or *"Akasha."* The common connection for all religions. The common connection to all of us. A sacred current that connects us as beings. It is the thing. Science recently began to understand this system as the *Millennium Run*. The ancient *Vedic* teachings call this *Nada Brahma*. Here we can clearly see an ancient text describing what science is just starting to understand. The science of 2022 AD, and the teachings of 1200 BCE. Three thousand years to scratch the surface of something we already knew. The Universe is vibration and so are you. As we open our internal life, we can understand the Universe by feeling it. It has a frequency.

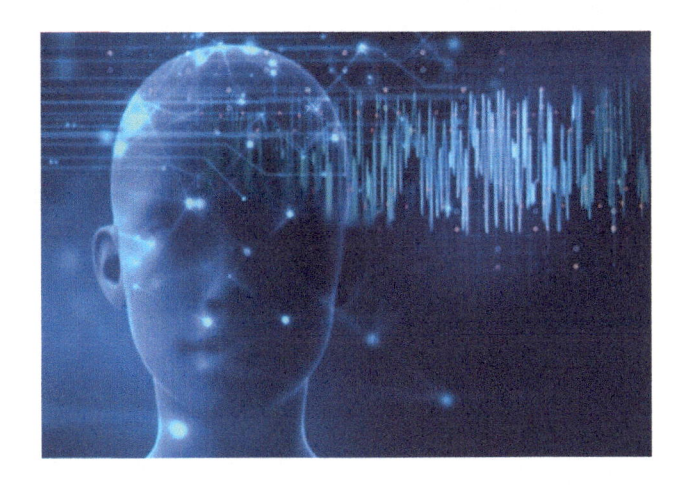

When people say, "raise your vibration" whether they know it or not, we are saying raise your frequency, which you can do. Higher frequency, higher self. Simple. So, with a curious soul, we went from *God* to *Om* to *Sound* to *Frequency to Vibration* to…to what? And then what? You meditate with that understanding and see what happens. You calm the mind…and then you wait and listen. When all seems silent, you start to feel the answer. Resonance.

Our words today were trying to describe *resonance*. That is what we've been calling *God* by so many names. A frequency that connects to *the all-knowing*. Suddenly the science around sound vibration shows us the basics of how the Universe was brought into creation. This is how things fall into place when you are dealing with the laws of *Universal Alignment*. They all work together, and they want to. You are becoming part of the *Sacred Geometry* yourself. This is a step of transcendence.

SACRED GEOMETRY

Everything in the Universe does not have an order it has a place. It is in unison. All these synchronicities align with what is in space, and what is in your body. This is how you were created, too.

We are trying so hard to understand the world from the outside, but the missing information we need is through the inside looking out. When we uncover these things, we thrive with them in our world-building and dream-making. Your own resonance as creation energy. Perhaps we will learn enough about our minds to ignite our *Psionic Energy* used for telepathy. Our minds have incredibly powerful tools in there, most of which we cannot currently access, but this stuff is like going to the gym. Just keep going to the gym, and your body will change on its own.

CHAPTER 16

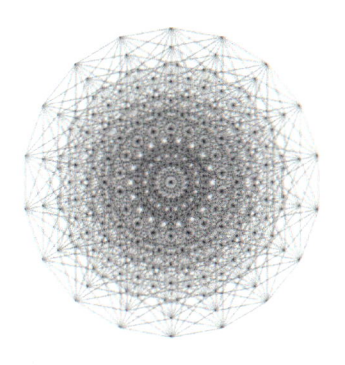

MULTIPLE DIMENSIONS

—

"The more that you read, the more things you will know. The more that you learn, the more places you'll go."

-*Dr. Seuss*

Take this little thought as a seed to plant the idea that in order to visit other dimensions, you have to become them. That is tricky for people at first. So, we make it easier and see the mirror of that process on a smaller scale. You are already doing it. You want "awareness," so you acknowledge your Soul Mind exists, then you stepped into awareness. You become awareness because you knew it was possible and you knew where to find it. Capiche?

We live in a particularly incredible Universe. To start understanding multiple dimensions, we have to stop trying to understand it with words. Picture the snow-globe. Shake it up. Now walk around it and describe to us what is in there. This is how the Universe perceives truth. There is no right answer because as you move around, the snow globe changes. *Dimensions are a culmination of vast perspectives.*

Dimensions also heavily affect our relationships! Today we say, uh, "I'm a Pisces and she's a Virgo." But now we can add more information. As we relate to specific chakras in our body that drive our outward lives, we also carry a dimensional energy around with us. Now you can unpack your partner in an entirely new way. Your partner could be a Pisces, with a life in the Matrix based on the first and fifth chakra, carrying a soul that is connected to the 11th chakra and has spent time in the ninth dimensional angel realm. This would mean your partner's primal self is feeling-based (Pisces) with a constant desire to make things and talk about it (chakra one and five) and a fifth dimensional perspective based in togetherness and family. Which means you're dating someone very emotional and painfully determined while being openly sensitive, who is also a giant ball of love inside, but with a heavy root chakra so they can also slay some dragons, or potentially slay you (on the inside.) If the world is polarity, then they would be a perfect fit for a Cancer, rooted in the fourth chakra, connected to their eight in the five of light. The opposing side of themselves. Match made.

    We live in the third dimension, and we are moving into the fourth dimensional energy, but we also live in all of them because they are all connected. All vibration is reflections and ripples in a giant grid. Therefore, we start building on the inside. We're creating channels and pathways in thought energy. Meditation works quite powerfully when you have a deep curiosity to know something and seek it out. If you wanted to go to the Akashic Records, you would learn how to get yourself to the 8th dimension. You can raise your frequency to match the hall of records and form access to your own file. All that has ever happened to you and every version of you. You cannot access other people's files and they cannot access yours. I always assumed this was some sort of cosmic protection. It is only now that I can understand that others don't go into your files because they are not becoming you, which would be required to see things from your perspective. If you work through a channel that can access these records, they only do so with your permission. (*Akasha* is the name for all creation and source in this Universe, so we are living in the *Akashic realm*.)

    The chances of most of us being from other dimensions and realms…is absolute. Thought from feelings has more power than anything else we can do. Realizing your power of loving thought, you start to comprehend the energy all around you and the possibility of communicating over what seems like impossible distances. Suddenly nothing is far, nothing is impossible and nothing is separate from you. Everything is connected and you are connected to it.

Which dimensions pull you in is usually a sign that you are connected to it in some way.

First Dimension

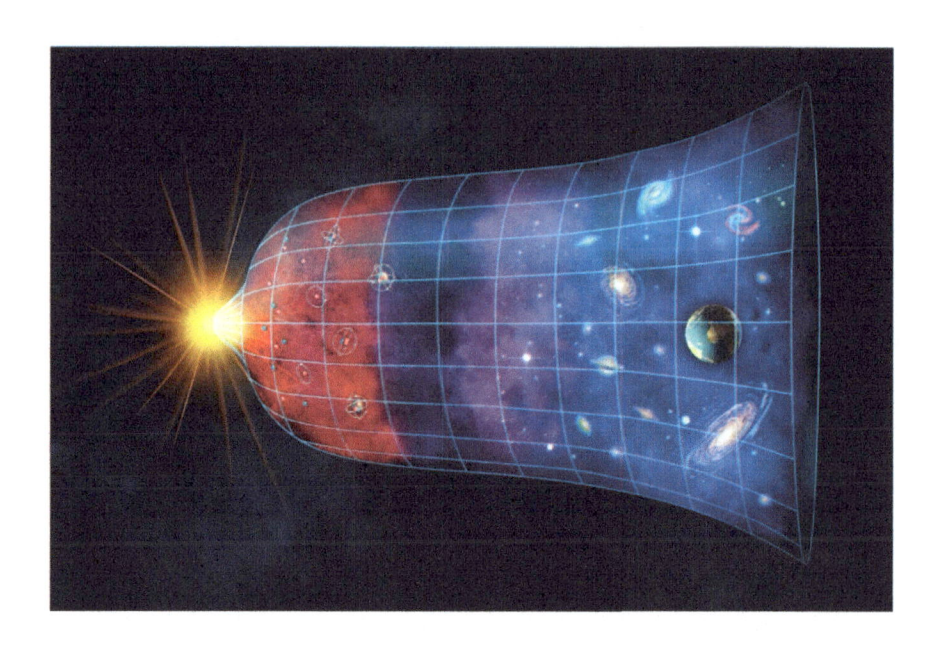

Pop. One particle of light. That is the real you. All alone in the dark. A thought floating in space. This is where *God* is. This is *Source* and it is the *beginning of our creation*. All there is, is there. What we would all refer to as, *The Void*. It is the place of the creation, a silent abyss to become. If you have removed hierarchy then you realize this doesn't mean just the first, it also means the last. A circle. This is the mind place. Where we started to ask, "What am I?" So, we moved into the second dimension and created…

Second Dimension

Pop. Two particles of light. Now you have a friend. Friction. This was our *polarity*. Polarity is what moves all things in the universe, and that polarity began when we split apart…love. We could not see ourselves, so we popped into two. This time wondering, "Hey, what are you?" and you said, "I don't know, what are you?" You see, we can't experience anything in a state of endless creation. So we made structure and that structure is *time manifested as nature*. Astounding.

Third Dimension

We created this dimension so we could manifest thought into a material world. We wanted to make planets so we did. All the light and all the dark. We are all so busy creating this, even if we aren't aware of it at the moment. The Universe is expanding from all the choices we are making here in this dimension. Then we made mistakes. Or, we wanted to try a different way. I'm not a bad person right? That was lovely, but so many suffered? I need to see more versions of this to know. I need to manipulate time to do this…

Fourth Dimension

This is where we created *time*, allowing you to go back and try to change things you had done. You are able to see our realities as a simulation of sorts…one you can effect. This helps you understand that you're not actually jumping through time, you're rotating around multiple perspectives of memory.

When we made the third dimension, the second dimension reacted and split into two and became the fourth dimension. It feels like looking at a snowflake. A geometric shape is charging itself into new things with thought and energy in vibrations. You see the dimensions beginning to replicate together and expand in complete mathematical symmetry. This is what I call one of the builder stages. 2, 4 and 6. Mechanical in nature. We wanted to manipulate the 3rd dimension, so we created a place to do that.

We can see different points in time because it's not a time jump, it's a perspective shift. If you learn that time is this beautiful cyclical energy in stages called *time* that we constructed in the middle of the Universe (that looks like a giant translucent donut in Space,) then you are free of it.

Fifth Dimension

The dimension or "perspective" you find when you leave self and start to think as everyone. This is a place of community consciousness and unity. A place of light. When we find our Trinity of mind, body and spirit, we create the fifth dimension. Now we can understand how existence works because we can see the entire process.

The more you understand every molecule of your body, brings you that much closer to the "perspective" of the fifth dimension. Think of dimensions as rooms around your mansion and they all play different music. Each room has a tone that represents what happens there. You can't join the band if you are playing the wrong tune, so you tune in when in meditation or just in spirit in your daily life. You are leaving "I" and becoming the vast paradise of "we." Think of this as more resonance than thought. That feeling of unconditional love.

Sixth Dimension

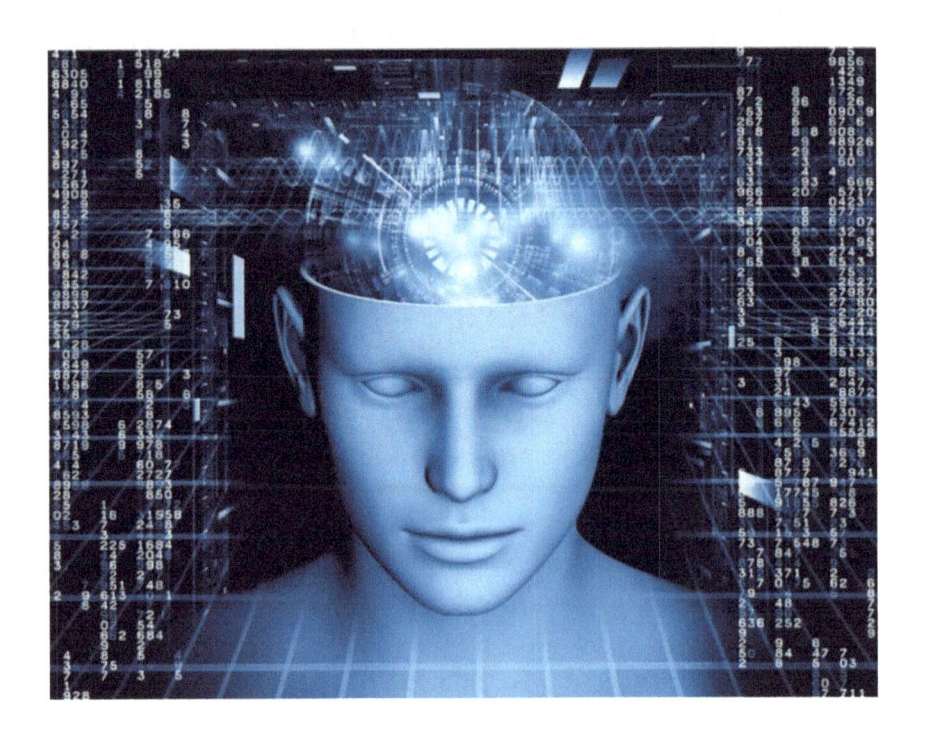

You can work with your past, present and future here. In the sixth dimension we are manifesting the creation of the geometry of the fourth dimension. With perspective of the fifth we can create sacred plans and send them into the Universal Matrix. This is what many refer to as the "Mental Realms." We become this in our Soul Mind.

We are able to revisit old wounds and heal them through understanding. Healing them is not to fix them, it is to understand the experience because that knowledge is the healing of the Universe. It brings it back to alignment too. Remember the Elohim? They are sixth dimensional planet architects—as in Archangel Michael. We learn to transform shapes and distort the light into rainbows of currents and redesign worlds.

Seventh Dimension

This one is my current fascination. The dimension of knowledge and Gods. The seventh dimension is interesting because it *is* the *Seven Laws of the Universe*. We can see them in the chakras. The seven chakras are the first dimension. The chakras all together would make what we call, *God/Source/Akasha*.

You have *God* inside you in seven pieces—which we now know to be seven perspectives. These spinning chakra wheels of energy inside you are split into seven because the laws of the universe are set in these seven truths, or as I say to no end, understandings. There are no laws, only agreed upon concepts based on synchronicity. If you understand all seven, you would have rejoined the seven back into the oneness we call *Source*.

Eighth Dimension

This is what we call the realm of information. It also holds our Akashic Records (later referred to in the Bible as The Book of Life). The data center of it all. We can attempt to access this from here and get a glimpse, but again, you would have to become the eighth dimension to be able to read all of the information. You see, it's ego proof. If you can completely stand in center, fueled by unconditional love and driven by soul curiosity, then you would resonate with 8.

If you want to see from that perspective, you must become that perspective. You have all these chakras and dimensions to play with. 8th dimension is a realm of possibilities. Image and create with endless amounts of information. This is the perspective that allows us to understand that "anything is possible" ...because it is.

Ninth Dimension

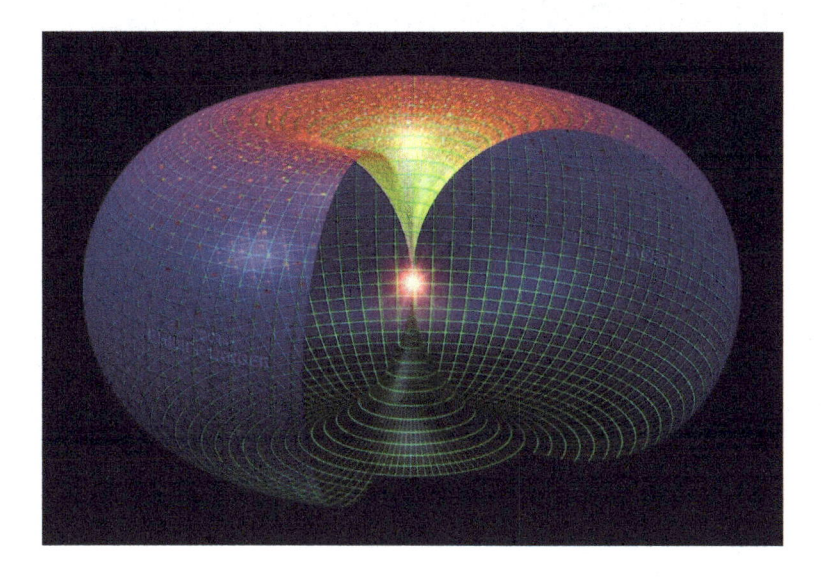

Prodicta. Oneness. Realization. A black hole. The transcendence of all things. This is where the truth resides. No "I", no "me", it just is. This is a place we start to weave back into the geometry. The 9th folds back into the 1st. All the old energy plugs back into the new. Our minds folded back into the first dimension, so we have immense thought energy connecting back. This is a keeper of information. It looks like a black hole. Like being on the inside of a Universal sized hard-drive.

This is where the truth of our truth is kept. Want to make your own Universe? You can do that here. This is your connection state after ascension to *Source* mind. The core of the 9th is the 6th. Remember 3-6-9. All geometry. This is all mathematically aligned so it's a very easy code to crack when science gets here. We understand ourselves in science as matter, this is the science of thoughts as energy.

Tenth+ Dimension

From here we move into forms of transcendence and light beings. It begins a new cycle and takes us onward to even more. (There is a collection of *twelfth dimensional (12D) beings* that operate in a light realm and they usher and guide your spirit from soul into body right before you are born. They are the spiritual storks of Earth who then become our shepherds of balance as we walk through this life in duality.

Dimensions without the smudged lens of Ego Mind become perspectives in beautiful geometry working together. Each realm is an expansion of the next, all relying on each other. Until we get there, and wonder, what's next?

THE ISH

My best friend Daniel and I spent thousands of hours writing scripts together. We would get to a "flow-state." Something we didn't really know how to describe, so we created one. It's the same thing you hear a musician talk about when they say, "The song…suddenly just came to me like one giant download." This is *the ISH*. The Information Super-Highway. (We had never heard the word *Akashic* at the time.) We pictured this as silvery rings of electric information spinning around the planet, rings filled with everyone's story from everyone who ever lived. It felt like if someone had a life moment they desperately needed to share with the world, they could shoot those signals out and see which writers caught them. We knew this to be true when we would have great ideas for a TV show and while we labored over the script, we would see a pilot episode on TV of the same idea we were working on. This happened to us enough that we decided when we have an idea, six other people just got the same idea so whoever does the work of translation first or hopefully most truthfully, that will be the shepherd of that story. We came to believe the playful idea that you could tap into *the ISH* if you were actively doing something with the information. If we wrote all the time, it was louder, particularly clear. If we didn't, the stream of creative thoughts would eventually dry up.

We know these things even when we don't. That feeling, that voice, that place where you write the greatest song, that is a place of connection to the *Source*. To feeling. The freedom comes when you learn one thing…live without ego. Fall back in love with this planet you are on. Fall back in love with yourself and remember that love and understanding will take you anywhere you want to go in the Universe. When the beauty of who you are expresses itself, the world becomes a more beautiful place to be.

'Once you eliminate the impossible, whatever remains, no matter how improbable, must be the truth"
  -Sherlock Holmes

CLOSING THOUGHTS

Take the leap of faith, let go. We are always safe. We are always okay. That's a soul promise from me to you.

Finding your truth is a tough and beautiful process. Hours spent staring at the back of eyelids in total darkness, to moments of clarity to help reveal something pivotal in our lives. We are changing from fear to a life of action. To change it, we become it. Always look for the loops so you can break them. Separation has led us to believe that we live, we die, and that's it. When really there's so much more to who we are. Messages from the ancient world give us clues because they were at the time untainted.

Be gentle when you wake up. You might feel the need to emotionally sucker punch everyone around you, but use your Daily Bread and Drain that Pain. Fall in love with your spiritual life because it only involves your endless soul. It is where you find your peace here. Who knows what magic you have inside. Learn to hear and feel the difference between authentic and inauthentic people. That is your guiding light. Talk to other civilizations, travel from the inside, or just become a happier but more whole person here, someone living in awareness. The world gets brighter. You can feel it again. But, this does not arrive in a life devoted to serving yourself. It is about letting go of Ego, to become whole again. This is the art of Emotional Intelligence,

This inner journey is a new adventure for all of us. You don't earn this ability, you go in search of it because it's already there. We now have step one. Death to Ego. The next steps are up to you. You are already expanding, or this is all bullshit. Be a journalist. Figure it out. Activate those Minds to guide your path.

Your life and *all* life are being created in this very moment. You are not in a movie, you are in the thing we make movies about. Wake up and help create it in a way you want to live it. By being open again, you come to these realizations in synchronistic symphony.

If you've gotten this far in the book, watch a television show called *The Good Place*. The one with Kristen Bell. If you get to the end of that show and you can truly understand what it means, not in the abstract but with full clarity and surrender, then you will fall back in love with your life here. The show's creator, Michael Shur, just so happened to align his story with the *Laws of The Universe* with playful exactitude—what a curious coincidence. When you see the final question Eleanor has to answer, you can ask yourself as well. Are you ready to stop? Are you done yet? Each of your lifetimes, a little like giving birth to a giant baby. Then, you jump out into bliss until you want to do it again because you missed something, and you want to go back. The less serious you take all of this, the further you will get. Less serious, more curious. *Amen*! Forget everything you know, and let's make some changes shall we, *Shakti*.

Ego will always exist here. It's part of what drives this entire experience. Live with authenticity and find your purpose that unlocks you from the shackles of this narrative. Find the loops of pain in the world and change them. There is no answer in the Matrix until you create one. You will have to create the new codes yourself.

Strive to build communities. Be active in your mind, but don't let it dominate your heart. Reconnect with your soul mind and let it flood you with wisdom once again. Life will go on, but this time we get to not just be intelligent animals, but now we can be the sentient Gods we already are inside. Live simply, love in abundance and use your vast resources to build a better world. A world in which you no longer live with the need to win or the desire to be right. After all of this research into the origins of our beings, I have only found one constant truth; *Love is why we are here.*

"We were more creator than human, and then we became more human than creator, and that's okay too, do with it what you will"

I don't like most of you from time to time, but that's only because I truly and deeply love all of you. We started this journey with, "What am I, what am I, what am I?" and we end with a feeling of, *I am*.

If this is the last thing I say.

Go, be free. See you on the other side. *Erin Dinsmore*

THE VOID

Rainer Maria Rilke from his "Poems to God"
Translated by Anita Barrows

I am too alone in the world, yet not alone enough
To make each hour holy
I am too small in the world, yet not small enough
To be simply in your presence like a thing, just as it is
I want to know my own will, and to move with it
And I want in the hushed moments, when the nameless draws near
To be among the wise ones or alone
I want to mirror your immensity
I want never to be too weak or too old
To bare the heavy lurching image of you
I want to unfold
Let no place in me hold itself closed
For where I am closed, I am false
I want to stay clear in your sight
I believe in all that has never yet been spoken
I want to free what waits within me
So that what no one has dared to wish for
May for once spring clear without my contriving
If this is arrogant, God, forgive me
But this is what I need to say
May what I do flow from me like a river
No forcing and no holding back
The way it is with children
Then in these swelling and ebbing currents
These deepening tides moving out and returning
I will sing you as no one ever has
Streaming through widening channels
Into the open sea.

"I am too alone in the world, yet not alone enough"

All these years wondering…he was describing Ego death. That lonely place between you and *Source*. Don't quit right before the miracle.

About the Author

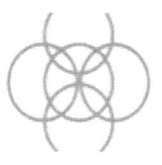

My mother always wondered why strangers came up to me all the time in school asking me to help them with a very complicated life situation. That continued to happen throughout my life. I often find myself in deep conversations with strangers about their most personal lives. Abortions, rape, to the pivotal life moments they cherished most. While I was having a heartfelt conversation, my soul was collecting data and forming insight, all based on, you. Always the emotional journalist looking for deeper answers to much bigger questions in hopes of making life here just a little bit better.

I was unknowingly born as an HSP, which is essentially a heightened sensory system to everything. An ability to see and feel all of life and its little curiosities with vast amounts of sensory data. I could sense our world on a multitude of levels; lights, smells, tastes, human behavior, feelings, tones of voice, body language--intuition and patterns were always developing. My brain was processing all of this through different channels in my highly activated nervous system, all-the-while, trying to understand…why we feel. I was a sensitive being in a society that rejected those attributes. The blessing and the curse. The purpose was set and I knew the road to the bright side was going to get a little darker first.

I loved life and it loved me back, but I didn't understand it here. Something deep down, was gutted. Something in us feels fundamentally broken. I was losing faith in who we are here. I tried so hard to pull myself out of the mud, but that mud always follows us around somehow. So, I needed to become it, to understand it. I was *Dumbledore* drinking darkness from a cup. I tore myself apart in hopes of understanding us a little better. A long road down into the darkness. I knew I needed to get to a place of nothing, so I could see who we really are. It's lonely there. Until, you find, it. The truth. Then everything changes. In that place of nothing, you find everything. *"When in darkness, light a match."* Awake. It was Ego Death, and it was just the beginning.

Made in the USA
Columbia, SC
14 October 2022